PRAGMATISM

*Philosophy
of Imperialism*

Pragmatism

Philosophy of Imperialism

BY HARRY K. WELLS

Essay Index Reprint Series

BOOKS FOR LIBRARIES PRESS
FREEPORT, NEW YORK

Copyright 1954 by International Publishers Co., Inc.

Reprinted 1971 by arrangement

For Cathy and Danny

INTERNATIONAL STANDARD BOOK NUMBER:
0-8369-2084-8

LIBRARY OF CONGRESS CATALOG CARD NUMBER:
74-128331

PRINTED IN THE UNITED STATES OF AMERICA

CONTENTS

INTRODUCTION

By Howard Selsam

THE PRESENT WORK represents a significant contribution to Marxist philosophy in the United States. Marxists have taught, written and fought against pragmatism for many years but here, for the first time, is a full-length exposition and criticism of this philosophy in its historical development, its basic premises and conclusions, its social-political role, and its impact on every phase of American life and thought.

The volume before us also represents a new stage in the development of its author. Three years ago Dr. Harry K. Wells gave us, in *Process and Unreality,* an effective critique of the philosophy of the late Alfred North Whitehead—an idol of certain sections of academic philosophers in the English speaking world. But whereas that work remained entirely in the conventional tradition of formal philosophical criticism, this one, while built around similar technical analyses, adds an entirely new dimension— that of social, political, economic criticism. It concerns itself, in short, not only with what the author regards as philosophically wrong with pragmatism, but with its class origins and social function: With what pragmatism *means* in actual practice.

This volume is designed to be of interest and concern not only to Marxists but to all teachers and students of philosophy, indeed, to all persons concerned with basic theoretical questions in the realms of natural science, economics, politics, the labor movement, education, law, culture, and world affairs. Especially must it be of concern to all people interested in preserving democracy in our country and peace in the world, for the philosophical questions at issue are directly reflected in the programs and policies currently being followed or advocated in the United States.

7

The basic questions before the reader must inevitably be: Is pragmatism what it claims to be? Is it, as Dewey claims, the philosophy of "modern science," natural and social? Is it the "intelligent," the "scientific" method for solving all social problems? Is it the ordinary person's "common-sense," "naturalistic" world outlook as opposed to both the idealist and "materialist" systems of previous philosophy? Or, is pragmatism what Dr. Wells maintains it is, following Marxist materialist principles and the Marxist dialectical method? He holds it to be the distinctive philosophy of imperialism, the philosophy of the "big stick," the philosophy of the sheerest expediency, of practice without theory, movement without direction, improvisation, getting-by, and the ultimate in American business creeds, "nothing succeeds like success."

Many leaders in American philosophy as well as in other fields have not been altogether comfortable about pragmatism, especially as carried forward in the writings of John Dewey. Some sensed its lack of any moral criteria or standards, others its inherent subjectivism and denial of objective reality. Many have felt and expressed doubts about its emphasis on "success" without adequate criteria and have feared its corrosive effect on objective principles in every sphere of life. Many, of course, have attacked it from a religious or an absolute idealist standpoint—attacks on which pragmatism has thrived and flourished, for opposition to religious orthodoxy and objective idealism has been pragmatism's stock-in-trade from its very beginning. But even much of this kind of criticism has had its positive aspect against pragmatism's lack of preciseness, principle and clarity. On many sides there has been dissatisfaction and even fear at the damage pragmatism has done to any objective theory of knowledge and truth, and to discipline in education and the arts. W. Y. Elliot, Morris R. Cohen, William E. Hocking, Alexander Meiklejohn, Roy W. Sellars, Arthur Murphy, Hans Reichenbach, and many others have criticized it for one or another of the above-named shortcomings.

None of these thinkers, however, has given us a full-length analysis of the philosophy of pragmatism. And although many have seen it as reflecting something wrong with the times, none even attempted to ask, as Dr. Wells has and as any Marxist must, whose philosophy is this? What class does it serve? Where does it stand in relation to the rise of U.S. imperialism and its present-day attempts at world-domination? Even on the purely philosophical level, none of the academic critics has asked where pragmatism stands in relation to the age-old struggle between materialism and idealism. Even those more inclined towards materialism were unable to see that pragmatism's destructiveness of both knowledge and values was due to its being a specially corrupt and cynical form of subjective idealism.

Unlike so many of their Latin American, European and Asian counterparts, the academic philosophers of the United States have consistently avoided, with the rarest exceptions, any real and serious study of Marxist philosophy. Only too often, like Dewey himself, they have regarded it as a peculiar aberration derived from the limited development of the natural and social sciences of the earlier part of the nineteenth century. They have failed to see that Marxist philosophy is in constant development and that in our own century the philosophical writings of Lenin have illuminated many philosophical questions. They have neglected to read and study Lenin's classic *Materialism and Empirio-Criticism,* which has been available in this country in English since 1927. If they had read Lenin they would have noticed that as early as 1908 he recognized the nature and roots of pragmatist philosophy from the reading of William James' *Pragmatism.*

The present volume makes a positive contribution to the issues long debated among our philosophers, as well as to questions facing the working class and the people generally. It merits the careful consideration of those who want to understand the philosophy embodied in U.S. foreign policy, expressed in the corruption of political life, in class-collaborationism in the labor movement, and in the disintegration of our national culture. It can help to clarify the thinking of all serious-minded people concerning the origins and influences of this distinctive philosophy of U.S. imperialism.

What are the chief features of pragmatism as opposed to a scientific materialist world-outlook? They are: 1. the denial of an objective reality, existing independent of any and all human experience and reflected in our minds through the medium of our senses; 2. the consequent denial of any objective necessity, any causality, any teaching that given such-and-such events and processes something else necessarily follows; 3. the denial of any objective knowledge or truth and hence of any real possibility of either prediction or control of natural and social phenomena; and 4. the assertion that the successful fulfillment of given aims, purposes, intentions is the only test of the validity of any ideas or principles and constitutes the sole meaning of their "truth."

Marxist scientific materialism holds the direct opposite of these basic teachings of pragmatism. Dialectical materialism teaches: 1. there is an objective, material reality which exists and is what it is whether our or any other minds experience it or not, and this reality is given us through our senses; 2. this reality has a structure, has laws of its development, so that given particular circumstances something else necessarily follows; 3. through our senses and reason we achieve real knowledge of reality, an approximation to absolute truth, and through this knowledge we can predict and control ever extending areas of nature and of our social relations; 4. although the test of the truth of our ideas is found solely in practice, they work, in the long run, only insofar as they are true and not as pragmatism holds that they are true because they work.

It is impossible to give a simple, plain definition of pragmatism, but wherever the four propositions ascribed to it above are found, there is pragmatism. Unfortunately, as Dr. Wells makes clear, the pragmatists seldom were at pains to state their position clearly and without ambiguity and equivocation. Dewey never said anything straight-forwardly if he could say it in a round-about way. With great effort and extraordinary skill Dr. Wells unravels the threads, cuts through the confusions and complexities to uncover the essence of pragmatism, whether in philosophy or in history, legal or educational theory, economic or political thought.

Basic here is the question of approach, and central to the Marxist approach is the question of class and social forces. How should we interpret a philosophy? What is more important, what it means to you or me? What it means to society at large? What it means to different social classes? Or are all these questions irrelevant and the sole question that of what a philosopher means to himself? To what extent are political and class considerations relevant in determining the meaning and evaluation of a philosophical doctrine? What is the relation between what a philosopher may have thought he was doing and what objectively, in terms of the history of ideology and class struggles, he was doing? These are a few of the questions this book raises and seeks to answer.

But Dr. Wells does not stop with such questions. He painstakingly shows that this philosophy is bad for the overwhelming masses of people, for the whole future of mankind, because *as a philosophy* it is anti-scientific, reactionary, obscurantist, anti-human. If the author sometimes seems blunt in his judgments the reader will soon find, by continued reading, that James and Dewey speak quite bluntly for themselves in Wells' quotations.

If the present volume teaches us to be wary when we hear such expressions as "be practical," "cut out the theory," "it's what you can get by with," etc., it will be worth while. If it leads to the study of other phases of American reactionary thought, as well as to more work in our great democratic tradition, it will be very good. But the least the readers can be asked is that they grasp enough of the essence of pragmatism to see it, day in and day out, as an insidious and pervasive enemy, ever to be fought, an enemy that insinuates itself into all of our activity, an enemy whose essence is *expedience* rather than *principle.*

For many years American Marxists have been challenging pragmatism and seeking to expose it as a socially corrosive force. With this book that challenge is raised to a new level through its historical treatment of pragmatism, the detailed analysis of its philosophy, and the study of its application in various fields. It shows that pragmatism is an enemy not only of the science of Marxism, but of peace and progress in the United States and throughout the world.

Jefferson School of Social Science
January, 1954

I. ROOTS OF PRAGMATISM

MAXIM GORKY well understood the pragmatic type of thinking when in one of his pamphlets he put into the mouth of an American millionaire the assertion that "It is not the method but the result that counts." This in essence is the basic principle of pragmatism, if it is possible to speak of principles in connection with a completely unprincipled philosophy.

Pragmatic thinking is the method of getting results regardless of the means employed. There is, for it, no objective measure of truth, thus the sole criterion is success. Anything goes, with no holds barred, so long as it "works." The only relevant question is, "Does it advantage me?" If it does it is called "true" and "good," if not, it is "false" and "bad."

President Eisenhower applies this pragmatic "principle" to the employment of atomic weapons: "To my mind the use of the atomic bomb would be on this basis. Does it advantage me, or does it not, when I get into a war? . . . If I thought the net was on my side, I would use it instantly. . . ." Does he decide whether "I get into a war" on the same basis? The philosophy of pragmatism offers no other.

It is this kind of thinking that is embodied in the formal philosophy of William James and John Dewey. It is elaborated in an almost endless variety of ways, but always the basic features are the same. In many cases it is camouflaged and yet, when the demagogic phrases are swept aside, the essence stands exposed in all its philistine crudity.

Pragmatism is a form of philosophical idealism. More specifically, it is a form of subjective idealism which asserts that only our mind really exists, that the natural and social world exists only in our sensa-

13

tions and ideas, will and emotions. It is a subjective idealist philosophy evolved within the concrete historical conditions of the United States. It was formulated principally by three philosophers: Charles S. Peirce, William James, and John Dewey. Peirce was its founder, James its popularizer, and Dewey its high priest.

But pragmatism is by no means simply an academic philosophy invented by professors at Harvard or Columbia Universities. It is the world outlook of the capitalist class first and the brainchild of bourgeois ideologists only secondarily. The formulated philosophy in turn acts back again on the general class outlook and on the life of society from which it originally sprang.

Philosophy is not an isolated phenomenon, cut off from the rest of life. It is an integral part of ideology, underlying it as the view of life and mode of thought of a class. In the *Eighteenth Brumaire Of Louis Bonaparte,* Marx spoke of the formation of ideology: "Upon the different forms of property, upon the social conditions of existence, rises an entire superstructure of distinct and characteristically formed sentiments, illusions, modes of thought and views of life. The entire class creates and forms them out of its material foundations and out of the corresponding social relations."[3] Pragmatism is the name which has come to signify the particular view of life and mode of thought created by the entire capitalist class in the United States out of its material foundations and out of its corresponding social relations. It is also the name for the academic formulation of the class-created world view made by the professional philosophers.

The first formulation of pragmatism, though the name was not used, was made by Charles Sanders Peirce in 1878. Peirce was the son of a Harvard professor and was a resident of Cambridge, Massachusetts, for the greater part of his life. He taught at Harvard and at Johns Hopkins but his regular employment was with the United States Coast Guard, working on the Geodetic Survey. He was a scientist trained in chemistry and physics who turned to philosophy under the impact of Charles Darwin, Charles Lyell and the new evolutionary content of science.

In two articles published in *The Popular Science Monthly* for January and February of 1878, Peirce developed the central thesis of pragmatism: "Consider what effects, which might conceivably have practical bearings, we conceive the object of our conception to have. Then, our conception of these effects is the whole of our conception of the object."[4] Bishop Berkeley had said "to be is to be perceived." Peirce gives this subjective idealist doctrine a revised and peculiarly American twist, for the essential meaning of the above thesis is that to be is to have practical effects, or *to be is to be useful.* A thing is what it is "good for" in practical human activity. If an object is not useful, it does not exist. A thing is nothing but how it works in practice.

This thesis contains in itself the kernel of subjective idealism, for it makes the object dependent on, not independent of, human beings and thus denies the objective material world. At the same time, it means that there is no such thing as truth, for there is no external world to which ideas in the mind can correspond. With no truth there is no knowledge, no theory, no science. An idea or a theory, therefore, cannot be true or false, it can only be useful or useless, and the only criterion is success in practical action.

Thus already by 1878 bourgeois philosophy in the United States had been given technical form. What were the economic, political and intellectual conditions which prepared the ground for this first formulation of pragmatism?

Political and Economic Background

In his classic work on imperialism, Lenin characterizes the decade 1860 to 1870 as the first of "the principal stages in the history of monopolies." It is the period in which "monopoly is in the barely discernible, embryonic stage." This first stage of the development of monopoly coincides with "the highest stage, the apex of development of free competition."[5] Through the process of competition itself, concentration of capital has reached the point at which monopoly is beginning to appear, though it is as yet "barely discernible." The second stage of development of monopolies begins "after the crisis of 1873" at which time there is "a wide zone of development of cartels; but they are still the exception. They are not yet durable."[6] Thus the years from 1860 to 1878 include the apex of free competition and the first stage and the opening of the second stage in the rise of monopolies.

Lenin was speaking of the development of monopolies in the capitalist world as a whole, but the United States was no exception.

The period between 1860 and 1878, when pragmatism was being

formulated, was one of rapid economic development and of sharp political struggle. In the economic base it was marked on the one side by a vastly heightened concentration of capital with the beginnings of monopolies, and on the other side by a large growth in the numbers of the proletariat. The political reflection of the changes of this period was characterized on the one hand by extension and consolidation of state power on the part of the capitalist class, and the ruthless wielding of this organized force and violence to subdue the workers, the farmers and the Negro people; on the other hand, by increasing militant resistance of the people through new forms of struggle, including national trade unions, national farm organizations, and independent farm and labor political parties.

On the international scene, the single event during this period which had the greatest impact on both capital and labor was the Paris Commune, following the Franco-Prussian War of 1870-71. It terrified the capitalist class by revealing in concrete form the doom of its system of exploitation and oppression through private ownership of the means of production. By the same token, it electrified the working class by revealing in a live flash the historic mission of the proletariat and its allies.

These economic and political developments had far reaching and profound effects on bourgeois ideology. In point of fact, the capitalist class, having seized full control of the state by eliminating the feudal-slave power of the South, had created for the first time in this country conditions which demanded the formation of a strictly entrenched capitalist class ideology. How were the economic and political developments of the late 'sixties and 'seventies reflected in the sphere of ideology? What was the ideological task facing the bourgeois philosopher?

First let us see what ideological developments we would expect to find following the full seizure of political power by the capitalist class. Here we have the earlier historical development in France and England to serve as a guide. Marx, in his preface to the second edition of *Capital*, draws in a few sentences the picture of what happened in these two countries:

In France and in England the bourgeoisie had conquered political power. Thenceforth, the class-struggle, practically as well as theoretically, took on more and more outspoken and threatening forms. It sounded the knell of scientific bourgeois economy. It was thenceforth no longer a question, whether this theorem or that was true, but whether it was useful to capital or harmful, expedient or inexpedient, politically dangerous or not. In place of disinterested enquirers, there were hired prize-fighters; in place of genuine scientific research, the bad conscience and the evil intent of apologetics.[7]

Although in this instance Marx is speaking with particular reference to economic theory, he is at the same time indicating the character of bourgeois ideology as a whole after the winning of state power. Expedient apologetics takes the place of scientific inquiry; usefulness to the class takes the place of truth.

Bourgeois apologists would claim that whereas this may be true of England and France, the United States is an "exception." But we would expect to find that capitalist ideology in this country is no exception, that it becomes apologetics at a new level after the Civil War. Furthermore, we would expect to find that U.S. bourgeois apologetics, developing, not as in England and France during the period of competitive capitalism, but during the rise of monopolies and imperialist tendencies, was from its inception the crudest and most decadent form of apologetics. Thus the doctrine of "American exceptionalism," in ideology as in other spheres, is not only completely contrary to fact but is the precise opposite of the truth. For the only "exception" in regard to ideology as apologetics is that the U.S. form is heightened and exaggerated. Far from being an exception to the laws of development of capitalism, the United States in the epoch of imperialism develops as a classic model of monopoly capitalism.

As we shall see, bourgeois ideologists in this country incorporated into the various phases of ideology the notions of *expediency* and *usefulness* as substitutes for science and truth. Expediency and usefulness were transformed from mere working dictums into broad philosophical "principles" which pervaded the entire ideology. In this way the essence of apologetics, which Marx characterized as expediency and usefulness to capital, became itself the philosophy, formulated as well as unformulated, of the capitalist class in the United States. It can be seen, therefore, that pragmatism, with its central doctrine of "to be is to be useful," constitutes decadent bourgeois apologetics in philosophy. In fact, pragmatism is the glorification and celebration of apologetics.

The story of the formulation of this philosophy and its pervasion of the whole ideology is the subject of this book. It is the story of the particular form given to the class content of apologetics with its key notions of expediency and usefulness. The form remains pragmatism from its inception down to the present time. The only essential progression is the movement from the open, unabashed versions developed in the late nineteenth century to the relatively camouflaged versions of the present. Accompanying the camouflage is a heightening of the decadence and degeneracy. The degree of camouflage is at the same time a more or less accurate reflection of the growth in organization and militancy of the working class and its allies.

The story begins in Cambridge, Massachusetts, in the year 1871, the year of the Paris Commune.

The "Metaphysical Club"

In Cambridge during the early 'seventies were concentrated a number of men who were to play a key role in the formulation of bourgeois ideology during the coming decades. All were instructors if not professors at one time or another in Harvard University, and all were in close personal and professional contact. There is considerable evidence that for a number of years, from 1871 to 1874, they met in an exclusive informal discussion group called, according to Charles S. Peirce, the "Metaphysical Club—a name chosen to alienate all whom it would alienate."[8]

In addition to Peirce, the group included Chauncey Wright, natural scientist, philosopher and psychologist; Oliver Wendell Holmes, Joseph B. Warner and Nicholas St. John Green, lawyer, judge and legal theorist respectively; John Fiske, historian; Francis Ellingwood Abbot, Protestant minister and theologian; and William James, physiologist later to become psychologist and philosopher. Of these, four were to play leading roles in their respective fields in the years to come; namely Peirce, Holmes, Fiske and James. The others, however, made by no means unimportant contributions in this early formative stage. In point of fact, the dominant figure in the group was Chauncey Wright, for it was he who furnished the *theory* which underlies the pragmatic *method,* while the method itself was given its germinal form by Nicholas St. John Green and Charles Peirce.

What was the common problem which brought this group of men

together? Throughout the first two-thirds of the nineteenth century theological or religious philosophy had been almost exclusively dominant. It had pervaded the ideology of the ruling classes of the North and the South. As long as slavery in the South and agriculture in both sections of the country were predominant, religion was adequate as a weapon. But with the great leap forward of capitalist industrial development following the victory of 1865, and the concomitant development of the proletariat with its forms of organized struggle, religion could no longer constitute the exclusive reliance. In this way, theology and religious philosophy generally were bound to be replaced by a more effective form, one which made room for and which utilized religion but which did not limit itself to that. The challenge of evolution to theology speeded up the process of the formulation of a strictly bourgeois philosophy, just as it speeded up the process of the liberation of the masses from religion. The common problem facing the Cambridge group was the double threat to established religion: from an aroused working class and from science, especially the theory of evolution.

Through their "solution" of this problem, the Cambridge intellectuals in fact formulated the pragmatic view of life and mode of thought and thus carried out an objective historical task.

Going on about them was a raging dispute between a handful of scientists championing evolution, led by the Harvard biologist, Asa Gray, and the whole angry pack of theologians and ministers led by another Harvard scientist, Louis Agassiz. It was a debate which could not be avoided by individuals, groups or institutions. It led to warring factions in schools and churches, in town meetings and legislatures. Echoes of the debate were still heard generations later, the most publicized being the Scopes trial in Tennessee of a teacher accused in 1925 of teaching evolution.

The members of the Metaphysical Club had before them the abortive attempts of the so-called "natural theologians" to assimilate evolution into church doctrine, to make science directly serve theology. Notable among these was Edward Hitchcock's attempt to theologize Lyell's theory of the evolution of the earth, and Paul Chadbourne's attempt to do the same with Darwin's *Origin of Species*. Hitchcock, a Calvinist theologian, president of Amherst College and professor of "geology and natural theology," wrote *The Religion of Geology and its Connected Sciences* which had gone through eleven printings by 1860. In it he advanced the

thesis that "geology has given great enlargement to our knowledge of
the divine plans and operations of the universe," and that the microscope
is "the sixth step in man's knowledge of Jehovah." Chadbourne wrote
the *Relations of Natural History and Natural Theology* in which he
tried to fit evolution into the doctrines of fixed species and special
creation by showing that it followed the "plan of creation." Evolution
in his view demonstrated "the instinct-like forethought which *is* the
law of growth of plants and animals" and proved the "adaptation of
means and ends such as justified itself to the Reason of man."[10]

The Cambridge group recognized the intellectual if not the political
inadequacy of all such open attempts at reconciliation of the new science
and theology. However, it was not as though they were defenders of
science and therefore resented its subordination to theology. On the
contrary, the theologians granted too much to science, for they accepted
the fact that Lyell and Darwin had discovered real laws of the objective
material world. Thus the Calvinist Hitchcock, for example, had held
that "geology expands our ideas of the time in which the material universe has been in existence."[11]

The alternative was to combat the materialism of science, and of the
working class under cover of an attack on all "metaphysics." By this
term they did not refer to metaphysics as it is defined by dialectical
materialism, namely, the mechanical method as opposed to the dialectical
method. On the contrary, they referred to any notion that there was
objective reference of ideas or theories to a reality existing independent
of human experience. In this way they could attack the concept of the
material world under cover of an attack on the theological conception
of a spiritual world which was independent of man's experience. Thus
the term "metaphysics" meant to them both the "belief" in the objective
material world and the "belief" in the objective spiritual world. By
means of this neat formula bourgeois philosophy could appear to line
up with science and the revolt of the working masses against religion,
and yet simultaneously reinstate at a far more vicious and degenerate
level the obscurantism which it had been the function of religion to
preach. By this two-pronged offensive it could at one and the same time
deny science, theory and truth, and conceal this denial under the camouflage of attack on theology. It would then be in a position to sneak
religion in the back door, for there would be no science to combat it.

It was a formula fully able to meet the historical requirements of the capitalist class after it had seized power and was steaming ahead in its never-ending drive for greater and greater profits. What was needed now was a technical theory and method which would attack materialism under the demagogy of an attack on theology. The theory must formulate the bourgeois view of life, namely, the denial of any objective necessity which could thwart the will of the class to accumulate profits and dominate the world forever. The method must formulate the notions of class expediency and class usefulness as substitutes for objective scientific understanding; the doctrine of any means to the class end was required.

The Philosophical Roots of Pragmatism

It was Chauncey Wright who formulated the capitalist view of life into the theory which was to constitute the ground on which the pragmatic method was erected. But he did not invent it out of the whole cloth. He borrowed from the classic philosophy of Berkeley, from the theories of John Stuart Mill, Jeremy Bentham and Alexander Bain, the utilitarians, and from Ernst Mach, Avenarius and Helmholtz, whom Lenin exposed in *Materialism and Empirio-Criticism* as nothing but Berkeleyan subjective idealists in modern dress.

The central doctrine Wright preached was that there was no necessity in nature or society. By denying necessity he denied that there were necessary laws of motion in the universe, that reality had a structure, that the development of nature and society follows general laws of motion. If there is no objective necessity then science cannot discover what is not there to be discovered. Thus what science calls laws of motion and development were to Wright only habits of human behavior.

The entire membership of the Metaphysical Club was indebted to Wright for stressing this doctrine of *no necessity*. It was at least half the clue to the solution of their problem. This indebtedness was fully conscious on the part of some of the members, as is shown in a proposal for a memorial made by Peirce to William James on the death of Wright in 1875. Peirce wrote in a letter to James that "His memory deserves it for he did a great deal for every one of us . . . . I mean you, Frank Abbot and myself."[12] What it was that he did for the members was stated by one of them, Oliver Wendell Holmes, fifty years after Wright's death: "Chauncey Wright, a nearly forgotten philosopher of real merit, taught me when young that I must not say *necessary* about the universe, that we don't know whether anything is necessary or not."[13] The denial of necessity runs consistently throughout the works of Peirce, Holmes, Fiske and James.

As Wright, himself, put it: "No *real* fate or necessity is indeed manifested anywhere in the universe,—only a phenomenal regularity."[14] To rationalize this repudiation of objective necessity, he had to appeal to British empiricism, and specifically to Berkeley. He had to make the whole of science a matter of *facts* alone, not laws; and he had to reduce these facts to useful practical instruments bearing on the "particular goods or ends of human life" and having nothing to do with objective truth. "True science," he writes, "deals with nothing but questions of facts: If the facts are determined, and, as far as may be, free from moral biases, then practical science comes in to determine what, in view of the facts, our feelings and rules of conduct ought to be; but practical science has no inherent postulates any more than speculative science. Its ultimate grounds are the particular goods or ends of human life."[15] The ultimate ground of science is not the correspondence with the objective material world, but is merely the practical effects. A "fact" is not true or false, but only useful or useless to the conduct of human life.

To Wright, science is science of the objects of knowledge, and the objects of knowledge are mental states. This is pure subjective idealism, pure Berkeley, as Wright well knew. In a letter written to Abbot in 1868 he answers a question put to him by the former: "Secondly, you surprise me by asking if Idealism is not 'the very negation of objective science?' . . . There is nothing in positive science, or the study of phenomena and their laws, which idealism conflicts with (See Berkeley). Astronomy is just as real a science, as true an account of phenomena and their laws, if phenomena are only mental states, as on the other theory."[16]

Abbot was, of course, right; the Wright-Berkeley idealism does constitute "the very negation of objective science." But Wright tries to cover this stubborn fact by the usual distinction between "phenomena and noumena" in which "phenomena" means effects on human beings, namely the object is what it is known as, or is what it is used for. In this way the phenomenal object is regarded as nothing but a mental state. Since this is all that can be known, it then becomes mere guess-work to posit a "real" object, a thing-in-itself, a noumenon, lying behind the mental object. Thus to the idealist, science is the science of mental objects, of phenomena, not of material objects, of real objects, as it is for the materialist. According to this one-sided, reactionary view all that human beings can know is their own ideas, the mental objects or mental states which exist only in their own minds. Wright makes this point perfectly clear in this same letter to Abbot when he speaks about "that important doctrine of positivism—the relativity of knowledge— that the only objects immediately known are really mental states, effects in us which we attribute, according to their connections, either to a self or to an external world, without further capacity for knowing more about their subjects."[17]

This is the heart of the theory on which pragmatism is based. It is the denial of science through the denial of the "external world." If science is simply the science of "mental states," of the "object" as it affects human beings, then there is no possibility of objective knowledge, that is, knowledge of external material objects as they exist independently of consciousness and experience. The theory of evolution, therefore, is reduced to a mere useful organization of mental states, and there can be no question of its truth or falsity, but only of whether or not as an idea it is in fact useful, or expedient, in leading toward "the particular goods or ends of human life."

The subjective idealist, positivist theory is the technical rationalization of the bourgeois denial of necessity in the world, in life and in society. The laws of development of the earth, the laws of development of living things, the laws of development of society are stripped of objective reference, are stripped of truth, and are only so many useful ways of organizing human experience. This frees the bourgeoisie from the necessity of thinking and acting on principle, and clears the way for their doctrine of expediency.

The subjective idealist theory, borrowed by Wright from Berkeley, Hume and British empiricism, likewise carries forward the spurious attack on all metaphysics. For if ideas in the mind have no external object with which to correspond, then the ideas of God, of immortality, of special creation, of external divine moral law, etc., also have no objective reference, and are, together with other ideas, simply useful ways of organizing mental states. They are ideas which "work" for certain purposes. It was this which was bothering Abbot, the theologian. He was worried about and was taking seriously what in reality was only camouflage of the primary target of the attack, the attack on science and materialism. Wright reassured him by saying that "Practical grounds are really the basis of belief in the doctrines of theology."[18] Wright was in effect telling Abbot that the only way theology and religion could continue to have a hold on people was by eliminating science as real knowledge of the real world. In this way superstition could be reinstated without fear of challenge from scientific theory.

Already by 1867 Wright had cleared the way for the formulation of the pragmatic method of expediency in means and ends. It was this clearing away of the concept of necessity together with its rationalization by means of subjective idealist, positivist theory, which Wright had to offer to the other members of the Metaphysical Club.

While the technical *theory* of pragmatism, the positivist rejection of necessity and the affirmation of subjective idealism, were borrowed from British empiricism, the technical formulation of the pragmatic *method* is borrowed primarily from German Idealism, and more particularly from Immanuel Kant, and secondarily from the utilitarianism of Alexander Bain. It was Peirce who brought the Kantian conception of practical knowledge to the club members; and it was Nicholas St. John Green who brought the teaching of Bain to them.

In the closing chapters of his *Critique of Pure Reason,* Kant pointed out that if you cannot have real knowledge on which to base action, and if you have to act, then the action can only be based on *belief.* In other words, if you have an established end or goal, but you do not know what means will of necessity lead to it, then you have to proceed on pragmatic belief; your only alternative is to *believe* that a certain means will reach a given goal. Here is Kant's definition of pragmatic belief:

The physician must do something for a patient in danger, but does not know the nature of his illness. He observes the symptoms, and if he can find no more likely alternative, judges it to be a case of phthisis. Now even in his own estimation his belief is contingent only; another observer might perhaps come to a sounder conclusion. Such contingent belief, which yet forms the ground for actual employment of means to certain actions, I entitle *pragmatic belief.*[19]

For Kant there were ways of knowing with certainty, and therefore pragmatic belief was not for him the only basis for action. For the members of the Metaphysical Club, however, with their formulation of the class view of life and mode of thought, the situation was different. In their formulation, there was *no necessity* in the world, and in fact there was no objective world, therefore there could be *no certainty* in knowledge, and, in fact, no knowledge. Thus the pragmatic theory makes the method of pragmatic belief the only possible one. What for Kant was an exception, became for the pragmatists the iron-clad rule. People would be forced to substitute belief for knowledge as the basis for action. Pragmatism is indeed the return to previous forms of ignorance, the reinstitution of superstition.

It was this Kantian doctrine which Peirce brought as his contribution to the technical formulation of bourgeois philosophy in the United States. But pragmatic belief combined with Berkeleyan subjective idealism was something professional philosophy had not seen before.

The pragmatic belief of Kant rooted in the subjective idealism of Berkeley and emerging as pragmatism was the technical, formulated philosophy most perfectly corresponding to the view of life and mode of thought of the rising monopoly capitalist class in the United States.

Of the character of the thinking of the members of the Metaphysical Club, Peirce wrote years later: "The type of our thought was decidedly British. I, alone of our number, had come upon the threshing-floor of philosophy through the doorway of Kant, and even my ideas were acquiring the British accent."[20] In short, Kant was becoming Berkeleyan, and Berkeley was becoming Kantian. The marriage has endured for some eighty years now.

The pragmatic method of belief in means to ends was also introduced to the group by Nicholas St. John Green. He kept insisting that Bain's definition of belief was highly pertinent. That definition of belief was "that upon which a man is prepared to act." Of Green, Peirce wrote: "In particular, he often urged the importance of applying Bain's definition of belief, as 'that upon which a man is prepared to act.' From this definition, pragmatism is scarce more than a corollary; so that I am disposed to think of him as the grandfather of pragmatism."[21] Kant and Peirce had pointed out that without knowledge action must be based on pragmatic belief. Now Green and Bain point out that belief means "that upon which a man is prepared to act." The latter, taken together with the Peirce-Kantian doctrine of pragmatic belief and the Wright-Berkeleyan doctrine of subjective idealism, rounds out the technical equipment required for formulating the philosophy of the U.S. capitalist class, for the working out of the formal philosophy of pragmatism. The task of putting all these elements together fell first to the lot of Peirce.

II. CHARLES S. PEIRCE:
THE THREE METHODS
OF PRAGMATISM

WE HAVE seen what economic, political and intellectual conditions preceded and prepared the way for Peirce's formulation of pragmatic philosophy. We turn to the two articles published in *The Popular Science Monthly* in the year 1878.[1]

The first of these articles is entitled "The Fixation of Belief." We are now in position to make sense of the title itself. For if there is no such thing as knowledge, and if people must act, as they must to go on living, then belief is the only possible ground for such action. But how can they know what to believe in? They can't *know*, and therefore the problem is how belief is fixed in people. This is obviously an important subject for the ruling class. How can belief of the *right kind* be fixed in people? We will see that it is precisely this question which is central in Peirce's thinking. The secondary question is how people can be prevented from believing in the *wrong kind* of thing. Wrong beliefs, in the eyes of the dominant economic element in a dying system, are those which are not simply beliefs but which are for the most part also truths. So the problem becomes how to prevent people from believing the truths of science, both natural and social. Both of these problems are dealt with in the two essays, the second of which is called "How to Make Our Ideas Clear." We will see that Peirce succeeds very well in making *his* ideas clear.

In the articles, Peirce is concerned not with knowledge and ignorance but with "the sensation of doubting and that of believing." For "Our beliefs guide our desires and shape our actions," while doubt blocks both. The guide to action is not theory but belief. The problem then is how to fix belief. But what is belief? We remember the definition given by Bain and Green that "belief is that upon which a man is prepared to act." Peirce gives it a slightly new twist. He says it is a "habit" which determines action. Belief is a habit of acting in a given way, while doubt is the interruption of such a habit. "The essence of belief," Peirce says, "is the establishment of a habit."[2] It is the establishmet of "some habit which will determine our actions."[3] Doubt disrupts the habit and "causes a struggle to attain a state of belief."[4] This struggle to move from doubt to belief so that habit may lead to action is what Peirce calls "inquiry" or "thought." The function of thought is not the attainment of knowledge but is solely "the settlement of opinion," the "fixation of belief."[5] The "production of belief," he says, "is the sole function of thought."[6]

Peirce's Theory of Truth

Where does truth come in? The answer is that it doesn't. What is believed in is what is called "the truth." To say that we should believe only the truth, is, according to Peirce and pragmatism, simply nonsense; it is circular or tautological reasoning. For the truth for us is what we believe, and what we believe is for us the truth. Thus he says: "Hence, the sole object of inquiry is the settlement of opinion. We may fancy that this is not enough for us, and that we seek not merely an opinion, but a true opinion. But put this fancy to the test, and it proves groundless; for as soon as a firm belief is reached we are entirely satisfied, whether the belief be false or true. . . ."[7] The settlement of opinion into belief is the goal of thought. We can call this "truth" if we want to, but it would merely be using a synonym. To speak of a "true belief" is simply redundant, for both terms have the same meaning. Belief is "truth" and "truth" is belief and belief is a habit of action; therefore "truth" is a habit of action, and nothing more nor less. The opposite of belief is doubt; but belief is "truth"; therefore the opposite of "truth" is not falsity but doubt. The function of thought or inquiry is to settle the struggle between doubt on the one side and belief, habit, and action on the other.

The fixation of belief means the fixation of a habit of action, and this is the function of inquiry, scientific, or otherwise.

"That the settlement of opinion is the sole end of inquiry," says Peirce, "is a very important proposition." This is, if anything, a gross understatement. It is indeed a highly important proposition, for inherent in it is the flat denial of the real function of scientific inquiry, namely, the discovery of objective truth. The proposition is the complete repudiation of scientific theory and truth; it is the rejection of any possibility of reflection in consciousness of the laws of development of objective material nature and society. The proposition *is* important, for it is imperative to grasp fully its reactionary and vicious significance. For example, if a group of people come to the agreement that they believe the lies of white chauvinism, that makes white chauvinism a truth, even though science and history prove their belief to be based on lies, to have no correspondence to objective fact.

Peirce, himself, throughout the remainder of the two articles demonstrates just how vicious and reactionary the doctrine is. He goes on to elaborate three methods of "fixation of belief" or of "settlement of opinion."

The Method of Tenacity

The first is what he calls "the method of tenacity." The essential content of this first method is that since there is no real knowledge or truth one might as well believe whatever one wants to believe. For there is nothing which could prove one wrong, nothing which could show that one's belief was not true. If belief is the whole goal of thought, and if there is no such thing as true or false, what can possibly stand in the way of believing whatever one *wills to believe?*

To the pragmatist the only possible criterion of the method of tenacity is whether it in fact succeeds, whether it works in fixing belief. If it works, or whenever and wherever it works, it is just as good as any other method. Philosophy has a name for this kind of thinking; it is called "voluntarism." It is the doctrine that if you believe what you want to believe with sufficient tenacity, it will come to exist for you. Voluntarism is the logical end product of the pragmatic method. Peirce describes it as follows: "If the settlement of opinion is the sole object of inquiry, and if belief is of the nature of a habit, why should we not attain the desired end, by taking any answer to a question, which we may fancy, and constantly reiterating it to ourselves, dwelling on all which may conduce to that belief, and learning to turn with contempt and hatred from anything which might disturb it?"[3]

He goes on to admit that if it succeeds there is nothing which could gainsay such a method: "A man may go through life, systematically keeping out of view all that might cause a change in his opinions, and if he only succeeds . . . I do not see what can be said against his doing so. It would be an egotistical impertinence to object that his procedure is irrational, for that only amounts to saying that his method of settling belief is not ours. . . . So let him think as he pleases."[9]

Anybody's opinion or belief is as good as anyone else's, for there is no truth. The above statement is a complete admission of the bankruptcy of pragmatism. It makes clear that pragmatism opens the way to any and all superstitious, obscurantist notions, with no basis on which to combat them. It will, and it must, accept anything if only it works for some one, for some group or some class. Believe anything that is useful, for there is nothing that can deny it or prove you wrong.

Peirce has an individual repugnance to the voluntarist method of tenacity. *He* would never follow such a method. He is an intellectual, a scientist. He writes of it with tongue in cheek. But this is completely irrelevant. What *is* relevant is that the pragmatic philosophy has to accept this method, along with the other two, which are even more anti-scientific, because pragmatic philosophy cannot combat ignorance or superstition even if it desired to. If this tenacity method works in fixing belief, what is to stop it? Certainly not Peirce or pragmatism or the capitalist class. All have a vested interest in both ignorance and superstition.

For Peirce and pragmatism there is only one thing which limits the effectiveness of the will to believe anything one wants. It does not always work. It runs into doubt because individuals meet others who do not share their beliefs. This sets up hesitations which may destroy the habit of action which is the belief. Only failure can limit the method of tenacity. And repeated failures have led to the necessity for a more effective method, one which is not limited to the individual but will be the fixation of belief in the community. The method of tenacity leads to doubt which can only be removed by fixing belief socially rather than individually. "So that," argues Peirce, "the problem becomes how to fix belief, not in the individual merely, but in the community."[10]

The second and third methods for the fixation of belief are methods of fixing it in the community. One is designed to fix belief in the great masses of the people and is called by Peirce "the method of authority."

The other is the method reserved for the select few, the intelligentsia, and is called ironically "the method of science."

The Method of Authority

The method of authority is the political fixation of beliefs backed by the organized force and violence of the state. Peirce's description of it reminds one of the great political struggles that took place in the period from 1860 to 1878, such as the attacks on the abolition movement, the labor strikes of the seventies and their brutal suppression, and the lynch offensive against the rising Negro nation in the South. It also sheds light on the comparatively minor question as to the awareness of the early formulators of pragmatism of what they in fact were doing. Here is Peirce's exposition of the fixation of belief through the method of authority:

> Let the will of the state act, then, instead of that of the individual. Let an institution be created which shall have for its object to keep correct doctrines before the attention of the people, to reiterate them perpetually, and to teach them to the young, having at the same time power to prevent contrary doctrines from being taught, advocated or expressed. Let all possible causes of a change of mind be removed from men's apprehensions. Let them be kept ignorant, lest they should learn of some reason to think otherwise than they do. Let their passions be enlisted, so that they may regard private and unusual opinions with hatred and horror. Then, let all men who reject the established belief be terrified into silence. Let the people turn out and tar and feather such men, or let inquisitions be made into the manner of thinking of suspected persons, and, when they are found guilty of forbidden beliefs, let them be subjected to some signal punishment. When complete agreement could not otherwise be reached, a general massacre of all who have not thought in a certain way has proved a very effective means of settling opinion in a country. If the power to do this be wanting, let a list of opinions be drawn up, to which no man of the least independence of thought can assent, and let the faithful be required to accept all these propositions, in order to segregate them as radically as possible from the influence of the rest of the world.[11]

It may be thought that Peirce is presenting the method of authority for the purpose of ridicule and rejection. But such a notion is a complete misunderstanding and underestimation of the character and role of pragmatism as the formulated philosophy of the capitalist class. If fixation of belief is the sole function of thought, and if this terrorist method of authority is effective in fixing belief, if, in short, it works, there is no other criterion, such as truth and progress and morality, which could provide a basis for rejecting it. For pragmatism and the capitalist class it is not only perfectly acceptable, but it is the best method, for it has proved in the past to be the most successful. Here we see the full viciousness of the philosophy. From its inception, pragmatism has within its character the potentiality of becoming the philosophy of fascism.

Though he does not indicate it in the articles, Peirce may have had a personal repugnance to the method of authority. Perhaps he would not have advocated it, as an individual. But certainly he never protested in actual life against its employment by the bourgeoisie. This is perfectly consistent with his philosophy, for on what principled basis as a pragmatist could he have voiced a protest or waged a struggle?

In these articles, far from castigating and repudiating the method of authority, Peirce has nothing but praise and commendation for it. He compares it to the method of tenacity, and as would be expected, the only basis for such comparison is the relative degree of success achieved by each method. He remarks: "In judging this method of fixing belief, which we may call the method of authority, we must in the first place, allow its immeasurable mental and moral superiority to the method of tenacity. Its success is proportionally greater; and in fact it has over and over again worked the most majestic results."[12] It is mentally and morally superior because it is more successful in fixing belief. The only "principle" of either morality or thought is expediency, namely the success in attaining the goal. The end, the fixation of belief, justifies any means whatever.

Peirce admits the class character of the method of authority: "Wherever there is aristocracy, or a guild, or any association of a class of men whose interests depend or are supposed to depend on certain propositions, there will be inevitably found some traces of this natural product of social feeling."[13] Reliance by ruling classes on the method of authority is both natural and inevitable, and there is nothing that can be done about it. Thus when pragmatism finds it expedient to talk in terms of natural inevitability, it forgets all about its underlying thesis that there is no such thing as necessity or inevitability. The terrorism of the ruling class is inevitably part of the nature of things, so the people must bow to it. The method of authority is always accompanied by cruelty and often by atrocities, but this is "natural." "Cruelties," writes Peirce, "always accompany this system; and when it is consistently carried out, they become atrocities of the most horrible kind in the eyes of any rational man."[14] Ruthlessness, cruelties and atrocities are the "natural product" of the fact that "the officer of a society does not feel justified in surrendering the interests of that society for the sake of mercy. It is natural therefore that sympathy and fellowship [presumably for the "interests of that society."—*H.K.W.*] should thus produce a most ruthless power."[15] The sympathy and fellowship of a class for itself *naturally* makes it dispense with mercy and rely instead on ruthless power.

Pragmatically evaluated, the method of authority is the best method for fixing in the minds of the people the beliefs required by the ruling class. It is the best because it is the most successful. It is the means to the end which works most efficiently. As Peirce puts it: "For the mass of mankind, then, there is perhaps no better method than this. If it is their highest impulse to be intellectual slaves, then slaves they ought to remain."[16] And pragmatism is the philosophy to help maintain slavery, economic and political as well as ideological.

Peirce sees the method of authority not as something which is resorted to only now and then, but as being the normal and *necessary* condition of social existence. The masses must always be governed by it. "The method of authority," he says, "will always govern the mass of mankind."[17] And he adds that "those who wield the various forms of organized force in the state will never be convinced that dangerous reasoning ought not to be suppressed in some way."[18] He concludes that "the method of authority is the path of peace!"[19] Here "peace," in the light of all the foregoing, is obviously a euphemism for keeping the people down and preventing progress.

The method of authority and the method of tenacity are two sides of one coin. They play neatly into one another. The will to believe prepares the way for belief on the basis of authority and terror. Both methods are rooted in a theory which denies that the function of thought is to gain knowledge and truth, and which substitutes the proposition that the sole function of thought is the fixation of belief. It is a philosophy which expresses and meets the requirements of U.S. imperialism. For in substituting the fixation of belief for the scientific discovery of truth, pragmatism tills the soil for the mass sowing of lies. By repetition, intimidation and terror, imperialism seeks to make people believe that war is peace and that police-state violence is democracy. Peirce's two methods of tenacity and violence constitute the intellectual reflection and justification of the actual methods employed by imperialism. The fixation of belief is the sole objective of imperialist ideology; the philosophy of pragmatism is its rationale.

The Method of Science

In these first two methods advanced by Peirce, he is open and unabashed in apologizing for the obscurantism required by the ruling class. But in the third and final one he tries to conceal the essence of what he is advocating. He resorts to demagogy. What he calls "the method of science" is designed to have us think that some beliefs can in fact be called "true or false." It is here that we find the camouflage flung over the character and role of pragmatic philosophy.

Peirce does not claim that the "scientific method" for the fixation of truth is ever to be an affair of the masses. Rather, it is reserved for the intellectual minority, the elite who are not satisfied with the crude methods either of tenacity or of authority. It is for those who travel and read and who thus come to know that there are other beliefs than those current in their own time and place. Such experience leads to doubt and thus to inhibition of action. But the ruling class requires that the intellectuals be prepared to think and act in the "right" way also, so that a different method of fixing belief in them is required. For these exceptional individuals "It is necessary that a method should be found by which our beliefs may be caused by nothing human, but by some external permanency—by something upon which our thinking has no effect."[20]

It appears at first sight that this third method of fixing belief, the fixing of belief in the intelligentsia, will be objective, based on scientific theory and on truth as a reflection of independent reality. And that is precisely what Peirce would have us think. But we must beware, for camouflage is being pulled over pragmatic obscurantism. Peirce is going to *talk* about "science," and about "truth" and even about "reality."

Thus Peirce speaks of belief being fixed, in "the method of science," "by some external permanency—by something upon which our thinking has no effect." It sounds almost like scientific materialism, almost as though an objective world with its reflection in human consciousness was being affirmed. But Peirce goes on to elaborate his meaning: "Our external permanency would not be external, in our sense, if it was restricted in its influence to one individual."[21] Notice that he speaks of "external, *in our sense,*" and then adds, "if it was restricted in its influence to one individual." Already in this one sentence we have the clue to the subterfuge he is to employ. It is the key to Peirce's formula for concealing the fact that his philosophy is the denial of external reality. It is his way out of the so-called egocentric predicament in which the world is simply "my" experience. What he seems to be saying is that the world is not *my* experience but *our* experience. In this way he would have us think that he is attacking and rejecting subjective idealism; namely, that to be is to be perceived by me. But in fact he is simply making a slight revision of the old form of subjective idealism by saying *to be is to be perceived by us*. Peirce is saying the world is not *my* creation but *our* creation. The essence of his formula is the substitution of mankind solipsism for individual or personal solipsism.*

It is easy to see that the simple substitution of "we" for "I," or of "our" for "my," does not make the world independent of human experience. To say that the world is my experience, or to say that it is our experience, is in each case to deny the objectivity of the real world. In either case there would be no objective material world and thus there would be no reflection of it in consciousness and no way of testing the truth or falsity of ideas by whether or not they correspond to objective reality.

Human or public solipsism and personal solipsim are, from the point of view of materialism and science, as alike as two peas. Both effectively eliminate science, theory and truth through the denial of objective reality. Hence, in the "method of science," as in the other methods, beliefs will be fixed without reference to knowledge, truth or reality. Once this step is taken, the "method of science" must, like the first two methods, end up in voluntarism, in what one wants to believe.

Opposed to the world view of subjective idealism with its primacy of sensation, experience, idea or belief, is the position of scientific materialism, the position of science and of "naive" humanity: There is an objectively existing material world independent of consciousness, and to which sensations, experiences, ideas and beliefs correspond if they

---

* Solipsism is the philosophical view that I alone exist, and that the rest of the world, including other people, have no objective existence but are creations of my consciousness.

are true. This is the reflection theory of knowledge, of materialism and of Marxism.

Of Peirce's formula for concealing subjective idealism with its egocentric predicament of solipsism, John Dewey wrote some fifty years later that "This is the pragmatic way out of the egocentric predicament."[22] And Peirce's formula is at the same time Dewey's. Neither Peirce nor Dewey can escape the self-created, or man-created universe. All they can do is to try to camouflage the degeneracy of their thinking.

Let us see how Peirce attempts to conceal the real meaning of his formula. This "method of science" involves two key concepts of pragmatism: (1) the pragmatic principle and (2) the definition of "reality" and "truth."

To examine the device Peirce employs to cloak his positivist theory we must return to what James called the "principle of pragmatism," cited at the beginning of the present chapter: An object is what effects it has on us through our sensations. Thus Peirce says, "Our idea of anything *is* our idea of its sensible effects."[23] But sensible effects are known only by the habits they produce. Thus the meaning of an object is its sensible effects, and the sensible effects lead to a habit of action which is a belief. The meaning of a thing is therefore the beliefs it evokes. Or another way of saying the same thing is, "what a thing means is simply what habits it involves."[24]

For example, if the question is concerned with the meaning of "fear," then, applying the pragmatic method, fear is defined by how it works in practice. It is how it affects human conduct. Thus it would be cold sweat, a choked-up feeling, running away, etc. Fear would not be defined as a reaction to something in the objective world which causes fear, such as unemployment, poverty and sickness, police brutality or lynching. It would rather be purely subjective. Fear would be what the sensation, via habits of action in the form of beliefs, leads one to do to express the fear. As a matter of fact, William James in his work on psychology develops this "theory" of the nature of emotions. The usefulness of such a theory to the ruling class is obvious.

This "principle of pragmatism" is the heart of Peirce's "method of science." While the principle itself is based upon a denial of the objective material world and truth, he nevertheless employs it to deny their existence.

Meaning of "Reality" and "Truth" for Peirce

Anxious to establish this "scientific" method for the intelligentsia "by which beliefs may be caused . . . by some external permanency," Peirce has already given us a clue as to the mankind solipsism which will supposedly free him from the egocentric predicament. Thus Peirce goes on to say of the external, "It must be something which affects, or might affect, every man."[25] He makes it clear here that external does not mean independent of human experience, but rather dependent on it. It means something which affects, not only myself, but others too.

He presents the "fundamental hypothesis" of the "method of science" for fixing beliefs, thus: "there are real things, whose characters are entirely independent of our opinions about them . . . we can ascertain by reasoning how things really are, and any man, if he have sufficient experience and reason enough about it, will be led to the one true conclusion."[26] It might appear that we were mistaken about Peirce. Here he is talking about reality and truth and "objects whose characters are entirely independent of our opinions about them." We must examine what he means by *reality* and *truth*.

Reality is the key concept, for without it there can be no such thing as truth. Without a reality which is independent of thought and experience, ideas and theories would have no external object with which to correspond, and truth would be eliminated.

Peirce recognizes the central role of the concept of reality when he remarks immediately following the above passage that "The new concept here involved is that of 'reality'."[27] He goes on to say that "It may be asked how I know that there are any realities."[28] Scientific materialism answers this question by pointing out first that the capitalist class has a basic political reason for raising the issue because of its fear of knowledge and truth in the hands of the people and particularly of the working class; and secondly, that the tremendous progress made by social labor in developing the forces of production, achieving greater and greater control over nature and society, is absolute and incontrovertible proof that human beings know the reality of the material world. But Peirce answers his own question with the enigmatic statement that "if investigation cannot be regarded as proving that there are real things, it at least does not lead to a contrary conclusion."[29] He might on this evidence alone be called an agnostic, one who does not know whether or not there is a real world, and who therefore leaves the way open for idealism and religion. We still do not know what he means by "reality." We must look further to find out.

He goes on to define the real: "Thus we may define the real as that whose characters are independent of what anybody may think them to be."[30] This again sounds materialist; there is, however, a "but." "But," says Peirce, "however satisfactory such a definition may be found, it would be a great mistake to suppose that it makes the idea of reality perfectly clear."[31] The definition was too clear. Peirce must go on to remove the materialist implication.

Applying the general rule of the pragmatic principle to the concept of reality, Peirce says: "Reality, like every other quality, consists in the peculiar sensible effects which things partaking of it produce. The only effect which real things have is to cause belief, for all the sensations which they excite emerge into consciousness in the form of beliefs."[32] Reality, then, is what reality makes people do. But action is the result of a "habit of action." Thus reality is a habit of action. But in turn, a habit of action is Peirce's definition of belief. Therefore, reality for Peirce can only be whatever is believed. Then whatever is belived, or is fixed as belief, is reality. *The real is what we believe and what we believe is real.* Reality is thus clearly dependent on human beings, on their beliefs. It is internal, not external to human nature. To have a belief is to have a habit of action; therefore, reality is a habit of action. We act as though a thing were real.

Thus, the fixation of belief could just as well be called the fixation of reality. For belief and reality, according to Peirce, are one and the same thing. *But for him a thing is real because we believe it; we do not believe it because it is real.*

This conclusion about reality as belief is identical with the method of tenacity, except for one little detail. The word "we" has been substituted for the "I" of the tenacity method. The real is what *we* believe, not simply what *I* believe. It is the fixation of public rather than private belief.

But what is the difference between the "method of science" and the "method of authority?" Both fix public belief. The difference is that one relies on force and violence and is the method which is "best for the masses," while the other relies on the "market-place of ideas," on the exchange of ideas or beliefs in the course of which perhaps some one or another idea gets settled on as a general belief by all who look into the matter. What is believed by the majority of the people in the intellectual market place is considered as true. *The criterion of truth is majority belief.* This, of course, is not the criterion of truth as materialists and scientists define it. By truth we mean that which corresponds to the objective material world regardless of whether the majority of people at any given moment recognize it to be true.

Thus, for Peirce, reality is what people who *think* agree to believe, after considerable thought and exchange, and after inquiring whether the beliefs are consistent with one another. The only question is one of self-consistency and non-contradiction, not one of correspondence or non-correspondence to objective reality.

Peirce's denial of reality lays the basis for his denial of truth. We would suspect that according to him truth, like reality, would be whatever is in fact believed. It would be belief, as a habit of action. Whatever is "real" is "true," and whatever is "true" is "real," and both "reality" and "truth" are whatever people believe.

What does Peirce actually say? "The opinion which is fated to be ultimately agreed to by all who investigate," he states, "is what we mean by the truth, and the object represented in this opinion is the real. That is the way I would explain reality."[33] "Truth" is what is fated to be believed by all who investigate, and reality is whatever is so believed. "Reality" is completely dependent on human consciousness, namely on belief or in other words on habits of action. Thus "truth" can have no meaning, for there is no reality to which ideas can correspond. Therefore "truth," "reality" and consciousness—in the form of beliefs—are all one and the same. "Reality" is a reflection of consciousness, not vice versa. The world is seen by Peirce as created by consciousness, not consciousness as a product of the material world. This is, of course, the central doctrine of subjective idealism.

Peirce anticipates the charge that his notion of "reality" is subjectivist and is therefore in contradiction with his previous definition of it as that which is "independent of what anybody may think of it." In attempting to meet the charge, he fully substantiates it:

But it may be said that this view is directly opposed to the abstract definition which we have given of reality, inasmuch as it makes the characters of the real depend on what is ultimately thought about them. But the answer to this is that, on the one hand, reality is independent not necessarily of thought in general, but only of what you or I or any finite number of men may think about it; and thus, on the other hand, though the object of the final opinion depends on what that opinion is, yet what that opinion is does not depend on what you or I or any man thinks.[34]

This is the closest approximation to a flat statement by a pragmatist that reality depends on thought in general. There can be no doubt about its meaning. "Reality" is independent solely of what you or I may think, but in no sense is it independent of thought or consciousness in general. It is entirely dependent on, and created by, human belief.

This is the crudest kind of solipsism. Man creates the universe, not vice versa. The public solipsism is itself a crude subtlety, for how does any individual know that other individuals exist? On the basis of Peirce's denial of reality, there can be no such knowledge. Thus an individual can only *believe* that others exist. *Therefore public solipsism collapses into personal solipsism;* and Dewey's statement about "pragmatism's way out of the egocentric predicament" blows up in his face. Public or shared belief only appears to be a way out of solipsism, or rather, it is simply an attempt to camouflage the subjectivist view, the pragmatic method, for only thus can the basis be laid for the fixation of belief as a substitute for genuine scientific method. With the denial of truth, knowledge, and science, the way is clear for the doctrine of sheer expediency in means and ends, the doctrine that the end justifies the use of any means.

All three methods for the fixation of belief are rooted in the non-existence of any reality or truth which could give the lie to what the ruling class finds it expedient that the people should believe. Thus Peirce has succeeded in formulating the view of life and mode of thought of the capitalist class, even though he may have thought of the project as one of meeting the challenge of evolution to the cherished doctrines of theology. In resolving the intellectual problem, he solved the ideological problem, the technical formulation of the bourgeois outlook as a weapon against the working class and its allies.

Peirce's formulation of pragmatism contains in itself the germ for all the formulations to follow. The three methods for the fixation of belief exhaust the possibilities of the pragmatic method. Those who followed after Peirce merely elaborated one or another of the three. William James developed the method of tenacity into the will to believe. John Dewey developed the "method of science" into his so-called "instrumentalist" brand of pragmatism. And finally, the method of authority is today the philosophy of U.S. fascism. From its inception with Peirce, the technical formulation of pragmatism was well adapted to serve any and all predatory purposes of the capitalist class in the era of imperialism.

But when the first formulation of pragmatism appeared in Peirce's two articles in 1878, the event was unheralded and the technical philosophy remained dormant for some twenty years. Not until it was rediscovered by William James in 1898 did the formal philosophy of pragmatism begin its spectacular career.

In his book, *Pragmatism,* published in 1907, James reviewed the historic destiny of what he called "The principle of Peirce, the principle of pragmatism": "It lay entirely unnoticed by any one for twenty years, until I, in an address before Professor Howison's philosophical union at the University of California, brought it forward again and made a special application of it to religion. By that date (1898) the times were ripe for its reception."[35] What had happened in the course of twenty years, the years between 1878 and 1898, that made "the times ripe" for the formulated philosophy of pragmatism? To discover the answer, we must turn to the economic, political and ideological developments that took place during this score of years.

III. JOHN FISKE:
APOLOGETICS IN HISTORY

As a bourgeois ideologist, William James had no way of understanding how it happened that the formal philosophy of pragmatism, still-born when introduced by Peirce in 1878, caught on like a prairie fire when he himself presented it in 1898. A real science of the history of ideas must look for the answer in changed historical conditions. What changes in the material and spiritual life of society took place during this period to make "the times ripe for its reception?"

This score of years saw the closing of the frontier, the continent "rounded out," the conquest of the internal market, and the Indian peoples mostly destroyed or confined to "reservations." The era of "free land and the trek west" was over. But most important, there had taken place a fundamental and far reaching change in the economic life of the nation. Competitive capitalism, through cut-throat competition itself, with the consequent tremendous growth of the social forces of production, had been concentrated in trusts to such an extent that by the turn of the century it was already a different kind of capitalism; it was monopoly capitalism. Likewise at the close of the century the United States made its inaugural into imperialist wars of aggression with its "intervention" in Cuba culminating in the annexation of Spanish colonial territories. In short, the year 1898 marked the advent of imperialism.

By 1898 the capitalist class with its monopoly combines and its full control of the state stood as the actual political and economic master of the United States. For three decades following the victorious conclusion of the Civil War it had been building and wielding this combined power at the terrible expense of the working population of the nation. Never before in history had there been such ruthless plunder and rape of a continent and a people by its home-grown ruling class.

But the robber-baron capitalists did not get away with all this rapine and plunder without opposition from the workers, the Negro people, the farmers and the small businessmen. The closing decades of the century witnessed some of the sharpest class struggles in history.

Altogether, the twenty years comprised a period of rapid development of monopoly concentration, exploitation and oppression, and of sharp class struggles against them. The interval between the obscure publication of Peirce's articles and the electric reception of James' formulation spanned the quantitative development of, and qualitative transformation into, monopoly capitalism. It was the period of the gestation and birth of U. S. imperialism.

Thus in the decades following the Civil War and up to the close of the century, the capitalist class expanded and consolidated its economic and political stranglehold on the continent and the people. The capitalists were the masters, but not the unchallenged masters of the nation. Throughout the period there was increasing need to protect their growing wealth and power. Their first line of defense was their full control and use of the powers of state. But even this was not enough. In addition the victorious capitalists required new ideological weapons to hold in check the rising tide of popular opposition and militant struggle.

By 1898 "the times were ripe" for the formal philosophy of pragmatism not only because of the fundamental economic and political changes, but also because of far reaching changes in the various phases of bourgeois ideology. Between 1878 and 1898 new theories were developed in most of the spheres of ideology. In each case, the theories developed were the embodiment of the pragmatic world view of the capitalist class.

The primary task of the pragmatists in all fields was to construct a new and more effective apologetics for the system and the class. To accomplish this task they all took a similar approach. The technique was to develop the following three-step argument: First they carried on a super-militant struggle against the absolute idealist or theological form of apologetics in their respective fields. Under the cover of this "struggle" they in fact cut the ground from under materialism and science. The first step thus prepares the way for the second, which is the substitution of the pragmatic method for the method of science. Once science and materialism have been "eliminated" the road is clear for expedience to take the place of truth. The final step is the reinstatement of the content, if not the precise form, of the previous theological type of apologetics. Thus all these ideologists are camouflaged salesmen of theology. They are hired prize-fighters of the capitalist class. In no sense are they seekers after truth.

Some such structure of argument is inevitable, given the class-appointed task of these ideologists. Above all they must apologize for the capitalist class. The problem facing each and everyone of them was that the old, exclusively theological form of bourgeois apology had become obsolete. The toiling masses as a whole could no longer be taken in by it. Thus the bourgeois theoreticians had to find a new form, one which would *appear* to combat the old, while at the same time retaining the essential features of it.

This three-step structure of partisan pragmatic argumentation will become clearer when we see it at work in the various fields. One of the first attempts to construct a new form of apologetics, one better adapted to the requirements of the capitalist class after it had won full control of the state following the Civil War, was made by John Fiske in the field of history. Fiske had been a member of Peirce's Metaphysical Club and thus had been a participant in the discussions which inaugurated the Cambridge school of pragmatism. He was strongly under the influence of the pragmatists including, in addition to Peirce, William James and Oliver Wendell Holmes. His theory of history, however, is not yet fully pragmatic, although it has many of the features of the philosophy.

Fiske's treatment of the subject constitutes something of a transition from the old, openly theological form of apologetics to the new pragmatic form. As such it is an important stage in the rise and development of pragmatism. His theory is particularly noteworthy because it is completely frank and open in its espousal of imperialist reaction. It thereby helps us to see through the demagogy of the later pragmatists.

In addition to pragmatism, Fiske's intellectual equipment included knowledge of the positivism of Comte and the evolutionism of Spencer. This is an interesting combination, the marriage of positivism and evolutionism, the one pseudo-materialist, the other pseudo-evolutionary. Fiske taught Comte's positivism at Harvard and at the same time championed the Spencerian teleological theory of evolution, namely, evolution toward a pre-ordained purposeful goal, with its notions of fate and destiny.

At first glance this combination of positivism and evolutionary destiny seems to be an irreconcilable contradiction. For the special feature of

Comtian positivism is the complete denial of all necessity, of all laws of natural and historical development and their reflection in scientific knowledge, while Spencerian evolutionary destiny holds that there is a necessary pre-ordained course in history. But the contradiction is only apparent, for if there is no real science of history, as positivism maintains, then there is nothing to prevent the assertion of divine planning and God-given destiny if such myths are deemed expedient. Thus Fiske's positivism clears the way for his fictional theory of evolutionary history.

Fiske's Theory of History

What is the structure, then of the three-step argument in Fiske's theory of history? The first step is the attack on the science of history masked under cover of an apparent attack on established theological theories of history. It is the establishment of positivism in the field of historiography. The second step is the establishment of the pragmatic method as a substitute for the scientific historical method. The pragmatic method in history is based on the freedom to invent whatever convenient fiction will serve the purposes of the bourgeoisie in its attempt to preserve and extend its class power. The third and final step in Fiske's argument is the actual fabrication of an historical fiction about "American destiny." This last step reinstates the essence of the theological theory of history, the notion of a divine plan unfolding toward a pre-established goal.

Fiske had been seriously shaken by the Paris Commune and wrote impassioned criticism of "communistic theories" in his book, *Cosmic Evolution*. He charged that communists would "regulate human concerns by *status* and not by contract," and would "smother all individualism under a social tyranny."[1]

Near the close of a century in which a real science of history had been developed, Marxist historical materialism, Fiske denies any possibility of such a science. Historical materialism maintains that history moves through evolution and revolution on the basis of change in the way people make a living. It holds that class struggles reflect the conflict between that which is dying and that which is coming into being in society. "It is not the consciousness of men that determines their existence but, on the contrary, their social existence determines their consciousness."[2] Marx continues: "At a certain stage of their development, the material

forces of production in society come in conflict with the existing relations of production, or—what is but a legal expression for the same
thing—with the property relations within which they had been at
work before. From forms of development of the forces of production
these relations turn into their fetters. Then comes a period of social revolution. With the change of the economic foundation the entire immense
superstructure is more or less rapidly transformed."[3]

Fiske must "destroy" the science of history before he can invent an
apologetic fictional theory. Thus he starts with the positivist denial of
objective historical necessity. He starts with the repudiation of even
the possibility of any science of history. In this way he would free himself
pragmatically to construct fictions serving the purpose at hand.

To see this "theory" of history in action, we turn to a little book
which was exceedingly popular when it first appeared in 1885, *American
Political Ideas,* by John Fiske.[4] Here Fiske begins with the statement
that "government of the United States is not the result of special creation,
but of evolution."[5] But he goes on to say that social evolution is development toward a "supreme end." This "supreme end" is "to insure peaceful
concerted action throughout the Whole, without infringing upon local
and individual freedom in the Parts."[6] And he adds "this has ever been
the chief aim of civilization, viewed on its political side; and we rate the
failure or success of nations politically according to their failure or
success in attaining this supreme end."[7] Where does this "chief aim of
civilization," this "supreme end" come from? From a scientific analysis
of history? From objective laws of social development? No, it is inherent
in "the Manifest Destiny of the Anglo-Saxon Race."[7] History is then
treated as a means to further this racist destiny. We turn to Fiske's
lecture on "Manifest Destiny" included in *American Political Ideas.* This
lecture was delivered several times in England and some forty-five times
in this country from 1880 to 1885.[9]

"Manifest Destiny of the Anglo-Saxon Race"

Fiske opens his lecture by relating a legendary tale of a dinner party
given in Paris by ex-patriate Americans to celebrate the 4th of July. In
the course of the dinner, three toasts were offered by three different
speakers:

"Here's to the United States," said the first speaker, "bounded on the north by British America, on the south by the Gulf of Mexico, on the east by the Atlantic, and on the west by the Pacific Ocean." "But," said the second speaker, "this is far too limited a view of the subject: in assigning our boundaries we must look to the great and glorious future which is prescribed for us by the Manifest Destiny of the Anglo-Saxon Race. Here's to the United States—bounded on the north by the North Pole, on the south by the South Pole, on the east by the rising and on the west by the setting sun." Emphatic applause greeted this aspiring prophecy. But here arose the third speaker—a very serious gentleman from the Far West. "If we are going," said this truly patriotic American, "to leave the historic past and present, and take our manifest destiny into account, why restrict ourselves within the narrow limits assigned by our fellow-countryman who has just sat down? I give you the United States—bounded on the north by the Aurora Borealis, on the south by the precession of the equinoxes, on the east by the primeval chaos, and on the west by the day of judgment!"[10]

The story is told in jest, but with a purpose. Fiske's own position is to be that of the second speaker. The third speaker with his fantastic claims, is merely a foil to make Fiske's proposals seem modest by comparison. Fiske reveals the "supreme end" of evolution as the domination of the world by "the Anglo-Saxon Race." It is in the light of this "Manifest Destiny" that he is going to interpret the course of history. Such a fictional interpretation is designed in turn to help achieve the end. What he is going to maintain is that the "Anglo-Saxon Race" is the guardian and embodiment of the "supreme end" of history, namely the political principle of "unity in the Whole and individualism in the Parts," later to be called the principle of "federalism." This is the "Anglo-Saxon" secret for world domination "from pole to pole and from rising to setting sun."

Two-thirds of the lecture is devoted to the reinterpretation of the history of "western civilization" to serve the end-in-view. His thesis is that the history of Europe and the United States is the story of the struggle of "superior" peoples against "inferior" peoples. Thus the first such struggle was the series of wars fought by Ancient Greece against the "inferior" Asiatic peoples of Persia. Then in turn it was up to the Ancient Romans to fight off the "hordes" of eastern "barbarians," and the Germanic peoples had to beat off the "lowly" Slavic peoples. Then at long last the great "super-race," the "Anglo-Saxons" come on the scene and it was their destiny to ward off the encroachment of the "inferior" French peoples. Finally there was the struggle for the North

American continent in the course of which the "Anglo-Saxons" not only had to eliminate the "inferior and barbaric" Indian peoples, but also the "inferior" Latin nations, the Spanish and the French. All this "evolution" was part of the destiny of the "Anglo-Saxons." As a matter of fact, we are told that the American Revolution of 1776 "only made it apparent to an astonished world that instead of *one* there were now *two Englands,* alike prepared to work with might and main toward the political regeneration of mankind."[11]

The Civil War was not fought to uproot chattel slavery, Fiske maintains, but to uphold the "principle of federalism." "Federalism," he says, "appears as one of the most important contributions that the English race has made to the general work of civilization."[12] What is this great contribution of the "superior race?" We are told:

The principle of federalism is just this:—that the people of a state shall have full and entire control of their own domestic affairs . . . but that as regards matters of common concern between a group of states, a decision shall in every case be reached, not by brutal warfare or by weary diplomacy, but by the systematic legislation of a central government . . . whose decisions can always be enforced, if necessary, by the combined physical power of all the states.[13]

The importance of the Civil War for "Universal History" was that it preserved this principle. "With this principle unimpaired," Fiske says, "there is no reason why any further increase of territory or of population should overtask the resources of our government."[14] Here at last we see why Fiske has established the principle of federalism as the "supreme end" of history. It is not only the gift of the "Anglo-Saxons," but it is far more importantly the formula for the political organization of the world. There is no reason, Fiske is saying, why the United States cannot continue to grow by employing this formula until it encompasses the entire globe.

White Supremacy

Fiske is fully aware that "Anglo-Saxon superiority" is part and parcel of the U.S. drive for world domination. But he is also fully aware of the inseparability of such superiority doctrines from white supremacy. Anglo-Saxon superiority and white supremacy are his twin ideological weapons for moving toward "Manifest Destiny." Speaking of Africa, Fiske says:

"Here is a vast country, rich in beautiful scenery and in resources of timber and minerals, with a salubrious climate and fertile soil, with great navigable rivers and inland lakes, which will not much longer be left in control of tawny lions and long-eared elephants and negro fetish-worshippers."[15] And he goes on to make a prophecy: "Who can doubt that within two or three centuries the African continent will be occupied by a mighty nation of English descent, and covered with populous cities and flourishing farms, with railroads and telegraphs and other devices of civilization as yet undreamed of."[16] Fiske and the imperialists cannot doubt such a sanguine "Manifest Destiny of the Anglo-Saxon Race."

Fiske speaks in the same way about Australia, "a country sparsely peopled by a race of irredeemable savages hardly above the level of brutes." He goes on to talk similarly of New Zealand and the Pacific Islands. Finally he sums up his "history" with further general predictions: "The day is at hand when four-fifths of the human race will trace its pedigree to English forefathers, as four-fifths of the white people in the United States trace their pedigree today. The race thus spread over both hemispheres, and from the rising to the setting sun, will not fail to keep that sovereignty of the sea and that commercial supremacy which it began to acquire when England first stretched its arm across the Atlantic to the shores of Virginia and Massachusetts."[17] Fiske closes this lecture on white supremacy, Anglo-Saxon superiority and world domination by visualizing a United States extending from pole to pole based on the principle of federation: "I believe that the time will come when such a state of things will exist upon the earth, when it will be possible (with our friends of the Paris dinner party) to speak of the UNITED STATES as stretching from pole to pole. . . . Only then can the world be said to be truly Christian."[18]

Such are the depths to which imperialist apologetics in the field of history descend. Fiske's fiction of "federation" and the "United States of Europe" were early versions of Winston Churchill's Council of Europe, Harry Truman's Marshall Plan and Atlantic Pact and imperialist cosmopolitanism, the contempt for national boundaries, peoples and cultures. With Fiske historical writing becomes apology for U.S. imperialist rapine and plunder, and expansion "rounding out" not only the continent but the entire world.

Thus having begun with an attack on the theological theory of history, Fiske ends by reinstating its content. The content of the theological theory is the embodiment of the interests and aims of the ruling class in "the very nature of things." The particular form given by theology to this content is that "the very nature of things" is the eternal will of God. Fiske retains the content but gives it a new form. With him "the very nature of things" becomes the pseudo-biological doctrine of racism. The "superiority" of the white Anglo-Saxon "race" takes the place of the will of God as the source of the "Manifest Destiny" of the ruling class to rule forever and to expand to the four corners of the earth.

For our purposes, the understanding of pragmatism, it is important to grasp the way in which Fiske's historiography expresses the pragmatic philosophy. The pragmatic view of life is expressed by the denial that the study of history must be a science of the objective laws of social development. Once the ground is thus cleared of all historical necessity, it is possible as Fiske does, to create a fictional course of history which will further the interests of the ruling class. The insatiable drive to more and more profit and world domination is held to be the inherent right and power of a "superior race." History has then become primarily apology for exploitation and oppression through the myths and lies of racism, with the central doctrines of "Anglo-Saxon superiority" and "white supremacy."

Fiske is one of those "hired prize-fighters" referred to by Marx who is not interested in truth but only in what is "useful to capital."

Fiske's repudiation of any scientific theory of the past or of the future strips day to day practice of any guidance. It is the doctrine of expediency with the only criterion being the prospect of success or failure in the immediate situation. This is the essence of pragmatism; but it was not invented by Fiske. Rather, he reflects the pragmatic outlook of the capitalist class as it enters the era of imperialism. Today this outlook, in the field of history, is expressed by innumerable "historians," among them Arthur M. Schlesinger, Jr. Schlesinger states the pragmatic approach to history in his *Age of Jackson.* Thus he says we must make "an earnest, tough-minded, pragmatic attempt to wrestle with new problems as they come, without being enslaved by a theory of the past, or by a theory of the future."[19] But this repudiation of real scientific theory is always a prelude to dreaming up expedient myths and lies about "western civilization," "communist imperialism," "red aggression," "third forces," and "America's responsibility for world leadership." This

historical myth-making is the counterpart of the rejection of genuine
historical theory and the meeting "new problems as they come" doctrine.

Charles A. Beard, at least in his later works, was essentially a pragmatic historian. After repudiating his economic determinist theory of
history, Beard came to the conclusion that there could be no such thing
as an historical science. He rejected the possibility of ascertaining true
reality or ultimate meaning. "Any selection and arrangement of facts,"
Beard said in his presidential address to the American Historical Association, "pertaining to any large area of history, either local or world,
race or class, is controlled inexorably by the frame of reference in the
mind of the selector and arranger."[20] Thus an historian uses facts to
invent whatever fictional historical effect he would produce. Written
history, Beard held, was not a science, but an "act of faith."[21] Henry Steele
Commager paraphrases Beard's later theory of history: "The historian
could not know the past; he could only reconstruct such fragments of
it as were fortuitously available to him according to some incoherent
plan which reflected the inescapable limitations of his own mind. . . .
The scientific method, bequeathed by Ranke and embroidered by a
thousand hands, was, Beard insisted, bankrupt, its champions confounded
and bewildered."[22]

If historians cannot know the past but can only weave facts into
plans spun in their minds, then this is indeed a pragmatic positivist approach to history. Facts can be arranged so as to fit any expedient purpose
of the bourgeoisie. Historians, as apologists for U.S. imperialism, can
fit the facts to suit white supremacy and global domination, euphemisti-
cally called "world leadership."

Pragmatism in historiography was a necessary development in shap-
ing an ideology suited to the growing imperialist giant. Fiske's pragmatic
treatment of history went a long way toward cultivating the ideological
ground for the reception of the formal philosophy of pragmatism when
it was presented by James in 1898.

IV. OLIVER WENDELL HOLMES:
APOLOGETICS IN LAW

FISKE WAS not the only member of Peirce's Metaphysical Club to make a contribution to bourgeois ideology. Oliver Wendell Holmes transformed legal theory through incorporating into it the pragmatic outlook.

That Holmes was a pragmatist in legal theory has long been recognized. Henry Steele Commager, for example, writes that Holmes was "the first, and remained the greatest, of legal pragmatists."[1]

In legal theory, as in philosophy and history, the formulation of a pragmatic approach was made under the appearance of meeting the challenge of evolution to traditional doctrine. Evolution, the argument went, had undermined the heretofore accepted theory of natural law. The latter taught that law was rooted in the very nature of things and that it expressed the will of God and divine reason. Blackstone's *Commentaries* were taken as the legal bible proclaiming that "upon the law of nature and the law of revelation depend all human laws." It was to natural law that the American Revolutionaries appealed in the Declaration of Independence and the Bill of Rights, and to which the Abolitionists appealed in the great struggle against chattel slavery. The Rights of Man were clearly declared to be natural rights, the right to life, liberty and the pursuit of happiness—the inalienable rights. The doctrine of natural law had been the theoretical justification and rallying cry of the bourgeois democratic revolutions of the 18th and 19th centuries. But it had not been employed solely as the theoretical justification of revolutions. It had been utilized also by victorious classes as a sanction for slavery, for legal robbery, for exploitation and oppression buttressed by law.

Following the Civil War, and at least by 1880, the capitalist class, on two counts, required a new legal theory. The old natural law doctrine was, on the one hand, no longer an adequate weapon against the growing proletariat with its rising militancy and its developing class consciousness. The working class, organizing in trade unions and political parties and with socialist fermentation, would not be taken in, as a class, by a doctrine which preached that the laws of the employers were in fact the laws of God and nature. On the other hand, the swiftly concentrating corporations and trusts had of necessity to undermine the doctrine of the natural rights of man. Jefferson and Lincoln in times of revoluionary upheaval had appealed to the natural rights of life, liberty and the pursuit of happiness. But to the capitalist class in full state power these rights had become revolutionary and highly explosive doctrines. That they were natural rights was an idea no longer to be tolerated.

New weapons were required in legal ideology. Regardless of what way the protagonists viewed their tasks, the upshot of their endeavors was to develop new forms of apologetics in legal theory which adequately met the requirements of the ruling class and which are still a most effective weapon against the workers.

Like Peirce in philosophy and Fiske in history, Holmes accomplishes the historic task by rooting his legal "theory" in the outlook and method of pragmatism. Here again, the first step is the positivist denial of objective necessity in law under cover of an attack on the theological theory. The second is the substitution of expediency. The third is the reinstatement of the essence of the theological justification.

Holmes' Bet-abilitarianism

We have already seen, in the previous chapter, that Holmes learned from Chauncey Wright that there is no such thing as the "kingdom of necessity" in the universe. Through Wright he was led to accept the subjective idealist teachings of British empiricism, particularly the doctrines of Berkeley and Hume. Thus he writes in a letter to Pollock: "The fact is that each has his more or less differing system; whether there is an objective reality in which is to be found the unity of our several compulsions or whether our taste in truth is as arbitrary as our taste in coffee and there is no objective truth at all, I leave to philosophers by profession."[2]

By leaving the question to professional philosophers, he leaves himself theoretically without either objective reality or objective truth. With the denial of reality and truth, the way is cleared for the doctrine of subjective experience, and of moving from one experience to another solely in terms of what appears expedient to subjective purpose or desire. Holmes develops his own version of James' voluntarist doctrine that "truth is what I can't help thinking." "My ultimate test of truth," he says, "is that I can't help believing so and so. I have learned by experience that this test is not infallible."[3] This doctrine is the denial of objective truth and is the counterpart of the repudiation of necessity in the universe. On the question of truth, he once wrote, "I used to say, when I was young, that truth was the majority vote of that nation that could lick all others."[4] This is an extension of the doctrine of "might makes right." For Holmes, might also could make "truth," since there was in fact no real truth.

Holmes labeled his own philosophy "bet-abilitarianism," meaning that since, as he learned from Wright, there is no necessity in the universe and hence no certain knowledge or objective truth, then all that can be done is to *bet* that such or such will happen. "So," he says, "I describe myself as a *bet*abilitarian. I believe that we can *bet* on the behavior of the universe in its contact with us. We bet we can know what it will be. That leaves a loophole for free will—in the miraculous sense—the creation of a new atom of force, although I don't in the least believe in it."[5] Elsewhere he defines a "*bet*abilitarian" as "one who thinks you can bet about it but not know."[6] It is this "know-nothing" theory which underlies all applications of the pragmatic method of expediency. In law it becomes the ability to bet on what the courts will really do. You can not know the structure of the state or of law, but on the basis of experience you can bet that judges will decide so and so in the light of "social convenience."

The structure of the law, which must be reflected in legal theory if it is to be scientific, is stated by Andrei Y. Vyshinsky in his *Law of the Soviet State*: "Law is the totality (a) of the rules of conduct, expressing the will of the dominant class and established in legal order, and (b) of customs and rules of community life sanctioned by state authority— their application being guaranteed by the compulsive force of the state in order to guard, secure, and develop social relationships and social orders advantageous and agreeable to the dominant class."[7]

It is this objectively real structure of the law, and the truthful reflection of it in legal theory, which Holmes and his followers deny. As a matter of fact, the central function of bourgeois legal theorists, whatever their subjective intent, is to conceal the class character of law under cover of phrases about the good of society as a whole. Thus Vyshinsky says: "Bourgeois theories of state and law—irrespective of the subjective aspirations and wishes of those who created those theories —serve the cause of exploitation. . . . [Bourgeois theories of law] disguise the class-exploiting character of bourgeois law. By phrases about 'the general welfare' and 'social' and 'popular' interests, they strive to conceal the fact that bourgeois law, that subtle and poisoned instrument which defends the interests of the exploiters, is oppressive and hostile to the people."[8]

Holmes, himself, was aware of what in fact he was doing, as we shall see when we cite some of his cynical admissions. Also we know that he read at least one book by Karl Marx, for in 1892 he wrote Pollock, saying "I have begun Karl Marx's book, but although he strikes me as a great man I can't imagine a combination less to my taste than Hegel and political economy." The reference to "Hegel and political economy" is interesting for the "Hegel" stands for *logic* or *structure,* which Holmes repudiated, while the political economy stands for the scientific understanding of capitalism and the inevitability of socialism, which Holmes feared and hated above all else.

Law Based on Expediency

In his first and perhaps most famous book, *The Common Law,* Holmes opens with the oft-quoted sentence: "The life of the law has not been logic, it has been experience."[9] This is a subtle statement and contains the heart of the pragmatic theory of the law. It is subtle because it can at first sight appear progressive. It would seem to be a repudiation of theological and absolutist metaphysical notions. But in fact it is an attack on all structure or logic within the law, not simply the traditional one. Thus under the cover of attack on all metaphysics, Holmes attacks the only conception which could make a science of legal theory, namely the *class structure* of the logic of the law.

If the "life of the law" is "experience" then it is whatever human experience wants it to be. It is what society finds to be "convenient": "The substance of the law at any given time pretty nearly corresponds, so far as it goes, with what is then understood to be convenient."[10] And standards of judgment about the law depend on "the degree to which it is able to work out desired results."[11] "Convenient" is another name for "expedient" and thus the life of the law is whatever is found to be expedient in the experience of the society. Holmes explains the evolution of the law by "considerations of what is expedient for the community concerned."[12] "Community" is a general term used to camouflage the class character of what Holmes is developing.

The law is not, for Holmes, what is expedient for the capitalist class, but "for the community concerned." The use of force by the law is related to public needs and welfare, not to class requirements: "The police power extends to all the great public needs. It may be put forth in aid of what is sanctioned by usage, or held by the *prevailing morality* or the *strong and preponderant opinion to be greatly and immediately necessary to the public welfare.*" There is law and a policing force to back it up because "when men live in society, a certain average of conduct, a sacrifice of individual peculiarities going beyond a certain point, is necessary to the general welfare."[14] The history of the law is the story of "every painful step and world-shaking contest by which mankind has fought and worked its way from savage isolation to organic social life."[15] The history of law is not an aspect of the history of class struggle, but is part of the unfolding of "organic social life." As such, laws are concerned with regulating the intercourse of individual and group members of the social organism in such a manner that there is the least amount of friction.

With the repudiation of any "metaphysical" or objective basis for law, either natural rights or class structure, Holmes roots it in sheer expediency. He points out that "the very considerations which judges most rarely mention, and always with an apology, are the secret roots from which the law draws all the juices of life. I mean, of course, considerations of what is expedient for the community concerned."[16] But expediency is a matter of means and ends.

If laws are to be means to ends, how are the ends established? To conceal the true end toward which laws are expedient, he says that, "The real justification of a rule of law is that it helps bring about a social end which we desire."[17] The ends are established by social desire, by "the community concerned." It is "the social end which is aimed at by a rule of law."[18] Thus the law is an instrument for social progress with the greatest good of the greatest number as its goal. It is "the public good" which sets the ends to be served by the law.[19] Thus would Holmes conceal the true nature of the law as an instrument of the dominant class to perpetuate, in a class society, its system of exploitation.

But having eliminated any scientific theory of the law and having substituted expediency, Holmes is free to advance fictional theories, just as Fiske did, which would be expedient or useful to capital. "The law," he says, "can ask no better justification than the deepest instincts of man."[20] So now he introduces the "instinct theory" of the law. And what is "the deepest instinct of man?" Naturally it is possession of private property. Thus in *The Common Law* he wrote: "Law, being a practical thing, must found itself on actual forces. It is quite enough, therefore, for the law, that man, by an instinct he shares with the domestic dog, and of which the seal gives a most striking example, will not allow himself to be dispossessed, either by force or fraud, of what he holds, without trying to get it back again. . . . As long as the instinct remains, it will be more comfortable for the law to satisfy it in an orderly manner, than to leave people to themselves."[21] Here we are told that one chief end of the law is the defense of the "instinct" of possession. Thus private property and its protection is an end which is established not by social desire of the community as a whole but by the biological instinct of the possessors. Holmes had made the statement that "the life of the law is experience," and now he says it is "instinct." The two are one side of the same coin. For once scientific theory reflecting the objective structure of the law is dissipated, the way is clear for the invention of any theory which is expedient.

The "instinct theory" of law reinstates the content of the old "natural law" theological doctrine. This content maintained that the laws of the ruling class were not class laws at all, but were legislated by "the nature of things." The particular theological form held that "the nature of things" is divinely ordained. Holmes and the legal pragmatists retained the content, but substituted a new form, one better adapted to modern conditions. They transferred "the nature of things" from the spiritual to the pseudo-biological realm. Inborn instincts became the source of the law.

Elsewhere, Holmes cynically demonstrates that he knows the true source of law and government, namely the dominant power in a community. Thus he reveals the camouflage character of his "public welfare" and "instinct" theories. In a paper on Montesquieu, he writes: "What proximate test of excellence can be found except correspondence to the actual equilibrium of force in the community—that is, conformity to the wishes of the dominant power? . . . the proximate test of a good government is that the dominant power has its way."[22] Elsewhere he explicitly states his class theory of legislation and the law: "The fact is that legislation in this country, as well as elsewhere, is empirical. It is necessarily made a means by which a body, having the power, puts burdens which are disagreeable to them on the shoulders of somebody else."[23] And in a letter he applied this doctrine specifically to the law: "So when it comes to the development of a *corpus juris* the ultimate question is what do the dominant forces in the community want and do they want it hard enough to disregard whatever inhibitions may stand in the way."[24] Holmes knew what kind of society he represented and what the source and origin of the law are, but his legal theory had as its main function the concealment of its class character.

Pragmatic Legal Practice

For our purposes, Holmes' general theory that the law is based on considerations of expediency or convenience for the community concerned, is of primary importance. But there is much more to his formulation of pragmatism in legal theory. He develops the pragmatic approach in the actual workings of the courts and in the arguing of cases. For example, a judge makes a decision, not as he may think on the basis of a body of pre-existing law and precedents, but by "prophesying" what the "social consequences" of his ruling will be. Thus the law does not look to *origins* but to *outcomes*. Rules of law and precedents are merely "sanctions added afterward" to justify the ruling.[25] In short, judges make their decisions on the basis of a prediction as to how they may *work* in practice. The decision is not based on principle but on possible success or failure in reaching the end in view. As Holmes puts it: "The primary rights and duties with which jurisprudence busies itself again are nothing but prophecies . . . a legal duty so called is nothing but a prediction that if a man does or omits certain things he will be made to suffer in this or that way ·by judgment of the court."[26] In this way, the courts are not so much instruments for applying set rules of law; they are rather legislative in function. Thus what cannot be legislated by congress can in fact be achieved by the courts in their decisions based on "social consequences." If the congress could not outlaw strikes and picketing, the courts by their prospective decisions could in fact accomplish it. This is what happened during the 'eighties and 'nineties and right down to the early 'thirties. Holmes in his legal theory is justifying this legislative power of the courts. In this connection, he gives a more precise pragmatic definition of the law as that which "the courts are likely to do in fact." "The prophecies of what the courts will do in fact, and nothing more pretentious, are what I mean by the law."[27] And what the courts will in fact do is determined by "considerations of expediency for the community concerned." And the word "community" is a euphemism to cover the fact that what the courts do depends on what "the dominant forces in the community" want and "how badly they want it."

For lawyers, Holmes' doctrine means that they must advise their clients of how the courts can be expected to act. They must prophesy what decision a judge will make in the light of "social expediency." A lawyer gives his client a "prophecy that if he does certain things he will be subjected to disagreeable consequences by way of imprisonment or compulsory payment of money."[28]

Thus Holmes washes the law "with cynical acid"[29] and strips it of all moral window dressing. He "dispels a confusion between morality and law"[30] and leaves the latter as nothing but expediency. This sounds like hard-headed, business-like realism, until we realize that the doctrine of expediency is meant to cut two ways. On the one hand, as "social expediency" it is the camouflaged doctrine of the law as an instrument of social progress; on the other, it frees the law theoretically from the traditional moral and natural rights doctrines and leaves it unimpeded at the service of the ruling class.

With one blow, Holmes had furnished the capitalist class with the new theoretical legal weapon it required. And he did this under cover of meeting the challenge of evolution to the old legal theories, and of applying "scientific method" to the study of law. What he in fact did was to incorporate the pragmatic view of life and mode of thought into legal theory.

Market Place of Ideas and
Clear and Present Danger

That pragmatism provides a theoretical justification for both bourgeois democracy and fascism is shown by two doctrines. These are "the market-place of ideas" and "the clear and present danger."*

Back in 1878, Peirce had defined truth as "the opinion which is fated to be ultimately agreed to by all who investigate."[31] Holmes developed this into the formula that "the best test of truth is the power of a thought to get itself accepted in the market."[32] Peirce and Holmes here give the subjective idealist test for truth as what is accepted or agreed to, as opposed to the scientific materialist test as the correspondence of an idea to reality tested by social practice.

Holmes utilized this doctrine to justify and veil the harsh class character of the law. He stated that "law embodies beliefs that have triumphed in the battle of ideas."[33] What kind of beliefs does the law embody? Holmes says they are "the felt necessities of the time, the prevalent moral and political theories, intuitions of public policy, avowed or unconscious, even the prejudices which judges share with their fellow men. . . ."[34]

This is Holmes' rationale for bourgeois democracy. With "the market-place of ideas" dominated by the monopolists through their control of the mass propaganda media, all prevailing ideas are termed true and can be made part of the law. Thus, the ruling class forces white chauvinism, male supremacy, religious hatred and other big lies upon the people and claims that these ideas have won out in "the battle of ideas." To give the appearance of a battle, the bourgeoisie permits a few opposition booths to be operated in the bourgeois-controlled market-place. They point to these limited civil liberties as "true freedom" and "American democracy" which they trumpet throughout the world.

When the masses of people, led by the working class, organize real struggles for extending their civil liberties, the monopolists vacillate between repression and concessions. The history of the 1930's in the United States shows how the masses of people wrested concessions from the bourgeoisie through sharp struggle. The legal pragmatists in the

---

* These doctrines can only be briefly discussed here, but a thorough examination of them is an urgent task.

Supreme Court at that time recognized the need for such concessions as vital for the maintenance of imperialist control in this country. Pragmatic legal theory with its central doctrine of expediency leaves room for such adjustments. These hard-won victories of the people were pointed to as further proof of the validity of the "market-place" doctrine. They created the illusion that the courts were an instrument for greater and greater reforms.

But "the market-place" doctrine is a double-edged sword. When the majority of the people begin to turn to true ideas, the monopolists begin to tremble. They fear the ideas of peace, of greater democracy and, above all, of socialism. Holmes recognized that class struggle and the increasing strength of the working class could oblige the ruling class under certain circumstances to close down the "market-place" to all ideas but its own. Thus he says: "The objection to class legislation is not that it favors a class, but either that it fails to benefit the legislators, or that it is danger-ous to them because a competing class has gained in power. . . ."[35]

No clearer proof of this can be furnished than the Supreme Court decision upholding the conviction of the Communist Party leaders and declaring the Smith Act constitutional. Holmes was, indeed, a valiant spokesman for monopoly capital as it developed and applied the law as a weapon against the people.

Holmes' Disciples

The pragmatic theory of law, first worked out by Holmes, was carried forward among others by Roscoe Pound, Benjamin N. Cardozo, Louis D. Brandeis, and Felix Frankfurter. In the decisions of the Supreme Court down to the mid-thirties, this group was represented primarily in dissent-ing opinions. But after Franklin D. Roosevelt's struggle with the "old guard" and the resulting changes in composition of the Court, the pragmatists finally came into a majority on the highest tribunal.

The leading theoretician among this group was Pound. He developed further the demagogic camouflage of the law "as an efficient instrument for social reconstruction."[36] Pound called his system "sociological juris-prudence," but he recognized that it was a pragmatic theory of law: "The sociological movement in jurisprudence is a movement for pragmatism as a philosophy of law; for the adjustment of principles and doctrines to the human conditions they are to govern rather than to assume first principles."[37] The central doctrine for Pound, as for Holmes, was "social expediency," with emphasis on the notion that "good law was what worked best for society."[38]

Commager, in *The American Mind*, sums up the "contribution" of this main-line school of legal theory: "Social jurisprudence was pragmatism. . . . It used law not as a shield to safeguard personal rights and liberties but as a cooperative instrument to satisfy social needs. It was a legal philosophy fitted to the realities of social life in an urban order, and of political life in an egalitarian order."[39]

A paraphrase of the closing sentence above, changing only two words, gives a true picture of the pragmatic theory of law: It was a legal philosophy fitted to the realities of social life in a capitalist order, and of political life in a class order.

Commager calls the 1937 changes in the Supreme Court "a constitutional revolution" which made the pragmatic "sociological jurisprudence . . . all but official doctrine of the court."[40]

What in fact did this "revolution" amount to? Nothing other than that the bourgeois legal theorists had succeeded in developing and getting accepted a new and peculiarly capitalist camouflage of the class character of U.S. law. By their own pragmatic standards, it has been a "good" theory, for it has had no small success in misleading the people, including dominant sections of the labor movement.

A corollary of this development of pragmatism in legal theory is the fact that those judges who have been considered the most liberal—Holmes, Pound, Cardozo, Brandeis and Frankfurter—are the very men who as legal theoreticians formulated the latest, most stream-lined theory of the law, one designed to conceal its reactionary class character. Their reputation as liberals stems not only from the demagogy in their theory, but also from the *concessions* embodied in some of their decisions. How they thought about these concessions is indicated by Frederick Pollock in a letter to Holmes in 1897. A year before, Holmes had upheld the right to peaceful picketing in a dissenting opinion. (Vegelahn v. Gunter.) The following year the English House of Lords sided with the Holmes view (Allen v. Flood.) Writing to Holmes about the latter case, Pollock says: "In the House of Lords Herschell, Watson and Davey are very well, but Macnaghten's is the judgment which posterity, if it be wise, will study side by side with yours in *Vegelahn v. Gunter.* . . . Only the organs of extreme capitalism (not having the wit to see that the contrary decision would have cut both ways) have expressed any dissatisfaction."[41]

In short, concessions made were concessions won, and constituted the most expedient way out for the capitalist class at the moment. To uphold peaceful picketing was at the time, in view of the militancy of the organized labor movement, the *judicious* thing to do. To rule against it would have "cut two ways." On the one hand it would have delivered a blow to labor and therefore was a decision to be desired by the bourgeoisie, but on the other it would have roused all unions to a new height of solidarity and struggle and therefore was a decision to be avoided. The pragmatic theory of law allows for such "adjustments" when found expedient. Legal pragmatists will be found on the side of concessions when that tactic is found expedient and on the side of repression when that is thought expedient.

Holmes once wrote to Pollock concerning the class role of philosophers: "I always think of a remark of Brooks Adams that the philosophers were hired by the comfortable class to prove that everything is all right."[42] A paraphrase of Adams' remark gives the true picture of Holmes and his colleagues: the jurists are hired by the comfortable class to see that everything remains all right.

Pragmatism in legal theory, as in other realms of ideology, is capitalist class expediency made to look like a consistent doctrine of "social progress."

V. WILLIAM JAMES:
APOLOGETICS IN PSYCHOLOGY

WILLIAM JAMES' *Principles of Psychology,* in two heavy volumes and fourteen hundred pages, was published in 1890. If there is one single work that is most important in the formulation of pragmatism, this is it. Here the pragmatic theory of knowledge, or more correctly, the theory of *no knowledge,* receives its intellectual foundation. Bourgeois authorities recognize this fact and pay tribute to it. But it is significant that none of them actually go into the *Principles of Psychology* and point out in what way James' work forms the basis for the theory of knowledge of pragmatism. To do so would be to give the show away.

James' psychological theories are typical of the bourgeois approach to consciousness. Bourgeois psychology approaches the psyche, not historically, but as the unchanging human nature of some sort of abstract, unhistoric "man in general." The development of the psyche is to be understood as a process of the unfolding of tendencies inherent in the nature of the mind. Thus it views the psyche in terms of innate instincts, drives and emotions. Further the fixed tendencies with which it deals are the "instincts," the "drives" and the "emotions" of bourgeois man, which are then assumed to be psychological features of "man in general." Work for wages, love of money, drive to war, economic competitiveness are presented as eternal characteristics of human nature. The general starting point for bourgeois psychology is the biological rather than the social level. Biological reductionism is utilized to transform the true science of psychology into an apologetic pseudo-science rooted in the philosophy of subjective idealism.

In psychology, as in other spheres of ideology, the pragmatic apologetic approach is worked out in the guise of meeting the challenge of evolution to the traditional, openly theological, doctrines. It is what James calls "the soul theory" which is under attack from the evolutionary science of Darwin and Lamarck. "This," says James, "is the orthodox 'spiritualistic' theory of scholasticism and of common sense."[1] It posits "a simple entity, the personal soul" which "manifests its faculty of Memory, now of Reasoning, now of Volition, or again its Imagination or its Appetite."[2] By the traditional soul theory, all these functions of mental life are "absolute god-given Faculties,"[3] eternal and unchanging. Under the impact of evolution, however, such notions can no longer be supported. Evolution includes the evolution of consciousness. After raising a number of questions which would cast doubt on the soul theory, for example, "drugs," "asphyxia," "fevers," and "brain surgery," James concludes: "Moreover, there is something grotesque and irrational in the supposition that the soul is equipped with elementary powers of such an ingeniously intricate sort. . . . Evidently, then, *the faculty does not exist absolutely, but works under conditions;* and *the quest of the conditions* becomes the psychologist's most interesting task."[4]

This statement has by now a familiar ring, for it is the same kind of statement made by Fiske and Holmes in history and law. It looks like a good beginning, but when a pragmatist makes such a formulation it is a mere camouflage flung over an attempt to destroy the materialist approach in order to reestablish the traditional doctrine at a different level. We have found this to be the case with Fiske and Holmes, and we would expect to find it true for James in his treatment of psychology. Let us see how the latter carries on his "quest of the conditions" under which consciousness exists and develops.

We would expect first that in the positivist manner he would deny the materialist and scientific structure of change; that he would then substitute expediency in its place; and that finally he would construct a fictitious theory which in essence would reestablish the *content,* if not the precise *form,* of the traditional theological doctrine.

That we will in fact find some such procedure in James, is indicated already in the Preface to his *Psychology* when he says that the work is written from a "strictly positivistic point of view" and that he owes a debt of "gratitude" to "the intellectual companionship of Chauncey Wright and Charles Peirce,"[5] among others.

The first step is to deny any scientific materialist structure as a basis for psychology, and to do so under cover of being ultra-"scientific" and under cover of an attack on theological psychology. The structure he must repudiate is the scientific materialist theory of consciousness as a developing reflection of reality through the medium of social practice. The immediate prerequisite for consciousness is a central nervous system with a highly developed brain, but consciousness cannot be reduced to its biological base. Consciousness is a social and not an exclusively biological phenomenon. If, however, one should want to maintain an appearance of scientific materialism, while at the same time denying its essence, one could deal with conscious life in terms solely of brain physiology. It is precisely this formula which James takes as his starting point.

In the preface, James states in one sentence what he develops at length in the opening chapters: "I have therefore treated our passing thoughts as integers, and regarded the mere laws of their coexistence with brain-states as the ultimate laws for our science."[6] On this basis, which has the appearance of being "terribly scientific," he says that "the brain is the one immediate bodily condition of the mental operations," and that "bodily experiences, therefore, and more particularly brain-experiences, must take a place amongst those conditions of the mental life of which psychology need take account."[7] On this physiological basis he lays down "the general law that *no mental modification ever occurs which is not accompanied or followed by a bodily change.*"[8] The question before us is how James utilizes this biological interpretation of consciousness to get rid of the genuine structure of the science of psychology.

James advances the doctrine that mental life is the reflection, not of objective reality through social practice, but of "bodily experiences, and more particularly of brain-experiences" through the medium of sensations. The problem is not one of correspondence between ideas and reality, but between ideas and brain states or bodily functions. Thus he says, "A science of the relations of mind and brain must show how the elementary ingredients of the former sensations (ideas and feelings) correspond to the elementary functions of the latter (nerve excitations)."[9] His slogan is "No psychosis without neurosis,"[10] which for James is not psychiatric terminology but means that consciousness (psychosis) is composed of sensations which in turn are the product of nerve stimulation (neurosis).

"Stream of Consciousness"

Sensations are caused by nerve excitations, but since the nerves send an unending stream of excitations to the brain, there is an unbroken stream of sensations corresponding to them. Thus the "elementary ingredients" of consciousness constitute "the primordial chaos of sensation."[11] Consciousness for James *is* the uninterrupted flow of sensations corresponding to the uninterrupted flow of nerve excitations.

In James' view, consciousness is a "stream of consciousness" reflecting "a stream of nervous stimulation." This stream is not broken up; it flows like a river: "Consciousness, then, does not appear to itself chopped up in bits. Such words as 'chain' or 'train' do not describe it fitly as it presents itself in the first instance. It is nothing jointed; it flows. A 'river' or a 'stream' are the metaphors by which it is most naturally described. *In talking of it hereafter, let us call it the stream of thought, of consciousness, or of subjective life.*"[12]

With this conception of what he calls "the wonderful stream of our consciousness,"[13] James has eliminated all genuine structure for a science of psychology. He now has a "primordial chaos of sensations," a sheer flux of thought, which he is free to treat in whatever expedient fashion suits his purposes. The next step is to establish the notion of expediency as the central "structure" of this "stream of consciousness." By use of a mechanical reductionist approach, he has cleared the way for his doctrine of ends and means.

To introduce the *expedient* character of consciousness, James says that while the stream is not broken up in the first place, we succeed in breaking it up in the course of life. We break it up into parts according to "interest" and "attention." "Millions of items," James says, "are present to my senses which never properly enter into my experience. Why? Because they have no *interest* for me. *My experience is what I agree to attend to.* Only those items which I *notice* shape my mind—without selective interest, experience is an utter chaos."[14]

I pay attention, he is saying, to what interests me within the flow of consciousness, and I select those sensations, combine them, and give them names. I select in the same way the relations between these named bundles of sensations. Thus I build *my* world out of *my* stream of consciousness. Out of "the primordial chaos of sensations" I construct, through attention and selection based on my interest, the world I live in:

The mind, in short, works on the data it receives very much as a sculptor works on his block of stone. In a sense the statue stood there from eternity. But there were a thousand different ones beside it, and the sculptor alone is to thank for having extricated this one from the rest. Just so the world of each of us, howsoever different our several views of it may be, all lay embedded in the primordial chaos of sensations, which gave the mere *matter* to the thought of all of us indifferently. . . . Other sculptors, other statues from the same stone! Other minds, other worlds from the same monotonous and inexpressive chaos! My world is but one in a million alike embedded, alike real to those who may abstract them.[15]

Thus, I select out of the chaos of sensations, out of the stream of consciousness, what I call reality. For my interest and attention make me believe that what I select is the real. Thus reality and belief are one and the same thing, for James as for Peirce. Both are rooted in the interests and emotions which determine their selection from the "blooming, buzzing confusion of sensations." *"In its inner nature,"* says James, *"belief, or the sense of reality, is a sort of feeling more allied to the emotions than to anything else."*[16]

James' Subjectivism and Voluntarism

In a chapter called "The Perception of Reality," James makes the subjective and voluntarist character of his psychology and his view of life perfectly plain. Since the Jamesian psychology is admitted to be the foundation of the pragmatic philosophy, it is little wonder that the pragmatic philosophers content themselves with paying tribute to, but never analyzing, James' psychological work. The entire chapter is replete with statements which confirm their circumspection in avoiding it. The following statement indicates the character of James' thought: *"Reality means simply relation to our emotional and active life. This is the only sense which the word ever has in the mouths of practical men. In this sense, whatever excites and stimulates our interest is real. . . . The foundation and origin of all reality, whether from the absolute or the practical point of view, is thus subjective, is ourselves."*[17]

He continues further on: *"We need only in cold blood ACT as if the thing in question were real, and keep acting as if it were real, and it will infallibly end by growing into such a connection with our life that it will become real. It will become so knit with habit and emotion that* our interests in it will be those which characterize belief. Those to whom 'God' and 'Duty' are now mere names can make them much more than that, if they make a little sacrifice to them every day."[18]

Thus does James clearly and unmistakably state the subjective idealist position of his psychology. All the hundreds of pages preceding the above conclusions merely prepare the way for them. On the basis of his biological reductionism and his resulting "stream of consciousness," with the selection of clusters of sensation for attention and belief, the only possible outcome is complete solipsism, the self-created world, together with complete voluntarism, believing what one wills to believe. In a very real sense it can be said that James' psychology *is* the theoretical foundation of pragmatism.

The unorganized stream of consciousness is organized by the self to meet its needs and interests. The selecting is done on the basis of what is useful or expedient to me. That which in the flow of sensations I pay attention to is what I believe, and what I attend to and believe is reality for me. James says, "The most compendious possible formula perhaps would be that *our belief and attention* are the same fact. For the moment, what we attend to is reality."[19]

For materialist psychology, sensations are necessary for consciousness; they are the sole source of knowledge. Without sensations, consciousness is impossible. But sensations are the path to reality, not reality itself. James, like all subjective idealists, makes sensations a barrier rather than an avenue to reality. Marxist scientific materialism holds that we know the world through our practice in it, that our social-historical practice makes the world more and more known to us. It is social practice—productive activity, class struggle, science—which is both the source and the test of knowledge.

Further, James holds that sensations are "a blooming, buzzing confusion," a "stream of consciousness." Far from limiting human consciousness within a flux of sensations, as does James, Marxism sees the dialectical character of the development of our knowledge of the world. In the Marxist theory of knowledge, it is the objective world which is represented to us in our sensations. We *perceive* various aspects of the world, we gain *impressions* of the surrounding world through our sensations. As Mao Tse-tung pointed out in his pamphlet *On Practice,* this is the first stage of knowledge, "the stage of sensations and impressions."[20] At this stage, people see "the external connection between things."[21] The second stage is that of rational knowledge which reflects "not only the appearance of things, separate aspects of things, their external connection, but constitutes mastery of the essence of things, the common character of things, the internal connection of things."[22]

Lenin summed up the Marxist theory of knowledge: "The materialist theory then, the theory of reflection of objects by our mind is here presented with perfect clearness: things exist outside of us. Our perceptions and representations are their images. The verification of these images, the distinction of true and false images, is given by practice."[23]

James had developed his subjectivist theory of knowledge as an attack against this materialist theory, but concealed by a mock offensive against the theological approach. Thus he cleared the way for the substitution of the pragmatic in the place of the scientific method. It remained for him to smuggle in an unchanging human consciousness, the content of the theological doctrine, to give his psychology its full class essence.

Unchanging Human Nature

The next and final step for James is to reestablish the traditional concept of the soul, or at least its essential content, namely an unchanging human nature. Thus far he has succeeded in theoretically eliminating any real structure of consciousness, and in substituting expedient selection according to interest and attention from the structureless stream of sensations. The question remains: where do interest and attention come from? They cannot come from the flux of the senses, for it is a sheer flow, without, in its primordial chaotic state, being broken up into what is interesting and what is not.

Interest must come from some other source than sense experience. The latter James calls "the front door" of consciousness: "The way of 'experience' proper is the front door, the door of the five senses."[24] "The front door" opens on the stream of consciousness. But what about "the original elements of consciousness" such as "1. elementary sorts of sensation, and feelings of personal activity; 2. emotions; desires; instincts; ideas of worth; aesthetic ideas; 3. ideas of time and space and number; 4. ideas of difference and resemblance, and of their degrees; 5. ideas of causal dependence among events; of end and means; of subject and attribute."[25] Where did they come from? "Why may they not have come into being," says James, "by the back-door method?"[26]

What does James mean by "the back-door" of consciousness? By it he means a hereditary "organic mental structure" of consciousness. The mind brings to the stream of consciousness an already formed body of instincts and emotions which is the unchanging human nature, the soul, of tradition. It is the original "mental structure," made up of instincts, emotions, and various primitive ideas, which determines the interest and attention, which in turn select from the stream of sensations. Thus in the last analysis, for James, the selection of my world is the product of my inborn instincts and emotions. These are what set the direction of my interest and attention on the basis of which I select from "the primordial chaos of sensations" and construct the world I live in. I am born with a certain "organic mental structure," a "native wealth of inner forms," which did not come from any sense experience, which did not come from "the front door," but entered through "the back door." "Here then," James says, "is a native wealth of inner forms whose origin is shrouded in mystery, and which at any rate were not simply 'impressed' from without, in any intelligible sense of the verb 'to impress'."[27]

James' Instinct Theory

What is the "elementary constitution of the instinctive life?"[28] An instinct is the "blind, automatic, and untaught" impulse toward an end. It is "teleological or purposive" action without foresight of the goal. *"Instinct is usually defined,"* James says, *"as the faculty of acting in such a way as to produce certain ends, without foresight of the ends, and without previous education in the performance."* And he continues: "Man has a far greater variety of *impulses* than any lower animal; and any one of these impulses, taken in itself, is as blind as the lowest instinct can be."[30]

What are some of the "human instincts?" James gives a long and exhaustive list, beginning with "the instincts of infancy" such as "sucking" and "biting" and ending with "the sexual instincts." But in between are included such "instincts" as the "ownership" or "proprietary instinct." Thus with James, as with Holmes, private property is the result of "instinct," not history. "Everyone knows," he says, "how difficult a thing it is not to covet whatever pleasing thing we see. . . . When another is in possession, the impulse to appropriate the thing often turns into the impulse to harm him."[31] Then there is "the collecting instinct," as a corollary of the "ownership instinct"; "A variety of the proprietary instinct is the impulse to form collections of the same sort of thing."[32] Collections of industries, railroads and banks, for example.

Another impulse is the "killing-instinct"[33] or "pugnacity." It is this instinct which, according to James, makes lynching, massacres and war inevitable:

> In many respects man is the most ruthlessly ferocious of beasts. . . . Hence the gory cradle, the *bellum omnium contra omnes* (the war of all against all), in which our race was reared; hence the fickleness of human ties, the ease with which the foe of yesterday becomes the ally of today, the friend of today the enemy of tomorrow; hence the fact that we the lineal representatives of the successful enactors of one scene of slaughter after another, must, whatever more pacific virtues we may also possess, still carry about with us, ready at any moment to burst into flame, the smouldering and sinister traits of character by means of which they lived through so many massacres, harming others, but themselves unharmed.[34]

Bourgeois "instincts" such as these comprise the "organic structure of the mind" in the "light" of which selection is made from the "stream of consciousness." The "instinctive mental structure" is "the back door" which determines all that is allowed to enter consciousness by "the front door" of experience.

The task of James and of bourgeois psychologists generally is to make characteristics acquired during the life of individuals in the particular capitalist form of society into innate and therefore eternal instincts. In this way, they can uphold "an unchanging human" and deny that society can change since human nature cannot. James develops a theory of the emotions which aids him in carrying out this task.

James' Theory of Emotions

The emotions are likewise part of the "back door" inborn structure of consciousness. But they are scarcely separable from "instincts." *"Instinctive reactions and emotional expressions thus shade imperceptibly into each other,"*[35] writes James. Both are "impulses" from within the mental structure and have the same physiological basis. They do not come from experience of the world, but rather from the established physiology of the body and the nervous system, especially the brain. James' theory of the emotions centers around the doctrine that a man is afraid because he runs, not *vice versa*. His emotions are the result not of reaction to the objective world, but to his physiological changes. They reflect, not external reality, but his bodily excitement and motion. Here is James' description of his theory: "My theory, on the contrary, is that *the bodily changes follow directly the perception of the exciting fact, and that our feeling of the same changes as they occur is the emotion. . . .* We feel sorry because we cry, angry because we strike, afraid because we tremble, and not that we cry, strike, or tremble, because we are sorry, angry, or fearful, as the case may be."[36]

For James, the emotions reflect bodily changes, just as consciousness in general reflects nervous excitation. In both cases, it is a formula to establish subjectivism under the cover of "hard-headed" physiological analysis.

The Soviet psychologist E. T. Chernakov exposed James' theory of emotions as subjectivist:

> To understand feelings or emotions materialistically, means to see them as nothing else but reflections of objective reality in our mind—in other words, as reflections of objects and events in the outside world in their real relationship to us. . . . Our feelings or emotions cannot be non-objective or non-conscious. It is impossible to feel or experience an unknown something. . . . Organic reactions which are external manifestations of emotions, such as fear, for example, cannot be considered as a basis for the emotion but only as a consequence of the consciousness of danger which threatens the individual.[37]

We can heighten our understanding of James' theory of the emotions if we take an objective event which has aroused the burning anger of the Negro people, the working class and their allies, the legal lynching of the Martinsville Seven, and see how James would treat the aroused emotion, or would have us treat it: "Refuse to express a passion, and it dies. Count ten before venting your anger, and its occasion seems ridiculous. . . . Smooth the brow, brighten the eye, contract the dorsal rather than the ventral aspect of the frame, and speak in a major key, pass the genial compliment, and your heart must be frigid indeed if it do not gradually thaw!"[38]

James' "theory" is an attempt to convince us that there are no objective reasons for such feelings as anger, fear, sadness, despair. To get over these emotions, we need not eliminate exploitation and oppression at the hands of the capitalist class. All we need to do is to smooth our brows and straighten our shoulders, smile and be happy. If we should follow James' advice, there would indeed be a certain group of people who would be exceedingly happy.

James' Theory of Habit

James postulates one other element of the "organic mental structure." In addition to instincts and emotions, there are habits. But habit is simply the particularization of instinct and emotion as they enter concretely into the life of individuals. *"Instincts,"* James says, *"are implanted for the sake of giving rise to habits."*[39] Thus there is the "instinct of ownership," which in a particular individual works itself out in the habit of owning, say, banks. Or the instinctive emotion of fear may become the habit of fearing, for example, unemployment or war. "Habit," says James, "is thus the enormous fly-wheel of society, its most precious conservative agent. It alone is what keeps us all within the bounds of ordinance, and saves the children of fortune from the envious uprisings of the poor."[40] Habit is a powerful class weapon, so powerful, with its roots in the unchangeable instincts, that the ruling class could not maintain its position without it: "It alone prevents the hardest and most repulsive walks of life from being deserted by those brought up to tread therein. It keeps the fisherman and the deck-hand at sea through the winter; it holds the miner in his darkness. . . . It keeps different social strata from mixing."[41]

Not the material conditions of life under capitalism, but habits expressing instincts and emotions keep the worker working and the capitalist exploiting, and the classes from mixing.

James envisages habit as the cement of capitalist society. For materialist psychology, habits develop in and through the social practice of the individual, his activity in a definite society. In capitalist society, bourgeois habits are forced upon the people. But as the contradiction in the material life of capitalism sharpens, the habits of the working class change. The habits bred by capitalism are opposed by new habits, by new traits: comradeship, solidarity, steadfastness, devotion to their unions and their political parties, struggle against oppression. James' ardent desire is to maintain habits—bourgeois habits—in order to maintain capitalism. But what James sees as the cement of capitalism is disintegrating through militant working class struggle. Habits depend on experience, not on inborn "instincts."

Instincts, emotions and habits form the unchanging and unchangeable structure of consciousness for James. For breaking up of the stream of consciousness, the chaos of sensations, is accomplished by all three through interest and attention. Reasoning is simply the process of selecting, in the light of instinct, emotion and habit, that part of the stream which will lead to the desired end. Thus, James says, that "All Reasoning depends on the ability of the mind to break up the totality of the phenomenon reasoned about, into parts, and to pick out from among these the particular one which, in our given emergency, may lead to the proper conclusion."[42] And he adds that "Reasoning is but another form of the selective activity of the mind."[43] What is selected is called a "thing" and is given a name; but in fact, "things" are only "groups of sensible qualities," or bundles of sensations given a certain organization for practical or esthetic purposes by the "organic mental structure":

But what are things? Nothing, as we shall abundantly see, but special groups of sensible qualities, which happen practically or aesthetically to interest us, to which we therefore give the substantive names, and which we exalt to this exclusive status of independence and dignity. . . . But all these essential characteristics, which for us form the genuine objectivity of the thing and are contrasted with what we call the subjective sensations it may yield us at a given moment, are mere sensations like the latter. The mind chooses to suit itself, and decides what particular sensations shall be held more real and valid than all the rest.[44]

We have seen that for "the mind to suit itself" means simply that it chooses on the basis of instinct, emotion and habit. Since both emotion and habit are reducible in the final analysis for James to instinct, it is clear that "reasoning," and mental activity generally, is simply the servant of the instincts. And, since the instincts include all those things that are vital to the capitalist class, like "the instinct of ownership" and of "killing," it follows that reasoning and thought are in essential effect servants of the bourgeoisie. This is the sum of James' *Principles of Psychology*. It is not science, but sheer apologetics.

What happens to the natural sciences when treated in James' psychological terms? They, too, are selected by the mind from the chaos of sensations, and therefore have more to do with the "organic mental structure" than with experience, not to mention the material world. The mind, with its instincts, emotions and habits, *invents* rather than discovers the laws of science:

At present I will pass to the so-called *pure* or *a priori sciences* of classification, Logic, and Mathematics. My thesis concerning these is that they are even less than the natural sciences effects of the order of the world as it comes to our experience. THE PURE SCIENCES EXPRESS RESULTS OF COMPARISON *exclusively; comparison is not a conceivable effect of the order in which outer impressions are experienced—it is one of the house-born (back-door) portions of our mental structure; therefore the pure sciences form a body of propositions with whose genesis experience has nothing to do.*[45]

Not experience, not social practice, is the origin of scientific knowledge, but the "mental structure," the instincts, emotions and habits. Thus science is the tool of expediency; it organizes the chaos in *useful* ways, but has nothing whatever to do with truth, the correspondence of laws and facts to reality.

James speaks of "spontaneous variations," thousands of which are produced by the mental structure, but only a few prove useful. It is this aspect of Darwinism which he employs to justify his theory of psychology. He rejects the Lamarckian theory of acquired characteristics, and embraces the theory of "sports" or "mutations." It is not the activity of man to change the environment, that changes human consciousness. Rather it is the "spontaneous variations" generated by "the organic mental structure" out of its own substance, which, by trial and error and by survival of the fittest, gradually builds up a body of instincts, emotions and habits which then do the selecting out of the stream of sensations to build a behavioral environment.

James' Appeal to Morgan-Weismann Genetics

It is significant that in a later edition James appeals to Weismann genetics in support of his theory of the origin of instincts. Thus in the closing chapter of *The Principles* in a revised edition, James writes:

I leave my text practically just as it was written in 1885. I proceeded at that time to draw a tentative conclusion to the effect that the origin of *most* of our instincts must certainly be deemed fruits of the back-door method of genesis, and not of ancestral experience in the proper meaning of the term. . . . Already before that time, however, Professor Weismann of Freiburg had begun a very serious attack upon the Lamarckian theory, and his polemic has at last excited such a widespread interest among naturalists that the whilom almost unhesitatingly accepted theory seems almost on the point of being abandoned.

I will therefore add some of Weismann's criticisms of the supposed evidence to my own.[46]

This question of inheritance is crucial for James, since on it rests his reestablishment of the eternal and unchanging human soul in the form of instincts. It is by no means accidental that he appeals to Morgan-Weismann genetics as the last refuge of the reconstituted "soul theory." It was under cover of an attack on this theory that he set out to formulate a "science" of psychology. But from the beginning his prime task was to make "science" itself preach the "soul theory," and to eliminate the possibility of knowledge, scientific theory and truth, by eliminating all but psychic reality.

James' psychology not only formed the theoretical basis for all subsequent pragmatic philosophy, but also smoothed the way for Freudian psycho-analysis to conquer the field in the United States. The latter is almost deducible as a corollary from James' system. Likewise, the dominant schools of psychology proper, behaviorism and gestaltism, are rooted in James' "pioneering" work. Not least, it had a tremendous influence on John Dewey, both on his philosophical thinking and on his theory of education. Speaking of James' *Psychology*, Dewey remarks:

> As far as I can discover (if there is) one specifiable philosophic factor which entered into my thinking so as to give it a new direction and quality, it is this one . . . it proceeded from his *Psychology* rather than from the essays collected in the volume called *Will To Believe, Pluralistic Universe*, or *Pragmatism*. . . . I may cite as an illustration the substitution of the term "stream of consciousness" for discrete elementary states. . . . It is my conviction that a great deal of our philosophizing needs to be done over again from this point of view, and there will ultimately result an integrated synthesis in a philosophy congruous with modern science and related to actual needs in education, morals and religion.[47]

How justified Dewey's tribute to James' influence is, we will see in the following chapter when we deal with the former's educational theories.

The Principles of Psychology by William James gives the lie to all the demagogic claims pragmatism makes to being "scientific," "naturalist," and "progressive." It replaces the soul theory with the unchanging, instinctive, human-nature theory of psychology. It is the skeleton in the closet of the formulated pragmatic philosophy. Little wonder that it is kept under lock and key by bourgeois ideologists.

VI. JOHN DEWEY:
APOLOGETICS IN EDUCATION

So FAR in this process of formulation of pragmatic apologetics we have been dealing with a group of apologists centering around Harvard University: Wright, James, Peirce, Fiske and Holmes. We now turn our attention to another group centering around the University of Chicago. The leading exponent of the Chicago School of pragmatism is John Dewey.

The University of Chicago was founded and funded by John D. Rockefeller in 1892 and its first president, William R. Harper, called Dewey from the University of Michigan to head his Department of Philosophy. Dewey came to Chicago in 1894, where for ten years he devoted his primary attention to the development of the pragmatic theory of education. Dewey developed his philosophy of education in conjunction with an experimental school appended as an annex to the university. This was the famous "University Elementary School." Dewey's first major book was *The School and Society*[1] in which he set forth the pragmatic theory of education together with the results of some six years of experimentation at the University School. This book, published in 1899, is still the theoretical foundation stone of pragmatism in education.

John Dewey and his followers, most notable of whom are Kilpatrick, Childs, and Counts, represent in their writings the only systematized and institutionally influential theory of education in this country, the pragmatic theory.

Dewey's pragmatic theory of education would conceal the essence of bourgeois education through making it appear as the unfolding of the innate instincts and impulses of the child; through making bourgeois indoctrination appear as the flowering of the inner being of the child.

Every thoughtful parent and sincere teacher wants above all to see the fullest possible development of the child through the educational process. But how is this development to take place? Where does the potential lie? Is it primarily in the internal, inborn nature of the child, as Dewey holds? Or is it primarily in the culture, knowledge and truth created and discovered by mankind down the ages? Humanism, including above all the teachings of Marxism, maintains that the potential for the fullest possible development of the child lies in society and must be brought to him by the home, the school and the life of the community. The growth of the child into a richly endowed adult human being requires his careful nurture in all that people throughout history have accomplished materially and spiritually. Thus child development is essentially a process of bringing to the child human knowing and feeling, values and emotions, traits of character as exemplified in the heroes of mankind, scientific understanding, love of people, dedication to a better, fuller life for all. A rounded person is first of all a product of what is brought to him from outside himself by the people with whom he lives, learns, plays and works.

Dewey's formula would withhold this social heritage. It would do this by making the instincts of the child rather than the humanism of mankind the source of education.

How does Dewey perpetrate this sell-out of the child?

Through the pages of *The School and Society* we can follow the line of Dewey's argument. He begins by pointing out that "It is radical conditions which have changed, and only an equally radical change in education suffices."[2] What is the change in radical conditions which requires a radical change in education?

The toiling masses have been brought into the educational system. This is the "change in radical conditions," according to Dewey, which requires a "radical change in education." But why does it require a change in education? Dewey answers that the "impulses," the "tendencies," the "dispositions" of "the great majority," are not "intellectual" but "narrowly practical." Therefore there must be a radical change of education from primary concern with the "intellectual" to primary concern with the "practical." To be concerned primarily with the "intellectual" was justified when only the minority ruling class was being educated. Why? Because the sons and daughters of the owners have "intellectual impulses, tendencies and dispositions," while the sons and daughters of the working class have only "narrowly practical impulses, tendencies, and dispositions."

The new education, designed for the public schools where the children of the masses are concentrated, must be transformed in such a way as to allow for the unfolding of "the practical impulses."[3]

What inference is to be drawn from such an argument? The only realistic inference is that workers are workers not because of the character of the capitalist system which deprives them of a living unless they sell their labor power to the owners of the factories and farms, but because of their own innate character with its practical "impulses, tendencies and dispositions." Workers are born workers, and owners are born owners. Thus the class structure of capitalism is not created by history but by human nature, by heredity. This is, of course, the favorite doctrine of all ruling classes in a class society. It is at least as old as Plato with his "royal lie" that the gods mixed gold in the rulers and bronze in the workers and the direst sin is the mixing of metals.

The cornerstone of Dewey's pragmatic theory of education is contained in his statement that "The simple facts of the case are that in the great majority of human beings the distinctively intellectual interest is not dominant."[4] They have the so-called "practical impulse and disposition." Substitute "toiling masses" for Dewey's "majority," and his real meaning becomes unmistakable. Dewey's reform of bourgeois education follows as a corollary from the above statement: "If we [the capitalist class] were to conceive our educational end and aim in a less exclusive way, if we were to introduce into educational processes the activities which appeal to those whose dominant interest [the interest of the toiling masses] is to do and to make [to produce profits for the owners], we should find the hold of the school [and the capitalist system] upon its members [the working class] to be more vital, more prolonged, containing more of culture"[5] (namely, more of what the ruling class requires in the way of ideas and attitudes). Dewey would make it appear that the interests and impulses of the workers are "to do and to make," which, when paraphrased, means to produce profits or to be wage slaves of the capitalists.

To allow for the fullest possible unfolding of this impulse to do and to make profits for the bosses, the school must center around the *occupations* which the capitalist class requires. In short, the public school must become primarily a vocational school teaching *how* jobs are to be done, but not the theory of *why*. *Know how,* but not *know why* is to be the subject-matter taught. In this way the "impulses" of the working class will be given full opportunity to develop. Dewey states that in the new education "occupations are made the articulating centers of school life."[6] The workers are to learn by doing "what comes naturally" to them; namely, the occupations which the capitalist class requires them to be able to fill. The public school, the working class, is not concerned with "the mere absorbing of facts and truth."[7] Certainly not, for facts and truth in the hands of the workers are dangerous weapons. For the great "majority," there is "no obvious social motive for the acquirement of mere learning, there is no clear social gain in success thereat." As a matter of fact, for the bourgeoisie there is a clear social threat in the acquirement of learning by the working class.

Speaking of such occupations within the school as "work in wood and metal, of weaving, sewing, and cooking,"[8] Dewey says: "It keeps them alert and active, instead of passive and receptive; it makes them more useful, more capable, and hence more inclined to be helpful at home; it prepares them to some extent for the practical duties of later life—the girls to be more efficient house managers, if not actually cooks and seamstresses; the boys (were our educational system only rounded out into trade schools) for their future vocations."[9]

Such, then, is the general character of Dewey's "radical change" in education designed to meet "the changed radical conditions."

He goes on to conceal the class nature of this theory of education by claiming that all people, or at least "most of us" are workers. Of course, some "of us" are "managers" while most "of us" are "subordinates." In any case, each should be so educated as to be satisfied with what he is doing. This satisfaction is to be achieved through understanding the "large and human significance" of the job one is occupied with. This means that the worker is to be satisfied to be exploited because he is to be kept from understanding that he *is* exploited. He is to be taught instead that he is performing a social service full of "large and human significance" when he works for the owner. The worker does not as yet fully understand this because he has not had the "opportunity to develop his imagination and his sympathetic insight as to the social and scientific values found in his work." Dewey would have the schools give such an "opportunity" to the worker, as a substitute naturally for working class militancy and proletarian consciousness. Let Dewey state his own position:

The world in which most of us live is a world in which everyone has a calling and occupation, something to do. Some are managers and others are subordinates. But the great thing for one as for the other is that each shall have had the education which enables him to see within his daily work all there is in it of large and human significance. How many of the employed are today mere appendages to the machines which they operate! This may be due in part to the machine itself or the regime which lays so much stress upon the products of the machine; but it is certainly due in large part to the fact that the worker has had no opportunity to develop his imagination and his sympathetic insight as to the social and scientific values found in his work.[10]

Through the "new education," Dewey would turn out workers who would be satisfied, if not over-joyed, to be "mere appendages to the machines which they operate." For he would have them well-indoctrinated with the "large and human significance" of low wages, speed-up, long hours, an army of unemployed and all those "social and scientific values" so close to the heart of the capitalist class.

Dewey claims that this type of education is the only road to the solution of the evils, the contradictions, of capitalism. Only by laying hold of the working class "instincts of construction" can progress be made in locating and dealing with "our economic evils." The "economic evils" are located in the undeveloped "instincts" of the working class. Education must center around the development of these "instincts"; from childhood they must be, "trained in social directions, enriched by historical interpretation, controlled and illuminated by scientific methods." Only with such guidance of working class "instincts" can the owners have "the deepest and best guaranty of a larger society which is worthy, lovely, and harmonious." If the schools could only imbue the workers with the idea that their deepest "instincts" are fulfilled in operating the machines which produce profits, then indeed the "evils" of the capitalist system, as the capitalist sees them, would be located and largely solved.

On locating and dealing with "our economic evils" in terms of laying hold of "instincts," Dewey states:

At present, the impulses which lie at the basis of the industrial system are either practically neglected or positively distorted during the school period. Until the instincts of construction and production are systematically laid hold of in the years of childhood and youth, until they are trained in social directions, enriched by historical interpretation, controlled and illuminated by scientific methods, we certainly are in no position even to locate the source of our economic evils, much less to deal with them effectively.[11]

It is not an historically constituted system of exploitation of man by man which "lies at the basis" of capitalism. Rather it is the "instinct of production" which is the foundation of the system. Thus capitalism is the product of "instinct"; it has a biological, not a social source.

With Dewey, as with James and Holmes, biological "instincts" take the place of the directly supernatural in guarantying the permanence of the economic system. It is simply a slight variation of the "human nature" theory of society. And when human nature is conceived as a mass of "instincts," then it follows that for all practical purposes "you can't change human nature." According to Dewey and the pragmatists generally it is human nature with its biological "instincts" which lies at the basis of society; not the forces of production, the way in which people make a living. The latter, the only scientific formulation, makes the structure of society a matter of social organization and therefore changeable with changing forces of production. The former, based on the ideology of the ruling class, makes the structure of the social system instinctive and permanent.

The Child-Centered School: An Instinct Theory

"Instincts" play the leading role in Dewey's pragmatic theory of education. All "impulses," tendencies, etc., are reducible in the final analysis to "original instincts" inherited through the Morgan-Weismann mechanism of gene genetics. Thus the Jamesian biologically oriented psychology forms the cornerstone of Dewey's "new education."

Under cover of an attack on traditional education, Dewey builds his theory on the foundation of "the immediate instincts and activities of the child himself."[12]

The theory was not original with Dewey. Froebel had developed the instinct theory of education in Germany a generation before. We will see that Dewey gives due credit to Froebel. Both speak of the child-centered school but make it clear that this is simply a high sounding name for what is in fact the instinct-centered school.

Dewey attacks the "old education" for some things which are worthy of attack. But in so doing, he throws the basic concept of education out along with what should be eliminated. He does this by identifying all that was bad in traditional education with the concept of education as coming from "outside the child." The old education located the source of education in the teacher, in the textbook, rather than "in the immediate instincts and activities of the child himself." Dewey maintains that learning is an internal process with its source within the child, and more particularly in the instincts. This reversal of theory he calls a "Copernican revolution." It *is* a Copernican revolution—in reverse! It makes society turn in an orbit around the instincts of the child. It is a counter-revolution which Dewey would perpetrate. The center of gravity of education is to be the child-instincts, not society, not the class which is doing the educating. Dewey would in this way make bourgeois indoctrination appear as a fountain of childhood instincts: "Now the change which is coming into our education is the shifting of the center of gravity. It is a change, a revolution, not unlike that introduced by Copernicus when the astronomical center shifted from the earth to the sun. In this case the child becomes the sun about which the appliances of education revolve; he is the center about which they are organized."[13]

The child with his instincts is to be the center of the school and so the problem of education is twofold: first, it must "lay hold" of "the rudimentary instincts of human nature"; and second, it must facilitate their expression "by supplying a proper medium." In this way education will achieve even better results in the way of "technical information and discipline" than the old education. This "assertion and growth" of "the rudimentary instincts" is what Dewey calls "the kingdom of heaven, educationally." Given the kingdom of heaven, everything that the bourgeoisie could desire in terms of "discipline," "culture" and "information" will follow "in their due season." "If we seek the kingdom of heaven, educationally, all other things shall be added unto us—which, being interpreted, is that if we identify ourselves with the real instincts and needs of childhood, and ask only after its fullest assertion and growth, the discipline and information and culture of adult life shall all come in their due season."[14]

Substitute the word "bourgeois" for the word "adult" in the closing sentence of the above passage and Dewey's meaning is interpreted. He is sensitive on this point, for his child-centered school with its learning by doing methodology had been sharply criticized in the bourgeois press and journals. The capitalist class had not yet fully understood

what a useful service this new apologist at the University of Chicago
was performing. They charged him with failing to allow for the things
which were central in the old education; namely, discipline, technical
information and indocrination with the bourgeois outlook, morality
and habits. Over and over again in *The School and Society* Dewey
stresses that his theory not only does what the old education did, but
does it better. Today, of course, the ruling class has long since recognized
the true character of Dewey's theory of education.

What is the *role of the teacher* in the child-centered school? The
teacher is "to get hold of the child's natural impulses and instincts, and
to utilize them so that the child is carried on to a higher plane of
perception and judgment, and equipped with more efficient habits."[15]
The teacher is to act as a guide to the unfolding of the instincts. In this
guidance process there are two factors. The first is "initiation in the
child's own impulse" and the second is "termination on a higher plane."[16]
With regard to the first factor, the greatest pedagogical sin in Dewey's
manual is for the teacher to take the initiative. The teacher must never
initiate any activity. The initiative must come from the child: "As a
general principle no activity should be *originated* by imitation. The
start must come from the child."[17] The teacher must know what instinct
is striving for utterance at a particular time in the development of the
child, and the sole function of the teacher should be to supply stimuli
and materials which will allow for its expression.

He continues: "As just intimated, it is the teacher's business to
know what powers are striving for utterance at a given period in the
child's development, and what sorts of activity will bring these to helpful expression, in order then to supply the requisite stimuli and needed
materials."[18] The teacher is to be a diviner of instincts and a supplier
of materials. But Dewey does not leave it at that. He slips in the "old"
concept of education from the outside, from the teacher, when he says:
"A sympathetic teacher is quite likely to know more clearlly than the
child himself what his own instincts are and mean. But the suggestion
must *fit in* with the dominant mode of growth in the child; it must
serve simply as stimulus to bring forth more adequately what the child
is already blindly striving to do."[19]

Here is the split between theory and practice; between the theory
which is designed to conceal from the toiling masses, and from the teacher
also, the fact that education is the process of imbuing students with the

ideas of the educator. The theory maintains that the child is to express its instincts, while the teacher is to make the materials for such expression available. But in practice, it works out that the teacher—the "sympathetic" teacher, and what teacher wants to be unsympathetic?—will know better what the child wants, or *should* want, and therefore will play an active role in imbuing the child with these "wants."

Thus, bourgeois indoctrination is made to *look* as if it came from the instincts of the child, rather than from outside imitation and suggestion. Dewey makes the latter secondary and the former primary. Imitation and suggestion, according to the theory, are supposed to be merely instruments to help the child carry out his wants and desires based on his instincts: "Imitation and suggestion come in naturally and inevitably, but only as instruments to help him carry out his own wishes and ideas."[20] But Dewey has already made it clear that the "sympathetic" teacher will know better than the child what the child wants. It follows that the wants, wishes, ideas, "instincts," and "impulses" of the child will be those of the teacher.

The aim of education, Dewey says, is "the full development of the child's powers."[21] But "powers" is simply another name for "instincts," "impulses," "wants," "interests," and "ideas." Since these come from the educator, as Dewey admits is the case with "sympathetic" teachers, then it follows that the aim of education is to imbue the child with the outlook which the teacher has been imbued with in his education and life. But the entire process is presented as the unfolding of the internal, instinctive, hereditary nature of the child himself.

The *practice* is bourgeois indoctrination while the *theory* is bourgeois demagogy to conceal the fact.

Every parent would like to think that the "full development" of his child was the central concern of the school. And teachers would like to think that they are concerned with the "full development" of the child as a human being. Conversely, few parents would like to think that their children are going to school to be imbued with the ideas of the class which oppresses and exploits them. And few teachers would like to think that they are instruments of ruling class indoctrination. Dewey's theory is well designed to conceal the unwelcome fact from both parents and teachers.

The theoretical fiction of the child-centered school would conceal the practical reality of the bourgeois-centered school.

Let us now examine the psychological basis of the pragmatic theory of education.

Psychological Basis

The heart of his theory of education, says Dewey, is "contemporary psychology"[22] by which he means the psychology of William James. He calls his experimental University Elementary School "a laboratory of applied psychology,"[23] and says that it is concerned with "the problem of viewing the education of the child in the light of the principles of mental activity and processes of growth made known by modern psychology."[24]

When we remember that James' psychology was primarily concerned with instincts and the phases of their growth, we can readily understand why Dewey, with his instinct theory of education, turns to James for his theoretical justification. The problem of education for Dewey is to discover the stages of growth of the instincts and impulses so that the proper materials or subject-matters can be introduced at the time when the natural history of the child is ready for them. These stages of psychological growth are primarily biological. But there is in fact no contradiction when we recall that James reduced psychology in large part to biology, and ended up with the Weismann theory of heredity. Dewey does the same thing, as we shall soon see.

Dewey states the problem of education as he sees it. The problem, he says, "takes the form of the construction of a course of study which harmonizes with the natural history of the growth of the child in capacity and experience. The question is the selection of the kind, variety, and due proportion of subjects, answering most definitely to the dominant needs and powers of a given period of growth, and of those modes of presentation that will cause the selected material to enter vitally into growth."[25] Subjects are to be introduced when the child is ready for them. To be ready for them means that the powers, needs, interests and habits are at a stage of development at which the subject can "enter vitally into the growth" of the child. But powers, interests, needs and habits are "based upon an original instinct." "In the first place, every interest grows out of some instinct or some habit that in turn is finally based upon an original instinct."[26] Those instincts which are most important for education, namely those connected with occupations, are the "instincts of construction and production."[27]

The study of psychology is to determine at what particular stage of development of the "instincts of construction and production" certain occupations, such as carpentry, weaving, cooking, and other trades, should be introduced into the "natural history" of the child.

The central question then becomes what can the psychology of the Jamesian variety tell us about the stages of growth of the child. Dewey asks the questions himself: "What, then, are the chief working hypotheses that have been adopted from psychology? What educational counterparts have been hit upon as in some degree in line with the adopted psychology?"[28]

He lists and discusses three hypotheses which he has taken over from James' psychology. In each case he poses the "new" hypotheses against the corresponding ones of the "old" psychology. And in each case he fights against something worthy of criticism, but goes on to throw out the good along with the bad. In this way he adopts a wholly reactionary psychology as a rationale for his theory of education. But he does it under the cover of an attack on some outmoded traditional notions.

Speaking of the hypotheses adopted from contemporary psychology, Dewey says: "The discussion of these questions may be approached by pointing out a contrast between contemporary psychology and the psychology of former days. The contrast is a triple one."[29]

The *first hypothesis* is directed against the "old" notion that the individual mind gets its ideas from contact with the external world. According to Dewey, the difficulty with this concept is that it sees the individual as completely isolated from society. This sounds good. But Dewey goes on to point out what he means by the relation of the ideas of the individual mind with society. The individual gets his ideas, his mental equipment, from society. This is true, but the important question is *how* this takes place. Marxists say that ideas come from the social practice of the individual, from his participation in society, both in productive and conscious social life. Thus mental equipment, consciousness, the psyche, are primarily *social* processes, though resting on a physiological basis of the brain and central nervous system. But with Dewey, as with James, the mind of the individual is determined primarily by biological heredity. Society, in the form of parents, passes biologically from generation to generation, not only the physiological equipment but also the mental equipment of the individual. The individual gets his

psyche, his consciousness, as an inborn inheritance from the "race."
Thus Dewey's attack on the old notion conceals the reactionary content
of what he would substitute. At the same time he has discarded what
must be retained of the old notion, namely that the individual mind is
formed through interaction with the external world. For Dewey, mind
is equipped from within, from individual heredity.

With his instinct theory of education, Dewey would have to find
a psychology which taught that the individual mind was formed primarily through inheritance of instincts, rather than through social
practice in the external world.

Thus he says: *"The idea of heredity has made familiar the notion
that the equipment of the individual, mental as well as physical, is an
inheritance from the race: a capital inherited by the individual from the
past and held in trust by him for the future."* The physical heredity
mentioned by Dewey is obviously a reference to the then "new" genetics
of Morgan-Weismann which regarded the organism simply as the
bearer of the gene which was passed unchanged from generation to
generation. The mental heredity, the inheritance of mental equipment,
mentioned by Dewey, is obviously the Jamesian extension of Weissmann
genetics to psychological phenomena.

The first hypothesis which Dewey takes over from the "new psychology" is, then, that mental equipment is a social phenomenon in the
sense that it is inherited and that the individual mind is simply a
middle-man between generations. The instincts and impulses are passed
through the individual mind to the following generations basically untouched.

The *second hypothesis* adopted into Dewey's theory of education
from psychology has to do with the substitution of activity for truth.
This comes directly and explicitly from James. But again it comes under
cover of an attack on the old notion, in this case that intellect or knowledge was the whole content of psychology, to the exclusion of emotion
and activity. This old notion is worthy of attack, but the use Dewey
puts it to is to conceal the fact that he makes emotions, impulses and
instincts the sole content of psychology to the exclusion of any real
knowledge of the real world. Along with James, he reduces the intellect
or knowledge to mere direction of activity apart from any concept of
truth about reality. Knowledge becomes simply the formula for moving
from desired ends to the means of their fulfillment. It is the substitution

of expediency for knowledge and truth. In Dewey's theory of education this becomes the rationale for his stress on the relation of means and ends as the subject-matter of learning.

Here is how Dewey poses the second hypothesis adopted from Jamesian psychology:

> In the second place, the older psychology was a psychology of knowledge, of intellect. Emotion and endeavor occupies but an incidental and derivative place. Much was said about sensations—next to nothing about movements. Now we believe, to use the words of Mr. James, that the intellect, the sphere of sensations and ideas, is but a "middle department which we sometimes take to be final, failing to see, amidst the monstrous diversity of the length and complications of the cogitations which may fill it, that it can have but one essential function—the function of defining the direction which our activity, immediate or remote, shall take".[31]

In throwing out the old notion of knowledge as having no relation to action, Dewey and James throw out that which alone would make it possible for knowledge to guide action, namely, that the knowledge be true knowledge, that the ideas correspond to the objective material world. This is the central crime of the pragmatists, as has been pointed out time and time again. They claim to unite theory and practice, true knowledge and action, but in the process they eliminate true theory or knowledge and thus leave practice without guidance, transforming practice into expediency in means and ends, improvisation and spontaneous trial and error. To guide action, knowledge must reflect the way things are and move in the real world. It is this latter aspect which the pragmatists repudiate. They say that knowledge is only and solely concerned with practice. It is a formula to eliminate guidance, for it destroys scientific theory. It is Dewey's apology for the elimination of intellectual knowledge from the public schools where the workers' children are educated. He is only going to teach *know-how*, the relation of means to ends which are desired; not knowledge of the real world in the form of truth accumulated by human beings throughout their history.

The second hypothesis adopted from James' psychology, is, then, the elimination of true knowledge and the substitution of expediency in means and ends as a "guide" to activity. It is the anti-intellectual, anti-theoretical feature of pragmatism in all fields.

The *third hypothesis* adopted from Jamesian psychology and incorporated into Dewey's theory of education is concerned with the stages of growth of the instincts and impulses of the child. But again the reactionary content of Dewey's thought is masked under cover of an offensive against a traditional notion which should be attacked. This time the offensive is directed against the old idea that the mind is un-changing, that it is given once and for all. But Dewey reinstates this concept after attacking it. He reestablishes it in the form of instincts and impulses which were present from the beginning but which simply unfold in stages. He is going to maintain that the mind is a growing process, not a fixed thing. But what he means by growth is the stages of unfolding instinct. From this he draws the inference for education that any course of study must be rooted in the instincts which are flowering at the particular stage of growth. Learning must be fed in accordance with the given stages. What can be fed at what stage can be discovered only by trying it out in practice. This process of trying out was the function of Dewey's experimental laboratory school in Chicago.

Here is Dewey's statement about the stages of growth:

> . . . *Now we believe in the mind as a growing affair, and hence as essentially changing, presenting distinctive phases of capacity and interest at different periods.* . . .
>
> If once more we are in earnest with the idea of mind as growth, this growth carrying with it typical features distinctive of its various stages, it is clear that an educational transformation is again indicated. *It is clear that the selection and grading of material in the course of study must be done with reference to proper nutrition of the dominant directions of activity in a given period,* not with refer-ence to chopped-up sections of a ready-made universe of knowledge. . . . (My italics.—H.K.W.) [32]

Since for Dewey interests have their source in "original instincts," the entire conception of "stages of growth" is based on a biological-psychological level. It is not the social relations a child enters into which will determine the stages of his growth; rather, for Dewey it is the unfolding of the inborn instincts. The stages are bio-genetic. Of course, the stages of growth which Dewey distinguishes are not actually bio-genetic, but are psychological stages stemming from the bourgeois relations into which the child enters.

In an article on Soviet psychology, A. N. Leontiev identifies this bio-genetic theory of stages of growth as the typical bourgeois approach to pedagogy:

It is well known that there are numerous bio-psychological divisions of the childhood into periods. Their general quality is evident from the fact that they all, despite their differences, start out from the metaphysical conception of the development of the psyche as a process of the unfolding of properties already existing in the child. Such theories explain this process by starting out from an illegal carrying over into child psychology of a so-called bio-genetic law: directly connecting the course of development of the child's psyche with its biological development and adducing to the support of their division into periods such criteria as the replacement of the milk teeth by the permanent teeth, or the development of the function of sexual desire. In general, all such attempts represent the development of the child's psyche as a simple function of his growth—as if unalterably connected steps of the process were tied to definite stages of growth.

The pseudo-scientific nature of these self-created pedagogical divisions of childhood into periods was self-evident.[33]

In opposition to this bourgeois bio-genetic theory of stages of growth, Soviet psychologists have "shown that what appeared to be fatalistic 'presence' of psychological characteristics in a specific case of growth was actually the product of the child's life in definite social relations, a product of instruction and education."[34] Thus what Dewey would have appear as bio-genetic stages of unfolding of instincts are in fact the product of life and schooling in capitalist society. Stages of learning are primarily social, not biological phenomena.

The third and final hypothesis adopted by Dewey from Jamesian psychology is, then, the bio-genetic theory of stages of growth. It is the stages of unfolding inherent "instinct," "tendencies," "impulses," "needs" and "interests."

The three hypotheses are interdependent. As a matter of fact, given the first, the other two follow logically. For if mental equipment is biologically inherited in the form of "instincts," "tendencies," etc., then it follows that "knowledge" is concerned with the means for the satisfaction of these inherent, innate drives, and that the latter unfold in a process of "growth." The three taken together have far-reaching implications for the theory of education. Dewey draws the inferences of the "new" psychology for education by starting from the third hypothesis, namely, that the "instincts" or "interests" unfold in stages of growth. He says: "In coming to speak of the educational answers which have been sought for the psychological hypotheses, it it convenient to start from the matter of the stages of growth."[35]

Through the medium of the bio-genetic stages of growth, Dewey introduces his entire theory of education. This theory centers about the introduction of a particular subject-matter into the "natural history" of the child's growth at the stage at which his "instincts" and "interests" are "ready" for it. But what is the "subject-matter?" It is the *means* which will satisfy, or give results, or will work in producing what the child, in the light of his "instincts" and "interests," wants. The entire subject-matter of pragmatic education is the relation of means to ends, and overcoming whatever obstacles lie in the way of success in the process.

Means and Ends in Place of Knowledge

To Dewey, the aim of education throughout all stages of growth is the relation of means to ends. "The general standpoint," he says, is "the adaptation of means to ends." The "ends" come supposedly from the "interest" which "grows out of some instinct or some habit that in turn is finally based upon an original instinct."[36] The aim of education, according to Dewey, is to discover what "end," "interest," etc. a child at a certain stage of growth has, whether or not he is aware of it, and to lead him to employ whatever means will give results in terms of the child's "interest." The aim is to have the child be able to discriminate and employ means which work in leading toward his goal.

Dewey speaks of only two stages, not because there are not more but because the University Elementary School has experimented with only two "age groups." "The first stage," he says, "found in the child say from four to eight years of age is characterized by directness of social and personal interests, and by directness and promptness of relationship between impressions, ideas, and action."[37] This age group does not yet discriminate between means and ends, action and ideas, but rather lives in a "vague unity of experience."[38] This "vague unity," however, demonstrates "the intimate connection between knowing and doing, so characteristic of this period of child life."[39]

It is not until the second stage of growth that education becomes primarily concerned with the "adaptation of means to ends." The age group "from eight or nine to eleven or twelve" is ready for the introduction of "rules of action—that is, of regular means appropriate to reaching permanent results." At this stage of growth the problem becomes one of bringing the child to the recognition of the "need of securing for himself practical and intellectual control of such methods of work and inquiry as will enable him to realize results for himself."[40] Not knowledge which reflects truthfully the processes in the objective external world, but simply any means that appear to work in leading toward the desired end is the content of education as Dewey would have us see it. Subjective satisfaction is substituted for truth. Anything that is useful, anything that works is called "true." In this manner would Dewey "educate" the sons and daughters of the working class. They would not be taught the accumulated knowledge and truth of mankind, which would be dangerous in their hands; rather, they are to be taught the "rules of action" which will make them good producers. And more important, they will be deprived of the weapon of truth which could combat the expedient lies and attitudes by which the ruling class binds them to the system of exploitation and oppression. Limiting education to "rules of action" leaves the way wide open for white supremacy, Anglo-Saxon superiority, for all the vicious ideological weapons of the imperialists.

As N. K. Goncharov in an article on U.S. education puts it:

It is well known that the pragmatists place at the basis of learning subjective experience, and the instrument of gaining experience is theory, knowledge, ideas, and convictions. In their opinion, ideas, science, and experience do not reflect the objective world, and are valuable only insofar as they are useful to mankind. "The criterion of the value of an idea," writes Dewey, "is its ability to solve the problem for which it was designed. Workability is the test, the measure or criterion of truth." Instead of objectivity of truth the pragmatists speak of usefulness of truth. Of course, such a "philosophy" suits very well the reactionary American bourgeoisie, since everything it finds useful is declared to be true. "The Marshall Plan" is useful to reactionaries, consequently it is true. Anti-labor laws are no less useful, so they too are true. By such sophistry one can prove anything at all, even that American war-mongers are innocent lambs, or that reactionary educators are benefactors of all mankind, precisely what they represent themselves to be.[41]

Whatever *means* are useful in reaching the *end-in-view* is the subject-matter of education. And this training is to begin when the child reaches the age of "eight or nine." If the end-in-view is to feel superior to people of a different color, then the problem is to find the means to satisfy this "impulse," "need," or "want" rooted in "an original instinct." Let it unfold and flower in the Ku Klux Klan. If it works in satisfying a want, it is "true." There is no objective truth which could give it the lie on the basis of pragmatic theories. Dewey does not, of course, make any such explicit statement, but it is the undeniable logic of his position.

Dewey describes the expedient means-end subject-matter and methodology which is to be introduced in the second stage of growth:

> In the second period, extending from eight or nine to eleven or twelve, the aim is to recognize and respond to the change which comes into the child from his growing sense of the possibility of more permanent and objective results and of the necessity for control of agencies for the skill necessary to reach these results. . . .
>
> *The problem on the side of method is an analogous one: to bring the child to recognize the necessity of a similar development within himself—the need of securing for himself practical and intellectual control of such methods of work and inquiry as will enable him to realize results for himself.* (My italics.— H.K.W.) [42]

The aim of education, Dewey says, is to give "rules of action" or "means appropriate to reaching permanent results" at the times when they are best suited to changes in the growth of the child. This "aim" might sound good if we did not know the difference between "rules of action" on the one hand and knowledge and truth on the other; if we did not know that Dewey is substituting expediency in means and ends for knowledge and truth. The expediency he and the schools will transmit to the child at appropriate stages of growth is, of course, whatever the bourgeoisie finds expedient at the time. Today it is war hysteria through the practice of A-bomb drills and red-baiting.

The educational method flows from the stated aim. It is to "bring the child to recognize . . . the need of securing for himself . . . such methods of work and inquiry as will enable him to realize results for himself." The child is to learn "that success is what counts," that whatever "works" has "cash-value," in the words of William James.

This "educational" process of learning "rules of action" which lead to success in "the adaptation of means to ends" continues also after the age of twelve. Since the experiments had not yet been performed in the laboratory school, Dewey merely outlines how the aim and method would work out in various traditional subjects such as history and science. In connection with the subject of history he says: "Since the aim is not 'covering the ground,' but knowledge of social processes used to secure social results, no attempt is made to go over the entire history, in chronological order, of America. . . . The aim is to present a variety of climatic and local conditions, to show the different sorts of obstacles and helps that people found, and a variety of historic traditions and customs and purposes of different people."[43]

History is studied to see what means have worked in the past to accomplish ends. It is not taught chronologically, but in bits and parts; which is an effective way of avoiding history with its class struggles and revolutions. Moreover, history is taught to see how people in the past have overcome obstacles, where the latter are not social and concerned with colonial oppression and war, but are natural obstacles such as "climatic and local conditions." It is clear that history taught as the study of past successful or unsuccessful means to ends is the elimination of history from the curriculum. Dewey's subject of "history" is designed to teach the sons and daughters of the working class that there is no such thing as history; that there are only varying means to given ends.

With regard to the subject of science, Dewey says: "The general standpoint—the adaptation of means to ends—controls also the work in science. The experimental side devotes itself to a study of processes which yield results of value to men. The activity of the child in the earlier period is directly productive, rather than investigative. His experiments are modes of active doing—almost as much as his play and games. Later he tries to find out how various materials or agencies are manipulated in order to give certain results.[44] Thus science is not a matter of facts and laws which correspond to the way in which things and processes move in the objective world. It is rather simply the "know-how," the "rules of action" which have been found to give desired results. This is not the teaching of science but a formula for the elimination of science from the curriculum. Again it is what we would expect from a bourgeois-apologist theoretician of education. For genuine science poses a threat to the ruling class, as does a genuine science of history, when put in the hands of the "great majority."

With regard to other subjects, Dewey says: "The relation of means to ends is emphasized also in other lines of work."[45] Among the "other lines of work" he mentions "art," "cooking," "sewing," "reading," etc. Throughout all the subjects in the curriculum, Dewey sees that "the specific principle of the conscious relation of means to ends has emerged as the unifying principle. . . ."[46] And he adds, "it is hoped that emphasis of this in all lines of work will have a decidely cumulative and unifying effect upon the child's development."[47] The emphasis on pragmatic expediency in means to ends as a substitute for knowledge and truth is indeed designed to have "a cumulative and unifying effect upon the child's development"; it is calculated to imbue him with the intellectual and moral bankruptcy which characterizes the capitalist class in the era of imperialism—and thus through "cumulative effect" to "unify" him, to make him submit to the bourgeois social order.

Conclusion

Finally, Dewey pays tribute to his spiritual master in the field of education. Froebel had developed the bio-genetic theory of stages of growth as the main thesis of his book, *The Education of Man,* published in Germany in 1826. Speaking of the University Elementary School, Dewey says, the "school endeavors throughout its whole course—now including children between four and thirteen—to carry into effect certain principles which Froebel was perhaps the first consciously to set forth."[48] Among the principles advanced by Froebel, Dewey paraphrases the one that is most central in his own theory: "That the primary root of all educative activity is in the instinctive, impulsive attitudes and activities of the child, and not in the presentation and application of external material, whether through the ideas of others or through the senses."[49]

This is the fundamental principle embodied in the pragmatic theory of education. It is the turning of education upside down, so that it stands on its head. It is crude subjective idealism. It makes education depend on the internal, mental instinctive equipment of the child rather than on the ideas and attitudes of the child depending on the education which comes from the outside, from the teacher, from books, and from life in society. In education as in all fields, the bourgeoisie requires subjective idealism in order to drug the people with its reactionary ideology. Just as Charles Peirce borrowed the subjective idealist philosophy from Berkeley and Hume in order to lay the basis for his formulation of the class-created pragmatic method, so Dewey borrowed the subjective "instinct" theory of education from Froebel in order to rationalize the pragmatic method of "adaptation of means to ends" in the field of pedagogy.

Dewey's pragmatic theory and method of education are summed up in his instructions to the teacher. There are two such general instructions. The first is rooted in the subjective "instinct" theory. When the teacher is considering to what occupation he should introduce the child, he must ask himself the following question: "Is it something of which he [the child] has the instinctive roots in himself, and which will mature the capacities that are struggling for manifestation in him?"[50]

The second general instruction to the teacher tells him that, once the occupation which corresponds to the child's stage of growth of "instincts" has been chosen, he must thereafter be concerned "with the development of a sense of more remote ends, and of the need of directing acts so as to make them means for those ends."[51]

Thus the subjective *instinct theory* paves the way for the *educational method of expediency* in means to ends.

Dewey's *School and Society* marked the formulation of the pragmatic apologetic theory of education in the United States. Since the turn of the century, his philosophy has become the guiding "light" of most of the leading teacher training institutions across the nation. The theory is not progressive. It is thoroughly reactionary. However, in the hands of sincere, devoted and capable teachers it has helped to undermine the old authoritarian, drillmaster type of education. This was an historically necessary task in the development of the theory and practice of education. The pragmatic approach likewise has permitted the teacher to carry on her work more freely and experimentally. It has focused attention on an important aspect of the educational process, the development of a child as an individual rather than as a parrot of the teacher. But with all this, the pragmatic theory has essentially served to mislead teachers and schools with regard to what is to replace the old drill-master system. Instead it has placed education in the United States in the service of the dominant interests, just as the old education did, but adapted to the conditions of the twentieth century.

Dewey and his followers—Counts, Childs, Kilpatrick, Keleher, Washburne, *et al.*—have substituted the "instinct" theory and the expedient methodology for authority and drill and have thus guaranteed that education will be the servant of imperialist reaction. As Goncharov described it: "Dewey, Counts and other educational theorists like them wage a most decisive struggle for the preservation of the bourgeois influence not only in economics but in ideology as well. They place pedagogy wholly in the service of the political interests of American reactionaries."[52]

With the publication of Dewey's *The School and Society,* culminating twenty years of development of pragmatic apologetics in various realms of ideology, the time was ripe for the popularization of philosophic pragmatism. William James, rediscovering the Peirce articles, had only to generalize from Fiske in history, Holmes in law, Dewey in education, as well as from his own psychology, to formulate the pragmatic philosophy. This he did, leaving no stones unturned. His philosophic writings, almost entirely devoid of demagogy, lay bare for all to see the crude essence of pragmatism. We turn now to an examination of these works.

VII. WILLIAM JAMES'
RADICAL EMPIRICISM

"'THE TRUE,' *to put it briefly, is only the expedient in the way of our thinking, just as 'the right' is only the expedient in the way of our behaving."* Thus does James, himself, expose the crude essence of the pragmatic formula. As if to underscore its decadence, he adds, "expedient in almost any fashion."

James is writing in 1907 during the decade of the first full flush of U.S. imperialism, the era of "Teddy" Roosevelt's "Big Stick." It was a period of braggadocio and the will to power when the American financiers were flexing their economic and military muscles and whetting their appetites for world domination. But it was also a time when labor was growing in class consciousness, though it did not as yet pose an immediate threat to the lust for superprofits. If only the working man could be "kept in his place" there seemed no limit to the possibilities opening before "the adolescent industrial giant of the new world." It would be the dawn of "The American Century."

Into the breach stepped William James gathering the various threads together, giving articulate expression to the imperialist outlook, unadorned and as brash as the times in which he wrote. In a single phrase he caught the temper of the class: "An idea is 'true' so long as to believe it is profitable to our lives."[2] The "will to believe," ideological counterpart of the will to power, takes the place of science, theory and truth, while whatever is "profitable to our lives," whatever has "practical cash-value," usurps the place of the objective material world and *is* "reality." Any demagogic claim Peirce had made to "scientific method" is stripped away and pragmatism stands nakedly exposed as the celebration and exaltation of sheer dollar expediency.

The closing decades of the 19th century had seen a sharp decline in the hold of religion on the masses. Until the eighties and nineties philosophy in the United States had been almost wholly absorbed in theology buttressed by an absolute idealism which preached that evil was relative and finite while the good God, the absolute ground of all things, was a perfection eternally complete. It was a religious philosophy rooted in the principle that "everything is for the best in the best of all possible worlds." This doctrine of resignation in the face of evil had obvious advantages for the capitalist class. The trouble, however, was that the working people as a whole would no longer be taken in by it. The evils had become too great; the illusion could not stand up against the brutal reality.

This posed a threat of major proportions to the ruling class. A fresh ideological weapon was required to stem the tide, one which would give a new basis for obscurantism, ignorance and superstition while appearing to be scientific. The reconciliation of science and religion was on the agenda of capitalist ideology.

William James was acutely aware of the gravity of the situation on the capitalist ideological front, as is made clear beyond any shadow of doubt in the opening chapter of his major work, *Pragmatism,* published in 1907. Here he shows that his primary concern is with what he calls the "revolt against the airy and shallow optimism of current religious philosophy."[3] He finds an example of this revolt in a little book entitled *Human Submission,* by Morrison I. Swift, an anarcho-syndicalist pamphleteer with a following in the current labor and socialist movements. James gave considerable space to the arguments of Swift, obviously feeling that they reflected the thinking of broad sections of the working people. He quotes several pages from Swift in which the latter, after building a case against capitalism by referring to newspaper items reporting unemployment, poverty, disease and starvation, concludes with the following statement:

> . . . The records of many more such cases lie before me . . . an encyclopedia might easily be filled with their kind. These few I cite as interpretation of the Universe. We are aware of the presence of God in his World, says a writer in a recent English review. . . . "The Absolute is the richer for every discord and for all the diversity which it embraces," says F. H. Bradley. He means that these slain men make the universe richer, and that is philosophy. But while Professors Royce and Bradley and a whole host of guileless thoroughfed thinkers are unveiling the Absolute and explaining away evil and pain, this is Reality and the condition of

the only beings known to us anywhere in the universe with a developed conscious-ness of what the universe is. What these people experience *is* Reality. The philoso-phers are dealing in shades, while those who live and feel know the truth. And the mind of mankind—not yet the mind of philosophers and of the proprietary class—but of the great mass of the silently thinking men and feeling men, is coming to this view. They are judging the universe as they have hitherto per-mitted the hierophants of religion and learning to judge them. . . .

These facts invincibly prove religion a nullity. Man will not give religion two thousand centuries or twenty centuries more to try itself and waste human time. Its time is up; its own record ends it. Mankind has not aeons and eternities to spare for trying out discredited systems![4]

With James' citation of this passage, can it be doubted that he was fully conscious of the situation facing the class of which he was a hereditary member? "The great mass of silently thinking men and feeling men" were coming to the view, in the light of their elemental experience of the evils of capitalism, that "these facts invincibly prove religion a nullity" and that time can no longer be wasted on discredited idealist systems. Knowledge of "these facts" must lead to action to change society and eliminate the evils. This testimony shook the foundations of the society which had given James all he could ask for. He draws the lesson for himself and his class: "Such is the reaction of an empiricist mind to the rationalist bill of fare. It is an absolute 'No, I thank you.' 'Religion,' says Mr. Swift, 'is like a sleep-walker to whom actual things are a blank!' . . . He becomes thus the judge of us philosophers. Tender or tough, he finds us wanting. *None of us may treat his verdicts disdainfully, for after all, his is the typically perfect mind, the mind the sum of whose demands is greatest, the mind whose criticisms and dissatisfactions are fatal in the long run.*"[5]

In short, James warns that to continue to rely on a philosophy which can no longer maintain the hold of religion on the masses is fatal both to the philosophy and to the social system. He says that what is required is a doctrine which will reconcile the hard facts of life with the fiction of religion, science with superstition, and thus help blunt the point of revolt. James concludes by offering a philosophy better suited to the temper of the times: "It is at this point that my own solution begins to appear. I offer the oddly-named thing pragmatism as a philosophy that can satisfy both kinds of demand. It can remain religious like the ration-alisms, but at the same time, like the empiricisms it can preserve the richest intimacy with facts."[6]

Pragmatism is offered as a solution to the problem facing the capitalist class. James is not entirely as frank as that, but his appeal to the testimony of Swift leaves no room for doubt that it is a conscious effort to supply a class need. It was not simply an "innocent" desire to reconcile science and religion, as Ralph Barton Perry, author of *The Thought and Character of William James,* would have us believe.*

As early as 1875, while James was teaching psychology at Harvard, he showed an acute awareness of the problem. He wanted to teach a course in philosophy but the board of the College was hesitant to have a "scientist" teach philosophy, which was at the time largely religious. To convince the trustees James wrote a letter to President Eliot in the course of which he argued that:

> A real science of man is now being built up out of the theory of evolution and the facts of archaeology, the nervous system and the senses. It has already a vast material extent, the papers and magazines are full of essays and articles having more or less to do with it. The question is, shall the students be left to the magazines, on the one hand, and to what languid attention professors educated in the exclusively literary way can pay to the subject? Or shall the College employ a man whose scientific training fits him fully to realize the force of all natural history arguments, whilst his concomitant familiarity with writers of a more introspective kind preserves him from certain crudities of reasoning which are extremely common in men of the laboratory pure and simple?[8]

There is not much subtlety in this argument, but translated it means that it would be far more effective in keeping the students from becoming thoroughly scientific and materialist (the certain "crudities") if the college hired a scientist who knew the philosophical subtleties and could turn science into religion (the "more introspective kind"). He won the trustees over to his way of thinking.

The real enemy for James was science and materialism. The counter-weapon was religion and idealism, but dressed up to look like their opposites. To accomplish this sleight-of-hand the philosophy of pragmatism was well adapted.

---

* Perry sees James' motivation growing out of his loving pity for his aged father, Henry James, Sr., who was an exponent of religious philosophy completely at odds with science. In a letter quoted by Perry, James writing shortly after his father's death, says: "As life closes, all a man had done seems like one cry or sentence. Father's cry was the single one that religion is real. The thing is so to 'voice' it that other ears shall hear—no easy task, but a worthy one, which in some shape I shall attempt." And he did, but for a more compelling reason.

Science and Religion

First, it is important to see how James places pragmatism in the history of philosophy as he views it. He forgets all about his remark that in 1898 "the times were ripe" for it, and states elsewhere: "The pragmatic movement, so-called—I do not like the name, but apparently it is too late to change it—seems to have rather suddenly precipitated itself out of the air."[9] How "the air" can give birth to a philosophy we are told in his conception of its history. "The history of philosophy," he writes, "is to a great extent that of a certain clash of human temperaments."[10] So "the air" was a euphemism for "human temperament." The philosophy a person invents or embraces is not determined by the society he lives in, the way he makes a living, the class of which he is a member or with which he identifies himself but depends on the temper of his personality. The history of philosophy is the history of the clash of "human temperaments." It turns out tat there are really only two personality tempers, one "tough" and "materialistic," and the other "tender" and "idealistic." Thus the historic struggle between the two philosophical camps of materialism and idealism is not the ideological front of the class struggle but the clash of incompatible temperaments.

Having set down the thesis that the history of philosophy is the history of the clash of human temperament, James proceeds to elaborate:

> Undignified as such treatment may seem to some of my colleagues, I shall have to take account of this clash and explain a good many of the divergencies of philosophers by it. Of whatever temperament a professional philosopher is, he tries, when philosophizing, to sink the fact of his temperament. Temperament is no conventionally recognized reason, so he urges impersonal reasons only for his conclusions. Yet his temperament really gives him a stronger bias than any of his more strictly objective premises. It loads the evidence for him one way or the other, making for a more sentimental or a more hard-hearted view of the universe, just as this fact or that principle would. He *trusts* his temperament. Wanting a universe that suits it, he believes in any representation of the universe that does suit it.[11]

This is the *temperament theory* of philosophy and history. It is a convenient theory, for it makes the material life of society and its reflection in social consciousness completely irrelevant. All that is necessary is to know what kind of temperament you are dealing with, tender or tough, and you have all that you need to know about Plato and Aristotle, Kant and Hegel, Marx and Engels. The question of where temperament comes from is not raised, for then it would be right back where it started. Temperament for James is obviously part of the immutable human nature, the instincts, with which one is born. It is a good formula for keeping the class struggle out of the understanding of philosophy, and for preventing its history from becoming a science.*[12] For philosophy and its history to be a science it is necessary to look outside of the individual to the development of the objectively existing natural and social world. But James' thesis makes the whole question of philosophy a purely subjective, individual matter. If you are tough you are a materialist, empiricist, a lover of facts. But if you are tender, you are an idealist, a rationalist, a lover of eternal principles. He sets down the traits of "the two types of mental make-up" in columns entitled "tender-minded" and "tough-minded" respectively:[13]

THE TENDER-MINDED	THE TOUGH-MINDED
Rationalistic (going by principles),	Empiricist (going by "facts"),
Intellectualistic,	Sensationalistic,
Idealistic,	Materialistic,
Optimistic,	Pessimistic,
Religious,	Irreligious,
Free-willist,	Fatalistic,
Monistic,	Pluralistic,
Dogmatical.	Skeptical.

Having catalogued the traits of the two kinds of people, James remarks that "No one can live an hour without both facts and principles"[14] and that "most of us have a hankering for the good things on both sides."[15] Thus he sets the stage for the reconciliation of the tough and the tender, materialism and idealism, science and religion, facts and fiction. He proposes to take the "good" things on each side. But which are good? Good

* For the history of philosophy the only scientific thesis is that most recently formulated by A. A. Zhdanov: ". . . The scientific history of philosophy is the history of the origin, rise and development of the scientific materialist world outlook and its laws. Inasmuch as materialism grew and developed in the struggle with idealist currents, the history of philosophy is simultaneously the history of the struggle of materialism with idealism."

for whom? James says, "He wants facts; he wants science; but he also wants a religion."[16] Who is "he"? The answer is obvious. Swift did not say he wanted religion. It is the capitalist class that requires both science and religion, and therefore their reconciliation, which is in point of fact no reconciliation but rather the undercutting of science to buttress religion.

James shifts the pronoun to "you." That makes it more personal. He says "you" are in a quandary. "You" want a mixture of tough and tender, the "good" on both sides, but all "you" can find in the way of a philosophy is either the one or the other. "You" want "facts" *and* "religion," but "you" are offered an exclusive choice. "You" find a sharp conflict between science and religion, materialism and idealism.

"Now what kind of philosophy do you find actually offered to meet your need?" asks James. "You find," he answers, "an empirical philosophy that is not religious enough, and a religious philosophy that is not empirical enough for your purposes."[17] And he goes on to elaborate:

> If you look to the quarter where facts are most considered you find the whole tough-minded program in operation, and the "conflict between science and religion" in full blast. Either it is that Rocky Mountain tough of a Haeckel with his materialistic monism, his ether-God and his jest at your God as a "gaseous vertebrate"; or it is Spencer treating the world's history as a redistribution of matter and motion solely, and bowing religion politely out at the front door. . . . You get, in short, a materialistic universe, in which only the tough-minded find themselves congenially at home.[18]

"You," of course, don't want that. "You" want some relation to "facts" but surely not materialism. And yet that is all "you" are offered on the one side.

On the other side all "you" get is religious philosophy out of touch with life. This "transcendental idealism" and other-wordly "theism" cannot meet "your" needs. The people, as Swift warned "you," will not take it. The objective idealists, the Greens, the Cairds, the Bosanquets, the Royces are no longer of use to "you." With them "you escape indeed the materialism that goes with the reigning empiricism; but you pay for your escape by losing contact with the concrete parts of life,"[19] and, James could have added, with the people. Absolute or transcendental idealism and theism, "these two systems are what you have to choose between if you turn to the tender-minded school . . . but both are equally remote and vacuous."[20]

Thus if "you" look to your philosophical defenses you find two "untenable" schools, materialism and old-fashioned, openly religious idealism. One is "your" enemy and the other no longer an adequate weapon. The "history" of philosophy is the clash of these products of the tough and tender-minded. But "you" do not want either a tough or a tender. What "you" want is a tough-tender or a tender-tough, or maybe a tender in tough clothing.

"You want a system," James tells the imperialists, "that will combine both things, the scientific loyalty to facts and willingness to take account of them, the spirit of adaptation and accommodation, in short, but also the old confidence in human values and the resultant spontaneity, whether of the religious or of the romantic type."[21] And so, says James, "I offer the oddly-named thing pragmatism as a philosophy that can satisfy both kinds of demand." It is tough-tender, the tender in tough get-up. It will serve "you" well in the long pull ahead. It is made to order for what "you" require. "I hope," he adds, "that I may lead you to find it [pragmatism] just the mediating way of thinking that you require."[22]

"The pragmatistic philosophy," James concludes, "preserves as cordial a relation with facts and, unlike Spencer's philosophy, it neither begins nor ends by turning positive religious constructions out of doors—it treats them cordially as well."[23]

The key to this whole business is the meaning of "you." Reading it as we have done in the sense of the monopoly capitalist class makes James' words not only clear, but in the nature of a confession. The justification for making this translation is given by James himself in his quotation from Morrison I. Swift. There is no mistaking his meaning that the old religious philosophy no longer holds the millions of "Swifts" in ideological bondage. To reestablish the hold of religion on the people, a new philosophical formula is required, and James assures his class that pragmatism is "just the mediating way." What is the character of this formula?

Under cover of an attack on absolute idealism and traditional religion he denies all necessity in the world and certainty in thought. He then substitutes expediency in the form of the will to believe; the will to believe *anything,* including God, free will, immortality, ghosts, etc., and thus he reinstates the content of religion and obscurantism through the back door.

James speaks of "the scope of pragmatism" as "first a method; and second, a genetic theory of what is meant by truth."[24] In point of fact he has the order reversed, for the pragmatic procedure requires the elimination of truth before it can be applied, and further, as was the case with Peirce, both the pragmatic method and the "theory of truth" presuppose a world view. Such being the case, we will treat them in their logical order: World view, theory of truth, and method.

World View

"For many years past," writes James in 1905, "my mind has been growing into a certain type of *Weltanschauung* [World View]. Rightly or wrongly, I have got to the point where I can hardly see things in any other pattern—I give the name 'radical empiricism' to my *Weltanschauung*".[25] What is "radical empiricism?" What kind of world view is it? He gives a surprisingly candid answer when he says that it is "absolutely nothing new." "Being nothing essentially new," he continues, "it harmonizes with many ancient, philosophic tendencies."[26]

We do not have to speculate about these tendencies; James himself, tells us what they are: "It agrees with nominalism for instance, in always appealing to particulars; with utilitarianism in emphasizing practical aspects; with positivism in its disdain for verbal solutions, useless questions and metaphysical abstractions."[27] In short, it is something of an eclectic hodge-podge of all those philosophies which deny the existence of the world by drawing down a curtain of sense experience without external reference, thus leaving consciousness to spin "reality" out of its own mental substance. The philosophies of Berkeley and Hume come to mind at once, and James does not fail to pay them homage.

That James agreed with the subjective idealism of Berkeley, indeed that he felt he did not carry it far enough, is clear when he says, "Neither Locke nor Berkeley thought his truth out into perfect clearness, but it seems to me that the conception I am defending does little more than consistently carry out the 'pragmatic' method which they were the first to use."[28] Speaking of his radical empiricism in relation to Hume, he says, "It is essentially a mosaic philosophy, a philosophy of plural facts, like that of Hume and his descendants who refer these facts neither to substance in which they inhere, not to absolute mind that creates them as its objects."[29]

The doctrine which James embraces is the fundamental position of subjective idealism formulated by Bishop Berkeley in the phrase *"esse est percipi"* or "to be is to be perceived." "Real" objects are fabricated out of the raw material of sensations which are not experience of any external world. It is only on the basis of such denial of independent reality that Peirce and James and pragmatism can paraphrase Berkeley in their thesis that *"to be is to be believed."* "Reality" cannot be whatever one believes, unless it is first repudiated in its only true meaning as the objective material world existing independently and prior to consciousness. It is the function of radical empiricism to execute this primary task of repudiation.

James further identifies the character of his world view by listing a number of his contemporaries who were exponents of the same "philosophical tendency." "If I mention the names of Sigwart, Mach, Ostwald, Pearson, Milhaud, Poincaré, Duhem, Ruyssen," he says, "those of you who are students will easily identify the tendency I speak of, and will think of additional names."[30] Lenin wrote a book exposing the philosophies of five of the eight men named by James. He lumped them together as proponents of one school which he called "Machism" or "Empirio-Criticism." "I shall use the term [Machian]," Lenin says, "as a synonym for the term empirio-criticist."[31] The five men named by James whose philosophies Lenin exposed were: Mach, Ostwald, Pearson, Poincaré and Duhem. Lenin demonstrated that this school "did not adduce even one argument which had not been put forth by Bishop Berkeley."*[32]

The essential philosophical question, as Lenin states it, is "whether we are to proceed from things to sensations and thought, or from sensations and thought to things?"[33] This is the great question which, as Engels said, divides all philosophy into two camps. "Engels," says Lenin,

* Lenin warns against the pose assumed by Berkeley, the positivists and Machians calling themselves "natural realists," forerunners of the "naturalism" employed by the pragmatists from Peirce to Dewey. Referring to the fact that Berkeley's doctrine had been called "natural realism," Lenin says: "This amusing terminology must by all means be noted, for it tells the tale of Berkeley's intention to pose as a realist. In our further exposition we will from time to time meet with 'recent positivists', who employ the same stratagem or guile. Berkeley does not deny the existence of real objects! Berkeley denies 'only' the teachings of the philosophers, their theory of knowledge, the teaching which takes as a starting point the recognition of the external world and the reflection thereof in the human mind. Berkeley does not deny natural science which has always adhered (mostly unconsciously) to the materialist theory of knowledge."

"sides with the first, materialism; Mach, with the second, idealism."[34] Lenin continues with a characterization which fits James as aptly as it does Mach: "No tricks, no sophistry will obscure the clear and undisputed fact that Ernst Mach's doctrine of things as complexes of sensations, is subjective idealism and a tedious repetition of Berkeleyanism. If with Mach, bodies are to be reduced to 'complexes of sensations' or with Berkeley, to 'combinations of sensations,' then from this it inevitably follows that the 'world is my idea.' Starting with such a supposition it is impossible to arrive at the existence of other selves except myself—and this is the purest solipsism."[35]

Peirce and James, no more than Berkeley and Mach, can escape the logical conclusion of their doctrine, solipsism, namely that "the world is my idea" and that, other people also being "my idea," I am completely suspended in a void; I alone exist. It is this which underlies the "will to believe," for if there is nothing but my mind or consciousness, there is nothing to prevent me from believing whatever it is expedient for me to put my faith in. Indeed, in such a predicament I would have to rely solely on my belief in order to go on living. Thus "purest solipsism" is the ground for the expedient voluntarism of the pragmatic philosophy. In this way, Berkeley's *"esse est percipi"* becomes pragmatism's "to be is to be believed." It is this to which James referred when he said that Berkeley did not think "his truth out into perfect clearness" and his, James', conception "does little more than consistently carry out the 'pragmatic' method which he [Berkeley] was the first to use." It evidently took the complete decadence of capitalism in the era of imperialism to carry the solipsism of subjective idealism under Berkeley to its logical conclusion of crude voluntarism at the hands of James. Thus does history elicit the full implications of a theory.

We have seen that James explicitly recognized the similarity of his philosophy to that of Berkeley and Mach. We have likewise seen that Lenin identifies Mach's doctrine with Berkeley's. We have now to see that Lenin ties the ends together with the recognition that James is in the same boat with Machism. Hence Lenin agrees with James on one point: that there is a direct line of descent from Berkeley through Mach to James. In a footnote Lenin shows the relation of James to Mach:

Here is an example of how the widespread currents of reactionary bourgeois philosophy make use of Machism. The "latest fashion" in recent American philosophy is "pragmatism" (from the Greek word "pragma"—action; that is a philosophy of action). The philosophical journals speak more of pragmatism than of anything else. Pragmatism ridicules the metaphysics of idealism and materialism, extols experience and only experience and recognizes practice as the only criterion of truth. It points to the positivistic movement in general, and *leans especially* upon Ostwald, Mach, Pearson, Poincaré, and Duhem in their belief that science is not an "absolute copy of reality" and in a convenient manner deduces a god for practical purposes, without any metaphysics, without leaving the grounds of experience (*cf.* William James: *Pragmatism. A New Name for Some Old Ways of Thinking*). The difference between Machism and pragmatism is as insignificant as is the distinction between empirio-criticism and empirio-monism.[36]

Having exposed the Machians and the pragmatists as nothing but Berkeleyan subjective idealists, Lenin sums up his polemic: "Taken as a whole, the professors of economics are nothing but scientific salesmen of the capitalist class, and the professors of philosophy are scientific salesmen of theology."[37]

How true this is of James and pragmatism we will soon see; indeed, with regard to them it is almost an understatement, for the pragmatists are salesmen of theosophy, ghosts and mediums as well.

Materialism, with its affirmation of the objective world, science, theory and truth, is recognized by James as the ideological enemy. He knows that "materialism is opposed to spiritualism or theism,"[38] for "the laws of physical nature are what run things, materialism says."[39] While "spiritualism says that mind not only witnesses and records things, but also runs and operates them."[40]

James opens a direct attack on materialism, on the objective material world and the possibility of knowing it. What could be more expedient for this purpose than Berkeley's doctrine? So he begins with it. To "prove" that matter does not exist is the goal.*[41]

The essential content of his argument is that the world is my

---

* James says: "Material substance was criticized by Berkeley with such telling effect that his name has reverberated through all subsequent philosophy. Berkeley's treatment of the notion of matter is so well known as to need hardly more than a mention: So far from denying the external world which we know, Berkeley corroborated it. It was the scholastic notion of a material substance unapproachable by us, behind the external world, deeper and more real than it, and needed to support it, which Berkeley maintained to be the most effective of all reducers of the external world to unreality. Abolish that substance, he said, believe that God, whom you can understand and approach, sends you the sensible world directly, and you confirm the latter and back it up by his divine authority. Berkeley's

sensation, my idea, my thought; that "thing" and "thought" are one and the same homogeneous "stuff." Thus James asks, "To begin with, are thought and thing as heterogenous as is commonly said?"[42] He answers by referring to "the essential homogeneity of thought with thing,"[43] and by maintaining that "thoughts are in the concrete made of the same stuff as things are."[44] What is the "stuff" of which both thought and things are made? "There is," he says, "only one primal stuff or material in the world, a stuff of which everything is composed—we call that stuff 'pure experience'."[45] Thoughts and things are "mere bits of pure experience," they are "single *thats* which act in one context as objects, and in another context figure as mental states."[46]

But what then is "pure experience?" "The instant field of the present is at all times what I call the 'pure experience,'" James answers. "It is only virtually or potentially either object or subject as yet."[47] "Pure experience" is the "instant field of the present." What is the present? The present of what? The present of "experience"; "pure experience" is "immediate experience."[48] Whose "immediate experience?" It doesn't really matter, for the "experience" and the "thing experienced" are discriminated out of the stuff of "pure" experience or "immediate" experience. Knower and known, subject and object, like thought and thing, are merely experience taken in two different ways. They are in fact one and the same thing, namely "pure experience." "One experience," says James, "would be the knower, the other the reality, known."[49] James' "world" is "a world where experience and reality come to the same thing."[50] It is a subjective world entirely dependent on immediate human experience. "Subject" and "object," "knower" and "known," are discriminations made in retrospective conceptual experience. They are experience "twice-taken."*[51]

criticism of 'matter' was consequently absolutely pragmatistic. Matter is known as our sensations of colour, figure, hardness and the like. They are the cash-value of the term. The difference matter makes to us by truly being is that we then get such sensations; by not being is that we lack them. These sensations then are its sole meaning. Berkeley doesn't deny matter, then; he simply tells us what it consists of. It is a true name for just so much in the way of sensations."

* James says: "As 'subjective' we say that the experience represents; as 'objective' it is represented. What represents and what is represented is here numerically the same; but we must remember that no dualism of being represented

Pure, immediate human experience forms one undifferentiated whole, a "blooming, buzzing confusion," "a primordial chaos of sensations," "a stream of consciousness," which when looked back upon from the vantage point of later experience is thought of in terms of a dualism of thought and thing, knower and known, subject and object. In fact, though, for James and pragmatism, there is only one stuff, subjective experience: *"Experience, I believe, has no such inner duplicity; and the separation of it into consciousness and content comes not by way of subtraction, but by way of addition. . . .* In a word, in one group it figures as a thought, in another group as a thing, and since it can figure in both groups simultaneously we have every right to speak of it as subjective and objective both at once."[52]

The main point is that experience is not experience *of* anything, for there *is* nothing but human experience. One experience can be related to another, but experience as a whole can have no relations beyond itself. As a matter of fact the relations connecting the various parts of experience must themselves be experiences. Thus he says, "The relations that connect experiences must themselves be experienced relations."[53] Experience, therefore, is self-contained, has no reference beyond itself, and leans on nothing. Referring to the Berkeley-Hume-Mach-Peirce-James philosophy as "humanism" he says, "The essential service of humanism, as I conceive the situation, is to have seen that though one part of our experience may lean upon another part to make it what it is in any one of several aspects in which it may be considered, experience as a whole is self-containing and leans on nothing."[54] All of which is an indirect way of saying that there is no such thing as the objective material world which is experienced. What is experience? For James that is either a meaningless question, or the answer must be that experience itself is experienced. Experience is not experience of external, independent reality, but rather is itself reality: "Experience and reality come to the same thing," he says.[55]

To hold as James does that this world is my (our) experience, is, as we concluded of Peirce's doctrine, only a slightly revised version of

and representing resides in the experience *per se*. In its pure state, or when isolated, there is no self-splitting of it, into consciousness and what the consciousness is 'of'. Its subjectivity and objectivity are functional attributes solely, realized only when the experience is 'taken', *i.e.* talked-of, twice, considered along with its two differing contexts respectively, by a new retrospective experience, of which that whole past complication now forms the fresh content."

Berkeley's "to be is to be perceived." If the world is nothing but our experience, including the knower and the known, what is knowledge? It must be the experienced relation between one and another part of experience. "Knowledge" would have to be some form of *experience of experience.**[56]

James distinguishes two parts of experience: conception or knowledge on the one hand; and sense-perception or sensations on the other. Knowledge is knowledge of sense-perception, but both are elements of pure experience. The connection between the two is itself an experience, or a series of experiences. If, as with James, experience is reality, then both knowledge and sense-perception are "real." But neither "reality" nor "knowledge" has any genuine meaning; they are merely synonyms for experience and its discriminated parts. Knowledge is wholly an intra-mural affair. It never can refer to anything which is independent of sensations or thought. It takes place completely within the walls of the human being, for it is fabricated of our experience: "Knowledge of sensible realities thus comes to life inside the tissue of experience. It is made; and made by relations that unroll themselves in time. Whenever certain intermediaries are given, such that, as they develop towards their terminus, there is experience from point to point of one direction followed, and finally of one process fulfilled, the result is that *their starting-point thereby becomes a knower and their terminus an object meant or known.* That is all that knowing can be known as, that is the whole of its nature, put into experiential terms."[57]

First, I have sensations of color, size and shape; second, I organize these sense-perceptions into known-objects or ideas; finally, I take the latter back to sense experience and try them out. All of this takes place

* "If the central humanistic thesis . . . (that experience is self-containing and leans on nothing), be accepted, it will follow that, if there be any such thing at all as knowledge, the knower and the object known must both be portions of experience. One part of experience must, therefore, either (1) Know another part of experience—in other words, parts must, as Professor Woodbridge says, represent *one another* instead of representing realities outside of 'consciousness'—this case is that of conceptual knowledge; or else (2) They must simply exist as so many ultimate thats or facts of being, in the first instance; and then, as a secondary complication and without doubling up its entitative singleness, any one and the same that must figure alternately as a thing known and as a knowledge of the thing, by reason of two divergent kinds of context into which, in the general course of experience it gets woven. This second case is that of sense-perception."

"inside the tissue of experience." In this vein, James speaks of his dog: "To call my present idea of my dog, for example, cognitive of the real dog means that, as the actual tissue of experience is constituted, the idea is capable of leading into a chain of other experiences on my part that go from next to next and terminate at the last in vivid sense-perceptions of a jumping, barking, hairy body. These are the real dog, the dog's full presence, for my common sense."[58]

The "dog" is my knowledge of certain sensations organized in a certain way. There is no problem of how I can know my dog, for all three, "I," the "knowing," and the "dog," are my experience discriminated into so many constitutive elements. As James puts it, "The whole question of how 'one' thing can know 'another' would cease to be a real one at all in a world where otherness itself was an illusion."[59]

There is, in short, no problem of knowledge, if knowledge itself does not exist. For it has no meaning if it is not knowledge of the external, independent world. There being no such world for James, he can assign no real meaning to knowledge. It becomes simply ways of organizing my sense-experience in order to satisfy subjective, or class, needs and desires.

Through this device of "pure experience" James would conceal the subjective character of his world view. By qualifying the term "experience" with the adjective "pure" he would have us believe that the former somehow ceases to be human experience, that it is not the experience of people but is just there, given. But if the term "experience" has any meaning it signifies some organism which is doing the experiencing. No qualification can eliminate this fact. Thus "pure experience" is still the experience of human beings, and James' world view collapses into subjective idealism, namely, the world *is* human experience. It is created by man out of the stuff of experience. James himself makes this clear with his doctrine of the "double-barreled" character of experience, as subject and object. Both experiencer and what is experienced are extracted from experience.

Lenin pointed out, long ago, that the use of the term "experience" without reference to whose experience is nothing but a shabby device to hide the essential Berkeley doctrine that "to be is to be perceived." It is clear that experience is not something, like the material world, which can stand by itself. It is always relative to an experiencer.

James' world view, including his conceptions of reality and knowledge, is subjective idealism in a slightly camouflaged form. For him reality is purely "my" experience and knowledge is what "I" will to believe. Pragmatism is indeed simply "a new name for some old ways of thinking." It is a new name for Berkeleyism-Machism.

With such a world view, what sense can James make of truth? We turn now to this crucial subject.

VIII. WILLIAM JAMES'
WILL TO BELIEVE

JAMES CAN make no more sense of truth than he can of reality or knowledge, since its only sensible meaning is correspondence between idea and the external world, which for him does not exist. Pragmatic truth has to be, like pragmatic reality and knowledge, a relation between various parts of subjective experience. It, too, would have to be "wholly inside the tissue of experience." "In no case, however," says James, "need truth consist in a relation between our experiences and something archetypal or trans-experiential."[1] On the contrary, "the 'truth' of our mental operations must always be an intra-experiential affair."[2] It must be a marriage of one part of experience with another for purposes of convenience. How is this contrived marriage to be arranged?

Theory of Truth

In his theory of truth James relies heavily on John Dewey and F. S. C. Schiller, the British pragmatist. Remarking on the fact that Mach, Ostwald and Poincaré had "driven divine necessity from scientific logic" and had substituted "human arbitrariness," James goes on to say: "Riding now on the front of this wave of scientific logic Messrs. Schiller and Dewey appear with their pragmatistic account of what truth everywhere signifies. Everywhere these teachers say, 'truth' in our ideas and beliefs means the same thing that it means in science. It means, they say, nothing but this, *that ideas (which themselves are but parts of our experience) become true just in so far as they help us to get into satisfactory relation with other parts of our experience.*"[3]

116

Truth means a "satisfactory relation" between one and another part of experience. What does "satisfactory relation" mean as a synonym for truth? James answers: "Any idea upon which we can ride, so to speak; any idea that will carry us prosperously from any one part of our experience to any other part, linking things satisfactorily, working securely, simplifying, saving labor; is true for just so much, true in so far forth, true *instrumentally*."[4] And he adds, "This is the 'instrumental' view of truth taught so successfully at Chicago, the view that truth in our ideas means their power to 'work'."[5]

Here radical empiricism and pragmatism unite. Once the objective world is eliminated and knowledge is reduced to a mockery, there can be no ground for truth. It can, then, mean only the expedient: "The true . . . is only the expedient in the way of our thinking."[6]

Speaking of the "pragmatist," James says, "Truth, for him, becomes a class-name for all sorts of definite, working-values in experience."[7] He rejects "the absolutely empty notion of a static relation of 'correspondence' between our minds and reality." He must do so because there is no such thing as reality. "Truth" is pragmatism's name for the marriage relation of one part of experience with another for the sake of expediency toward felt goals. There is then, no such thing as objective truth. "Purely objective truth," says James, "truth in whose establishment the function of giving human satisfaction in marrying previous parts of experience with newer parts played no role whatever, is nowhere to be found."[8] Eliminate the clause in opposition, and James says flatly "Purely objective truth— is nowhere to be found." What other kind than objective truth can there be? Obviously none. Only the *term* can be retained in an attempt to conceal the atrocity. "The reasons why we call things true," James continues, "is the reason why they are true, for 'to be true' *means* only to perform this marriage-function,"[9] between bits of experience. There is no such thing for pragmatism as "truth independent; truth that we find merely"; "truth" is man-made, tailor-made, for practical, expedient purposes—like perpetuating exploitation and white supremacy, or selling atomic war in the guise of "aggression for peace." "Truth," in short, is not discovered, it is manufactured out of the whole cloth of "experience." It is invented, not found. "Truth," says James, "is *made*."[10] That sounds more like a definition of lying, but such a definition suits imperialism very well.

"An idea is 'true' so long as to believe it is profitable to our lives."[11]

Here it becomes clear that what pragmatism calls "truth" is merely another name for the valuative judgment of good or bad. The further question of good *for whom* is not mentioned, but if fascism is good for finance capital then it is "true"; if the theory of saving the "free world" from "red aggression" is good for Wall Street and the munitions makers, it is "true." It is Charles E. Wilson's doctrine that "What is good for General Motors is good for the country," and therefore "true."

James says: "You touch here upon the very central point of Messrs. Schiller's, Dewey's and my own doctrine of truth . . . truth is *one species of good,* and not, as is usually supposed, a category distinct from good, and co-ordinate with it. *The true is the name of whatever proves itself to be good in the way of belief, and good, too, for definite, assignable reasons.*"[12]

The converse of this is that if a genuinely true idea were not good for me, if it were bad for a person or a class, then it should be rejected, and something more expedient substituted. Truth should in that case be circumvented. The corollary is that a false idea or lie should replace it. That this is not simply an implication of pragmatism, but an explicit element of the doctrine is made clear when James says, "if there were no good for life in true ideas, or if the knowledge of them were positively disadvantageous and false ideas the only useful ones, then . . . our duty would be to shun truth, rather."[13] For radical empiricism, having "proved" that there is no reality, knowledge or truth, there could be no theoretical basis for challenging the falsity and lying. If they "worked," they would be "true for just so much, true in so far forth, true instrumentally."[14] "True" ideas are those that are agreeable to think about, but more important, they are those that are helpful in the struggles of life, the class struggle especially. "So certain ideas," says James, "are not only agreeable to think about, or agreeable as supporting other ideas that we are fond of, but they are also helpful in life's practical struggles."[15] Could there be a philosophy better suited to the ideological requirements of imperialism? Lying propaganda, the big lie, is given its "theoretical" basis, with the ground within the system cut from under any possibility of confronting it with science, knowledge and truth. Pragmatism is, indeed, the philosophy of U.S. imperialism, and with a vengeance.

"Truth" is defined by pragmatism as whatever is found to be useful for whatever purpose. The only hitch in believing whatever is useful is not that it might contradict the actual facts and laws of motion of the objective world, but the possibility that one "belief-truth" might clash with others which are equally useful. This is the only condition put upon the will-to-believe. "If there be any life that is really better we should lead," says James, "and if there be any idea which, if believed in, would help us to lead that life, then it would be really better for us to believe in that idea, *unless, indeed, belief in it incidentally clashed with other greater vital benefits.*"[16] And James continues: "Now in real life what vital benefits is any particular belief of ours most liable to clash with? What indeed except the vital benefits yielded by *other beliefs* when these prove incompatible with the first ones? In other words, the greatest enemy of any one of our truths may be the rest of our truths."[17]

Here James makes his closest approximation to a "principled" stand, but it is the exception that proves the rule of pragmatic unprincipled doctrine. He says that most people do not worry about clashing and incompatible beliefs; they believe whatever they want regardless of whether their beliefs are consistent one with another. They believe whatever "suits the temptations of successive hours. . . . But some of us are more than mere laymen in philosophy. We are worthy of the name of amateur athletes and are vexed by too much inconsistency and vacilla- tion in our creed. We cannot preserve a good intellectual conscience so long as we keep mixing incompatibles. . . ."[18] So if some beliefs do not "fit in" with others, James either gives them up "or else as a professional philosopher," he says without a blush, "I try to justify them by some other principle."[19] Amateur athlete indeed! That is the pragmatic method of preserving a "good intellectual conscience." Thus his one lone attempt at a principled stand turns into its opposite.

How could pragmatism and its formulators make a principled stand of any kind when they are dedicated to the extermination of man's most prized and valued possession, the great fund of truth built up through thousands of years of hard work, suffering and struggle. They would take from human beings their key to unlock the doors to a better society and to control over nature.

Pragmatic Method

"Truth," then, for pragmatism, is what would be better for us to believe. Thus the theory of truth merges with the pragmatic method. " 'What would be better for us to believe'! This sounds very like a definition of truth," James says, and he adds: "It comes very near to saying 'what we *ought*' to believe: and in *that* definition none of you would find any oddity. Ought we ever not to believe what it is *better for us* to believe? And can we keep the notion of what is better for us, and what is true for us, permanently apart? Pragmatism says no, and I fully agree with her."[20]

The confusion of "ought" with "what would be better" is merely an attempt to make the pill slightly more palatable. Notice that he drops it as soon as he raises it. The question now is what kind of things "would be better for us to believe?" The answer is anything and everything. The gates are wide open with no principles, no criteria of right or wrong, true or false, real or fictitious. Anything goes as long as it meets some kind of felt need or desire, as long as it apparently "works" for some useful purpose in day-to-day experience, as long as it "succeeds," as long as it has "practical effects." It does not matter what the goal is or how you get there, or whether you do, no matter what the end or means, as long as you are on the way, as long as you act. A pragmatist, says James, is one who "turns towards concreteness and adequacy, towards facts, towards action and towards power."[21]

For example, pragmatism "has no *a priori* prejudices against theology," James says, *"If theological ideas prove to have a value for concrete life, they will be true, for pragmatism, in the sense of being good for so much. For how much more they are true, will depend entirely on their relations to the other truths that also have to be acknowledged."*[22] But elsewhere he points out that if other "truths" do not "fit in" with theological ideas, in particular with the idea of God, then they must be altered so that they will combine harmoniously. In short, science must be reconciled with religion. "On pragmatist principles," James states, "if the hypothesis of God works satisfactorily in the widest sense of the word, it is true. Now whatever its residual difficulties may be, experience shows that it certainly does work, and that the problem is to build it out and determine it so that it will combine satisfactorily with all the other working truths."[23] Here is that "amateur athlete" again placating his "intellectual conscience." Yes, pragmatism will tolerate anything. As a matter of fact, it will foster anything.

As a case in point, James discusses the Absolute of transcendental idealism. He has for seventy pages been railing against it as well as against materialism. Now he smuggles it in by the back door of the pragmatic method, demonstrating thereby that his war on two fronts is mere window-dressing, as specious as any middle-ground or third-force in current politics. He has only one enemy, not two; and thorough-going materialism with its incorruptible defense of science, knowledge and truth is it: "First I called it [the Absolute] majestic and said it yielded religious comfort to a class of minds, and then I accused it of remoteness and sterility. But so far as it affords such comfort, it surely is not sterile; it has that amount of value; it performs a concrete function. As a good pragmatist, I myself ought to call the Absolute true 'in so far forth,' then; and I unhesitatingly now do so."[24]

Why is James at such pains to readmit the Absolute of transcendental idealism? The reason is soon made clear when he asks the question, "What do believers in the Absolute mean by saying their belief affords them comfort?" and answers it as follows: "They mean that since, in the Absolute finite evil is 'overruled' already, we may, therefore, when-ever we wish, treat the temporal as if it were potentially the eternal, be sure that we can trust its outcome, and, without sin, dismiss our fear and drop the worry of our finite responsibility. In short, they mean that we have a right ever and anon to take a moral holiday, to let the world wag in its own way, feeling that its issues are in better hands than ours and are none of our business."[25]

Such a belief *is* useful; the owners can wash their hands of responsi-bility for the evils of their system and the workers can look for pie in the sky while they suffer on earth in silent adoration. Such a belief is useful to the capitalist class; and if it is useful, if it is better for them to believe it and cultivate it, if it "works," then the Absolute with its "moral holidays" is "true in so far forth." God, the Absolute, with his granting of the "don't care mood,"[26] is in heaven and all is well, evil is really good; and "that," says James of the Absolute God "is his cash-value when he is pragmatically interpreted."[27] "If the Absolute means this," he adds, "and means no more than this, who can possibly deny the truth of it? To deny it would mean that men should never relax, and that holidays are never in order."[28] Was Lenin overstating the case when he called the bourgeois professors of philosophy, among them James, "salesmen of theology?"

But pragmatism does not limit itself to selling theology; it sells the label of "truth" to any and all comers:

You see by this what I meant when I called pragmatism a mediator and reconciler and said, borrowing the word from Papini, that she "unstiffens" our theories. She has in fact no prejudices whatever, no obstructive dogmas, no rigid canons of what shall count as proof. She is completely genial. She will entertain any hypothesis, she will consider any evidence.

... In short, she widens the field of search for God. Rationalism sticks to logic and the empyrean. Empiricism sticks to the external senses. Pragmatism is willing to take anything, to follow either logic or the senses and to count the humblest and most personal experiences. She will count mystical experiences if they have practical consequences. She will take a God who lives in the very dirt of private fact—if that should seem a likely place to find him.

Her only test of probable truth is what works best and combines with the collectivity of experience's demands, nothing being omitted. If theological ideas should do this, if the notion of God, in particular, should prove to do it, how could pragmatism possibly deny God's existence? She could see no meaning in treating as "not true" a notion that was pragmatically so successful.[29]

Here pragmatism, by the pen of one of its foremost spokesmen, is stripped of all pretense. It stands exposed as the incredibly shoddy, contemptible and utterly degenerate monstrosity, and at the same time, dangerous weapon that it is. Current pragmatists, Dewey in particular, would conceal and deny the fact that such is the sum and substance of this so-called "philosophy," but the putrefaction is too great to be covered by any aromatic scent.

There is, in the above passage from James, both a negative and positive formulation of the upshot of pragmatism. The negative is in the form of a question, "How could pragmatism possibly deny God's existence?" or any other superstitious notion, we might add. With reality, and truth, knowledge, and science, eliminated, there is indeed no ground for combating obscurantism in any form. The negative thus clears the way for the positive, the affirmation of mysticism: "Pragmatism is willing to take anything, to follow either logic or the senses and to count the humblest and most personal experiences. She will count mystical experiences, if they have practical consequences."

The only criterion for accepting beliefs, whatever they may be, is, do they have "practical consequences." A little judicious editing will reveal the essence: "Pragmatism is willing to take anything—if it has practical consequences." The key is the pragmatic meaning of the phrase "practical consequences." Since there is no objective reality independent of my experience it cannot mean changes in the world. It can only mean that whatever is in question affects my experience, makes me feel or think or act differently. I will believe, according to James, whatever makes me feel, think or act the way I want to. A person is to believe, to take as "true" and as "real," anything which appears in his immediate experience to lead toward the object of his desire, his subjective goal. In short, any means to my end. It is a simple process to transfer this from a personal to a class basis: a class is then justified in resorting to any means to its end. It is clear that for pragmatism "reality," truth, and "practical consequences," are synonyms; they are one and the same thing, namely, "success." James is candid to the point when he says that "truth" is "what works best in the way of leading us" and that pragmatism is "completely genial. She will entertain any hypothesis, she will consider any evidence." But the only evidence is "personal experiences," with "nothing being omitted."*[30]

Returning now to his statement that pragmatism "will count mystical experiences if they have practical consequences," we can paraphrase it as "pragmatism accepts mystical experiences because they obviously do affect personal experiences." They most certainly do have "practical consequences" within James' subjective meaning of the term, and highly useful ones for any predatory ruling class.

Thus mysticism is "true," as "true" as any other notion, since it "works"; it has practical consequences; it makes a difference in personal belief and conduct. Pragmatism tolerates anything if only it makes a difference in a person's actual life.

The only criterion to differentiate one belief from another is the effect it has on personal experience. James formulates the criterion as the "usual question" posed by pragmatism. It is the heart of the pragmatic method: "Pragmatism, on the other hand asks its usual question. 'Grant an idea or belief to be true,' it says, 'what concrete difference will its being true make in any one's actual life? How will the truth be realized? What experiences will be different from those which would obtain if the belief were false? What in short is the truth's cash-value in experimental terms?' "[31]

The pragmatic method means, James says, *"The attitude of looking*

---

* He is less candid when in speaking of "truth" as whatever is "pragmatically so successful," he says, "what other kind of truth could there be, for her, than all this agreement with concrete reality?" However, we are not taken in by reference to "concrete reality," for we have demonstrated that he means by it only "practical consequences" within "personal experiences."

away from first things, principles, 'categories,' supposed necessities; and of looking towards last things, fruits, consequences, facts."[32] You can only look toward what fruits and consequences you find useful if you look away from principles and necessity. In short, pragmatism with its stress on desired effects, must ignore objective causal necessity, which might demonstrate the futility and falsity of what one thinks one wants. Without causality, there could be no prediction of consequences; and causality and prediction are essential attributes of science. It may sound good to talk about concentrating on effects. It sounds hard-headed and "realistic." But when it is accompanied by "the attitude of looking away from first things, principles, 'categories,' supposed necessities," it reduces the effects to "practical consequences" within personal experiences which are completely subjective, irrational and unpredictable. Hence the pragmatic method opens the way to acceptance of anything which tempts the will to believe it.

It is a neat and vicious trick that James and pragmatism would palm off. In affirming effects and repudiating causes, it in reality also repudiates any real effects. Effects become influences on human conduct. Effects are what cause us to act. In short, they are "beliefs" or "habits of action." Thus James says, "I conclude, then, that real effectual causation as an ultimate nature, as a 'category,' if you like, or reality, is *just what we feel it to be,* just that kind of conjunction which our own activity-series reveal."[33] What does "our own activity-series reveal" about causality? James answers: "Sustaining, persevering, striving, paying with effort as we go, hanging on, and finally achieving our intention—this is action, this is effectuation in the only shape in which, by pure-experience-philosophy the whereabouts of it anywhere can be discussed—here is causality at work."[34] It is clear that by causality James means human beliefs, habits, and actions in leading toward desired goals. There is no reference to causality independent of human thought or will or action, to material causes acting in the material world. There is no conception of causality as the spatial and temporal interconnections which produce the changes in the objective world. But we could not expect James or pragmatism to deal with genuine causality, since for them there is no material world within which it could operate. Causality for pragmatism could be only the subjective relations within experience, within "our own activity-series."

The denial of objective causal necessity, as James himself admits, is the counterpart of the pragmatic method. It is the essential element which unites the method to the end-product of the philosophy, the "will-to-believe" what it is expedient to believe. In such a view, "science" is not opposed to "metaphysics," obscurantism and religion; it cannot combat them since there are no real causal interconnections. Thus "Science and metaphysics," says James, "would come much nearer together, would in fact work absolutely hand in hand."[35] The laws of science are themselves simply man-made formulas, handy rules for finding our way among experiences, and not in any sense reflections of reality. "But as the sciences have developed farther," he says, "the notion has gained ground that most, perhaps all, of our laws are only approximations . . . no theory is absolutely a transcript of reality, but that any one of them may from some point of view be useful. . . . They are only a made-made language, a conceptual shorthand, as some one calls them, in which we write our reports of nature; and languages, as is well known, tolerate much choice of expression and many dialects."[36]

The laws and theories of science are not "transcripts of reality," are not concerned with truth; they are merely a short-hand language useful for practical purposes. They are means to ends, not truths. *"Theories,"* he says, *"thus become instruments, not answers to enigmas, in which we can rest."*[37]

If "science" is concerned, not with reality and truth, but simply with useful ways of getting from one experience to another, then what is the criterion of what is to be accepted as scientific? Obviously, by the pragmatic method, whatever satisfies my "scientific tastes or desires," whatever works for me in this way, is "scientific truth." James himself draws the conclusion: "Truth in science is what gives us the maximum sum of satisfactions, taste included."[38] Thus does he apply his radical empiricism and pragmatic method to destroy the theoretical basis of science. He reduces it to ways of organizing experience which have "cash-value." Science goes the way of reality, knowledge, causality and truth. For pragmatism, none of them really exist. We "can proceed as if" they were real, "but we mustn't think so literally."

But can we proceed "as if" they were real, if they are not? Does it make no difference whether or not they exist? On the contrary, it makes all the difference, for if, as with pragmatism they are not real, then the only recourse is "the will to believe" whatever it is expedient to believe, and there is nothing to combat false belief within the limits of the philosophy. There is no material world, no causality, no truth. There is nothing but myself, my desires and will. Expediency then becomes the only "principle"; and ends determining and justifying means become the only procedure. Solipsistic voluntarism or voluntaristic solipsism take the place of the objective material world and its reflection in the natural and social sciences. In short, superstition is reinstated by pragmatism in the place of science as guide of human practice. Thus would James and his philosophy set the clock of social and intellectual history back; how far back we will soon see.

James sums up the pragmatic method of repudiating causality and science by repeating that it turns away "from looking backward on principles" and "shifts the emphasis and looks forward into facts themselves."[39] The pragmatic philosophy "looks forward" that the *status quo* may be preserved, while Marxism-Leninism looks back to understand the laws of development so that the *status quo* may in fact be transformed. Short of principles and laws of development nothing remains but to rely on wishful thinking. James makes this perfectly clear when he says:

> But if one talks of rationality and of reasons for things, and insists that they can't just come in spots, what *kind* of a reason can there ultimately be why anything should come at all? Talk of logic and necessity and categories and the absolute and the contents of the whole philosophical machine-shop as you will, the only *real* reason I can think of why anything should ever come is that *some one wishes it to be here*. It is *demanded,* demanded, it maybe, to give relief to no matter how small a fraction of the world's mass. This is *living reason,* and compared with it material causes and logical necessities are spectral things.[40]

Such is the upside down, Alice-in-Wonderland outlook that pragmatism would sell to the American people. Wishes are "real," while material causes and necessities are "spectral things." The way is indeed open to believe what the ruling class finds it expedient for the working people to believe. Of the elements of the pragmatic doctrine outlined above, James says, *"All these, you see, are anti-intellectualist tendencies."*[41] This is a true statement. One of the features of pragmatism is its violent anti-intellectualism, its anti-theoretical orientation. That practice without theory is blind and leads into the swamp of obscurantism is amply demonstrated by James as he draws the inferences of his philosophical position.

The Will to Believe

In essay after essay, and chapter after chapter, filling many volumes, James reveals the logical conclusions of radical empiricism and the pragmatic method. But the most popular essay, the one that has been most highly publicized, is the title piece in the book called, *The Will To Believe.* It has had a tremendous influence and is thus worthy of examination.

In the opening paragraph James introduces his subject with these words: "I have brought with me tonight something like a sermon on justification by faith to read to you—I mean an essay *in* justification of faith, a defense of our right to adopt a believing attitude in religious matters, in spite of the fact that our merely logical intellect may not have been coerced. 'The Will to Believe' accordingly, is the title of my paper."[42]

With this frank admission of purpose, James goes on to implement it. He spends a number of pages "proving" that "No test of what is really true has ever been agreed upon,"[43] and then plunges into his main topic, namely, "that we have the right to believe at our own risk any hypothesis that is live enough to tempt our will."[44] The two propositions complement one another, for if there is no truth, there can only be willful belief and if there is only willful belief, there can be no truth. James calls this by its rightful name. It is, he says, "The freedom to 'believe what we will.' "[45] This is the final outcome of pragmatism, its inevitable conclusion. It is the doctrine that "faith in a fact can help create the fact."[46] The complete passage in which James draws this conclusion reads as follows: "There are, then, cases where a fact cannot come at all unless a preliminary faith exists in its coming. And *where faith in a fact can help create the fact,* that would be an insane logic which should say that faith running ahead of scientific evidence is the 'lowest kind of immorality' into which a thinking being can fall. Yet such is the logic by which our scientific absolutists pretend to regulate our lives."[47]

James, by inference, admits that what he is recommending is that people be duped, or dupe themselves, with lies. He refers to the "scientific absolutist" who holds it is "better to go without belief forever than believe a lie," and states, "For my part, I have also a horror of being duped; but I can believe that worse things than being duped may happen to a man in this world."[48]

Under the dupery of "believing what you will" and "faith creating the fact," James reinstates all the articles of faith of the theology he had pretended to combat: "God," "free-will," "immortality," the "Absolute," and "teleology" or design in the universe. Each "takes its place with other religious doctrines," he says. "Between them, they build up the old wastes and repair the former desolations."[49] In other words, the destruction of superstition at the hands of science and materialism is checked and reversed, and the wastes and desolations of obscurantism are repaired and rebuilt by pragmatism: "Pragmatism alone can read a positive meaning into it, and for that she turns her back upon the intellectualist point of view altogether. 'God's in his heaven; all's right with the world!'— *That's* the real heart of your theology, and for that you need no rationalist definition."[50]

But the philosophy rooted in the principle that "faith based on desire is certainly a lawful and possibly an indispensable thing,"[51] does not stop with theology and religion. Indeed, it could not stop short of the lowest depths, for there is nothing within the system to stop it. So we should not be surprised to find that James treats with respectful credulity "divinations, inspirations, demoniacal possessions, apparitions, trances, ecstasies, miraculous healings and productions of disease, and occult powers possessed by peculiar individuals over persons and things in their neighborhood."[52] Mysticism in any and all forms is the logical outcome of pragmatism. Thus James says: "Repugnant as the mystical style of philosophizing may be (especially when self-complacent), there is no sort of doubt that it goes with a gift for meeting with certain kinds of phenomenal experience. The writer of these pages has been forced in the past few years to this admission; and he now believes that he who will pay attention to facts of the sort dear to mystics, while reflecting upon them in academic-scientific ways, will be in the best possible position to help philosophy."[53]

What James' "scientific-academic" way of dealing with haunted houses and ghosts amounts to, we will see in an essay called "what Psychical Research Has Accomplished," only one among many by James on the subject. He is reviewing the work of the Society for Psychical Research, which organization, he says, has as its purpose "first, carry on systematic experimentation with hypnotic subjects, mediums, clairvoyants, and others; and secondly, to collect evidence concerning apparitions, haunted houses and similar phenomena. . . ."[54] He has nothing but praise for the society and its published proceedings, and sees it as someday becoming one of the accepted learned societies.

James goes on to summarize "cases" under the various headings of "thought transference," "apparitions," "mediumship," "slate writing" and "table tipping." He weighs the evidence for each with an appearance of "objectivity." But then in the closing pages of the essay he makes his own position, and the position of pragmatism quite clear. The passages are long, and yet worth quoting with some deletions because they reveal as perhaps nothing else could the complete degeneracy and utter intellectual bankruptcy and decadence of the pragmatic philosophy of U.S. imperialism. What James has to say speaks for itself:

In the trances of this medium (Mrs. Piper), I cannot resist the conviction that knowledge appears which she has never gained by the ordinary waking use of her eyes and ears and wits. What the source of this knowledge may be I know not, and have not the glimmer of an explanatory suggestion to make; but from admitting the fact of such knowledge I can see no escape. *So when I turn to the rest of the evidence, ghosts and all, I cannot carry with me the irreversible, negative bias of the "rigorously scientific" mind, with its presumption as to what the true order of nature ought to be. . . .*

We all, scientists and non-scientists, live on some inclined plane of credulity. The plane tips one way in one man, another way in another; and may he whose plane tips in no way be the first to cast a stone. *As a matter of fact, the trances I speak of have broken down for my own mind the limits of the admitted order of nature. Science, so far as science denies such exceptional occurrences, lies prostrate in the dust for me; and the most urgent intellectual need which I feel at present is that science be built up again in a form in which such things may have a positive place. . . .*

Through my slight participation in the investigations of the S.P.R. I have become acquainted with numbers of persons of this sort, for whom the very word "science" has become a name of reproach, for reasons that I now both understand and respect. . . . I confess that it is on this, its humanizing mission that the society's best claim to the gratitude of our generation seems to me to depend. *It has shown some reasonable basis for the most superstitious aberrations of the foretime. . . .* (My italics.—H.K.W.)[55]

The only comment on this that need be made is a warning that in no primary sense can William James as an individual be held solely responsible. On the contrary, superstition, from organized religion to witchcraft, haunted houses and ghosts, is inherent in pragmatism, whether or not any given pragmatist carries the philosophy to this logical end.

If there is no world independent of personality, consciousness, desire and will, then "the universe" is a human invention and we are free to invent whatever "tempts our will." Here indeed is a "Copernican revolution," but in reverse and at a different level, it is counter-revolution: the world revolves, not around the sun, but around the "instincts" and "emotions" of man. For James "the trail of the human serpent is thus over everything."[56] and there is no such thing as "truth independent; truth that we *find* merely."[57] "The true," then, "is only the expedient in the way of our thinking"; it is what is "profitable to our lives," whatever has "cash-value."

How could pragmatism possibly oppose concentration camps or war when the imperialists find them so expediently full of cash-value? They are "true" and "good" if they are "expedient." Little wonder that Mussolini hailed James as his "teacher": "The pragmatism of William James was of great use to me in my political career. James taught me that an action should be judged rather by its results than by its doctrinary basis. I learned of James that faith in action, that ardent will to live and fight, to which fascism owes a great part of its success. For me the essential was to act."[58]

William James presents pragmatism unadorned. With John Dewey, however, we deal with a bird of another feather. The primary task in exposing Dewey's brand of pragmatism is to cut away the formal variations and reveal the same essential content. We turn our attention to this peculiar present-day phenomenon, a man who is the leading philosopher both of U.S. imperialism and of its special pleaders, the social democrats.

IX. JOHN DEWEY'S
INSTRUMENTALISM

NEVER HAS a philosopher been more idolized by the class he serves than has the late John Dewey. Nor can it be denied that he fully deserved this homage.

In his practical politics, as in his philosophy, he left little room for complaint. He extolled Theodore Roosevelt and the "Big Stick" policies of U.S. imperialism. He fought to get this country into the First World War. He scurried to the defense of Leon Trotsky. And through a twenty-year campaign of vilification he helped fabricate the big lie of "Soviet imperialism." He came out in support of the Korean War and contributed substantially to the doctrine of the "inevitability of World War III."

But his greatest service to reaction lies in his general philosophy. As pragmatism is today the main-line philosophy of U.S. imperialism, so Dewey is its leading and most influential exponent. His "instrumentalism" is the pragmatism of Peirce and James masquerading under another name. It is pragmatism under demagogic wraps.

That the distinctive feature of Dewey's pragmatism is its protective coloration is by no means simply the result of personal preference or individual peculiarity. It is rather the result of changed historical conditions. The great bulk of Dewey's work in philosophy, including his most important books, appeared in the wake of the Russian Revolution of 1917. James and Peirce did not live to have their work affected by the elimination of exploitation over one-sixth of the earth's surface. The class character of pragmatism was relatively open and undisguised in their hands. They were not forced to meet the challenge posed by the existence of the first socialist country, by the great upsurge of the world working class and the rise of the modern Communist Parties following the First World War. Peirce and James lived and wrote in the era of false optimism and security of the imperialist powers, not yet fully confronted with the inevitability of their own total elimination. After 1917 the handwriting was plain for all to see.

Dewey, on the other hand, had to furnish apologetics for capitalism in general crisis, hopelessly enmeshed in its own internal contradictions, and exposed by the building of socialism in the Soviet Union. His work was not merely influenced by this situation, but was primarily directed against its logical and historical inferences.

Hence Dewey wrote his chief philosophical tracts under conditions quite different from the period of either Peirce or James. The latter wrote in a general way against the *specter* of socialism; Dewey wrote against the *reality*. Yet the content of his thinking is identical with that of his predecessors. Only the form is altered.

John Dewey is in the first place the leading philosopher of U.S. imperialism, and in the second place he is the leading philosopher of social democracy in the United States. Social democracy is the prime agency of imperialism operating within the ranks of the working class and its allies. There is thus no real contradiction in the fact that one philosopher can function in both capacities. Particularly is this true in our country where there is not such a sharp line between bourgeois democratic and social democratic demagogy. Dewey employs both: now the demagogy of a Truman or an Eisenhower, now of a Walter Reuther or of a Norman Thomas.

This double role of Dewey was dramatized and publicized in the celebrations of his ninetieth birthday during the month of October, 1949. A dinner given in his honor at the Waldorf-Astoria Hotel was sponsored by "hundreds of leading citizens from all walks of life," namely from two: from the capitalist class and its labor lieutenants. Leaders of the trusts and their two political parties were joined by the misleaders of labor and representatives of the Liberal, Socialist and Socialist Labor parties in a carnival of jingoism and its counterpart, red-baiting and anti-Sovietism. In newspapers from coast to coast Dewey was hailed as "spiritual savior and defender" of "Western civilization" from "atheistic, materialistic communism." He was eulogized as "a great leader in the worldwide struggle for the minds of men." Special issues of the *New*

Republic and the *New Leader* were devoted to "Commemoration of Dewey's Ninetieth Birthday." *Time, Life, The Saturday Review of Literature, U.S. News And World Report* and *News Week,* among others, added article and editorial space to the canonization. There were congratulatory messages from President Truman, Sir Oliver Franks, then U.S. Ambassador of the Labor Party government of Great Britain, and from Giuseppe Saragat, then right-wing socialist Vice Premier of Italy.

Three years later, at the age of ninety-two, Dewey was dead, and *The New York Times* editorialized:

> Two university professors stand out as having infused philosophy with new life and a new relevance to this scientific age. They are William James and John Dewey. Both were pragmatists, but of the two John Dewey exerted the greater influence on American philosophy. Pragmatism is older than either James or Dewey. Its pioneer American expositor was the mathematician Peirce, who preached a philosophy of "common-sensism," but it was Dewey who, in the end, proved to be the apostle of pragmatism—that is, of the kind of experience on which ordinary men supposedly base their judgments. . . .[1]

Dewey's instrumental pragmatism does, in fact, present itself as a philosophy of *experience.*

Dewey wrote of his philosophy of "experience" in two ways, one popular and the other technical. We turn first to an example of the former. In an essay included in a volume entitled *Living Philosophies,* with the subtitle "A Series of Intimate Credos,"[2] he gives a bird's eye view of his "faith."

An Intimate Credo

Dewey opens the article with an attack on the traditional meaning of "faith" as "a definite body of intellectual propositions, acceptance being based upon authority—preferably that of revelation from on high."[3] In its place he advances his own definition: "Faith is tendency toward action."[4] Peirce had said that belief is a "habit of action" which in turn was a paraphasing of the utilitarian doctrine that "belief is that upon which a man is ready to act." Already Dewey strikes a familiar note.

He goes on to point out the implications of this definition in the light of the philosophy of experience: "Change from the one conception of faith to the other is indicative of a profound alteration. Adherence to any body of doctrines and dogmas based upon a specific authority signifies distrust in the power of experience to provide, in its own ongoing movement, the needed principles of belief and action. Faith in its newer sense signifies that experience itself is the sole ultimate authority. Such a faith has in it all the elements of a philosophy."[5] It does definitely have in it all the essential elements of Dewey's philosophy. This may not be readily apparent at first reading. But what would be the effect if the second sentence above read "Adherence to *any* body of doctrines based upon a specific authority, whether that authority be science or religion, signifies distrust in the power of day-to-day experience to provide, in its own ongoing movement, the needed principles of belief and action?" The meaning is clear. To eliminate the authoritative doctrines of science is to strip experience, or practice, of any principles that could guide it, and thus to leave it to improvised means to meet each situation as it arises. This is, of course, the central feature of pragmatism. By what right do we make the interpolations introduced in the paraphrased sentence? Are we not simply cutting and patching to fit Dewey to the custom-made pragmatic suit? Let us take a closer look at what he actually wrote.

He condemns "adherence to *any* body of doctrines . . . based upon a specific authority." The teachings of science are most assuredly a "body of doctrines" based upon the "specific authority" of carefully verified experimentation and the ability of labor to produce, guided by these doctrines. But Dewey does not want the reader to think of scientific doctrines, so he includes what the propaganda psychologists call "an emotionally charged word," namely, "dogmas." This is calculated to steer the reader's thoughts to religious rather than scientific doctrines. Dewey has already put the bait in this trap, for remember that he opened the article with an attack on the old notion of faith "based upon authority—preferably that of revelation on high." By this little trick he would condition the reader to think of religious doctrines and thus would conceal the real object of his attack. Internal evidence, therefore, supplies the justification for altering Dewey's original sentence so as to indicate what is included when he rejects "adherence to any body of doctrines." The full justification for our reading of the sentence, however, must await examination of his technical philosophy. There abundant evidence is forthcoming.

The only other change made in our paraphrase of Dewey's sentence was the qualifying of his term "experience" by "day-to-day." This is an attack on one of the subtlest and most crucial points in Dewey's philosophy. For the term "experience" can have a double meaning. It can mean immediate day-to-day experience and it can mean the tested, generalized experience accumulated by society in the course of human history. In the former sense, it is simple individual activity; in the latter it is another name for knowledge and truth, another name for scientific theory. Marxism employs the term "experience" in both senses when it demands the unity of theory and practice and holds that theory without practice is sterile and practice without theory is blind. Dewey, on the other hand, in rejecting the authority of scientific doctrines under cover of rejecting "dogmas," in fact rejects the accumulated social experience of mankind, and at the same time embraces immediate, day-to-day experience as "the sole ultimate authority." We will have occasion, later on, to investigate Dewey's concept of experience in considerable detail. At the moment it is sufficient to indicate an important conclusion flowing from it.

If the working class were to follow the teachings of Dewey, it would cast aside the generalized experience of the class embodied in the science of Marxism-Leninism, and would rely in its strategy and tactics solely on the power of its day-to-day experience to provide, in its own ongoing movement, the needed principles of class struggle. There would be no science of society, no science of political economy, no scientific socialism to guide working class practice. There would be only the rules-of-thumb of trade unionism, pure and simple.

In the remainder of the article Dewey tries "to indicate what a philosophy based on experience as the ultimate authority in knowledge and conduct means in the present state of civilization, what its reactions are on what is thought and done."[6] Noting that the natural sciences and technology have established that change is the essential feature of the world, he attacks economics, politics, morals and religion for rejecting change and defending "fixity" or the *status quo*: "Nevertheless, although the idea of movement and change has made itself at home in the physical sciences, it has had comparatively little influence on the popular mind as the latter looks at religion, morals, economics and politics. In these fields it is still supposed that our choice is between confusion, anarchy, and something fixed and immutable."[7]

He goes on to cite three examples of what he means: "It is assumed that Christianity is the final religion; Jesus the complete and unchanging embodiment of the divine and the human. It is assumed that our present economic regime, at least in principle, expresses something final, something to endure—with, it is incidentally hoped, some improvements in detail. It is assumed, in spite of evident flux in the actual situation, that the institutions of marriage and family that developed in medieval Europe are the last and unchanging word."[8]

In opposition, he states his own view: "These examples hint at the extent to which ideals of fixity persist in a moving world. A philosophy of experience will accept at its full value the fact that social and moral existences are, like physical existences, in a state of continuous if obscure change. It will not try to cover up the fact of inevitable modification, and will make no attempt to set fixed limits to the extent of changes that are to occur."[9]

For defense of the *status quo* he substitutes intelligent direction of change. This is his famous concept of "intelligence." Thus he says: "For the futile effort to achieve security and anchorage in something fixed, it will substitute the effort to determine the character of changes that are going on and to give them in the affairs that concern us most some measure of intelligent direction."[10]

It appears from this that Dewey is on the side of science and progress. Perhaps we were mistaken in our earlier analysis?

The lengths to which he goes can be seen in his treatment of the economic situation: "The greatest obstacle that exists to the apprehension and actualization of the possibilities of experience is found in our economic regime. . . . As long as the supreme effort of those who influence thought and set the conditions under which men act is directed toward maintenance of the existing money economy and private profit, faith in the possibilities of an abundant and significant experience, participated in by all, will remain merely philosophic."[11] Is it possible to call a man who advocates breaking out of the profit system a reactionary?

Dewey concludes the article: "It is in such a context that a thoroughgoing philosophy of experience, framed in the light of science and technique, has its significance. For it, the breakdown of traditional ideas is an opportunity."[12]

The real question before us is what kind of an opportunity does Dewey see in the breakdown of traditional ideas of divine fixity in the realms of economics, politics, morals and religion. The above passages would have us believe that he sees in it an opportunity to develop a forward-looking, realistic philosophy which could give intelligent direction to social change. On the other hand, if Dewey is truly a pragmatist, we would expect that he would see in the breakdown of traditional ideas an opportunity to reestablish the old theological content but in a new form.

To discover the essential character of his philosophy of experience with its instrumental intelligence we must examine his technical philosophy together with its application in the fields of science, social theory, ethics and religion.

Dewey's Philosophy of Experience

In the light of our examination of other pragmatic ideologists, what would we expect to find in Dewey? We would expect to find a three-step argument in which the third step is the reinstatement of what had supposedly been repudiated in the first. The pattern has repeated itself with monotonous regularity in every case we have investigated.

Perhaps this is because we have come to the analysis of pragmatism with a preconceived notion? The answer is "no." The reason we find this same pattern throughout lies in historical conditions and class requirements. The reason is objective, not subjective. Why must they follow this three-step procedure?

Each one of the pragmatists whom we have considered, whether in philosophy or in less abstract realms of ideology, has been combatting the threat of science, particularly the threat of evolution, to the traditional moral and religious doctrines. Thus each has had to appear, in the *first step,* to side with science against the old and obsolescent notions. But at the same time, each is an ideologist of a ruling class. Therefore, he must somehow reestablish the same old obscurantist weapons which, in their more obvious religious form, science and the rising class consciousness of the proletariat have rendered relatively ineffective. *The only way this can be attempted is by trying to prove that scientific knowledge is not true knowledge of the objective world.* This is the first step in the pragmatic argument. But it cannot be carried through openly. It has to be concealed under cover of a "truly militant" struggle against whatever it is that science and the working class are challenging in a particular field. For example, in legal theory the butt of the pragmatists' attack is the doctrine of divine law, in psychology it is the God-given eternal soul. In each case, however, the real object of attack is the scientific materialist understanding of the law and the human psyche.

Once science has been theoretically emasculated, the way is clear to take *the second step, namely, the substitution of pragmatic expediency in means and ends for the genuine method of science.* This in turn clears the way for *the third and final step, the reinstatement of the content of the very obscurantist fictions which had been the ostensible object of attack in the first place.* For example, in legal theory class law is once again clothed in the traditional absolute and unchangeable armor, not as God's law, but as laws rooted in immutable human instincts. Or again, in psychology the eternal soul attacked in the first step becomes, in the third, the inborn "organic mental structure" passed from generation to generation in Morgan-Weismann genetic rigidity. What formerly had been eternalized through objective idealism is eternalized once again, this time through subjective idealism. In each case the third step readmits by the back door what in the first step had been ejected by the front door.

We would expect to find some variation of this pattern in Dewey's philosophy of experience.

Dewey's Three-Step Argument

To discover the particular form of Dewey's three-step argument, we have in the first place to find out what it is that he is waging a "militant struggle" against. It is not far to seek, for he repeats it over and over again throughout his philosophical writings. He charges all previous philosophy with having as its prime task the reconciliation of science with religion. Why has this been the case? Dewey replies that philosophy has had to reconcile science and religion in order to serve whatever class was in power at the time. The central function of philosophy, he maintains, has been to demonstrate that science is really powerless to challenge such "values" as the right of private property, the superiority of a few people over the masses, the right of the few to rule, salvation in the next world, etc. According to Dewey, almost all philosophy prior to the rise of pragmatism has tried to prove that these values were eternally ordained by God and the divine order of things.

It is at once apparent that Dewey's form of the argument is to be of a different character than that of any of his pragmatic predecessors. He takes over a pseudo-class analysis of previous philosophies to help conceal what he himself is about to do. If he follows the general pattern, he will end by making a new reconciliation of science and religion to meet the requirements of the capitalist class in the United States in the era of imperialism.

Now that we have an idea of the objective of his "militant struggle," we can proceed to follow him through the three steps of argument. To do this we go to his works on general philosophy. Dewey wrote three books in which he set forth his over-all system. All three were written during the nineteen-twenties: *Reconstruction in Philosophy*, 1920; *Experience and Nature*, 1925; and the *Quest For Certainty*, 1929. His other writings are for the most part excursions into various fields in an attempt to apply the general philosophy. We will follow the argument as it is developed in these three volumes.

The first step in Dewey's three-step argument is an attack on science and the material world under cover of an attack on all metaphysics.

Dewey's point of departure is an attack on idealist metaphysics. He carries on a running fight against the doctrine that moral and religious beliefs are rooted in some "antecedent Being" existing prior to and independent of human experience. He is going to maintain, on the other hand, that traditional beliefs are the product of "practical activity" and have nothing whatever to do with *any* independent reality. In this way he maintains that there can be no threat of science to "ideas about values," another word in Dewey's lexicon for morality and religion: "If men had associated their ideas about values with practical activity instead of with cognition of antecedent Being, they would *not* have been troubled by the findings of science."[13] What he is saying is that if people had not identified religious and moral values with independent reality, existing antecedent to human experience, there would have been no conflict between science and religion and therefore also no need for philosophy to have the task of reconciling the two: "The problem of reconciliation arises and persists for one reason only. As long as the notion persists that knowledge is a disclosure of reality, of reality prior to and independent of knowing, and that knowledge is independent of a purpose to control the quality of experienced objects, the failure of natural science to disclose significant values in its objects will come as a shock."[14]

This appears to be an attack on revelation and on pure reason apart from the concrete world. But the second sentence says that there will be the necessity for reconciliation of science and religion "as long as the notion persists that knowledge is a disclosure of reality, of reality prior to and independent of knowing. . . ." Dewey wants the reader to think that he is talking solely about a particular kind of knowledge, namely, revelation or pure disembodied reason. Notice, however, that he does not qualify the term "knowledge." He is saying that "the problem of reconciliation" will remain so long as *any* knowledge, religious or scientific, is thought to be a disclosure of reality prior to and independent of knowing. This makes reality dependent on human thought. In short, he is denying that there is any objective world at all, any world which is prior to and independent of the human being, of human knowledge and of human activity. Thus, under the cover of denying supernatural knowledge, Dewey is denying all knowledge, for without independent reality there can be no real knowledge and no correspondence of idea to its object, therefore no truth. What happens to science when objective reality is denied? Obviously, there can be no genuine science.

Dewey did not really mean it when he said that if people only recognized that values are the product of practical activity there would be no need to reconcile religion and science. This was a cover for the further attack on science and materialism through attack on all reality. Dewey makes this clear when he goes on to talk about the issue of modern philosophy: "This then is the fundamental issue for present philosophy. Is the doctrine justified that knowledge is valid in the degree in which is it a revelation of antecedent existences or Being?"[15]

His attack on supernatural "antecedent Being" is now widened into a general attack on all "antecedent existences." From this attack Dewey is bound to hold that to be real is to be known; or to be real is to be a subject of action. This is but a paraphrasing of Bishop Berkeley with his "to be is to be perceived." Any such definition makes "reality" dependent on human experience. And any such human dependence is a form of subjective idealism in which people are the center of the world, or, more correctly, are world creators. The world is my idea, my activity, my experience.

It is this formula, as old as Berkeley, Hume, Ernst Mach, and Peirce that Dewey employs to destroy science and materialism. And he does it, just as the others before him did, under the cover of an attack on the metaphysics of the supernatural. There is essential identity between the theories of Berkeley, Hume, Mach, Peirce, James and Dewey. All are but one form of idealism, namely subjective idealism. The only difference lies in the *manner* in which they establish subjectivity. Berkeley, Hume and Mach follow the atomic sensational path. To a certain extent both

James and Peirce retain this basic sensationalistic approach but with the added element of practical activity as the final source of meaning of ideas. With Dewey, however, there is a far more subtle argument. It is more subtle because it is introduced as an attack, not only on Plato, but also on Berkeley. The camouflage includes an attack on subjective as well as objective idealism. What is Dewey's particular road to subjective idealism?

Dewey and "Experience"

The key concept is experience. What he means by "experience" is the cornerstone of his philosophical system. Here again we will find, as in every case with Dewey, that his real activity is concealed behind an apparently worthy battle against a reactionary doctrine. With regard to the concept of experience the doctrine against which he wages a super-militant struggle is *passive experience*. That is the basis for his mock attack on Berkeley. In fighting against this concept of passive experience Dewey is going to destroy the basis for a scientific approach. There is no question that Dewey makes experience active, but in doing so he makes it over-active; so active in fact that it eliminates genuine experience just as effectively as the old passivity doctrine of Berkeley.

For Berkeley, man passively received sense experience and could know only his own sensations. Far from the sensations being an avenue to knowledge, they stood in the way of knowledge. Sense experience was thus a curtain drawn down between man and an unknowable reality.

Dewey takes issue with this position. Speaking of his own philosophy, he says: "It points to faith in experience when intelligently used as a means of disclosing the realities of nature. It finds that nature and experience are not enemies or alien. Experience is not a veil that shuts man off from nature; it is a means of penetrating continually further into the heart of nature."[6]

On its face value, this statement is one with which no materialist could take serious issue. Only through further examination of what Dewey means by such terms as "nature" and "experience" is it possible to understand his true position. For example, the closing phrase above carries within it the device by which Dewey transforms his opposition to Berkeley into an alternate route to Berkeleyan subjective idealism. With Dewey, experience is not a veil separating man from nature. Far from it. On the contrary, man is inseparably linked with nature and nature with man. The connection is so close, indeed, that nature is identical with human experience. Experience penetrates so deeply into nature that the latter has no independent existence at all. In this way Dewey denies objective reality and clears the way for his "instrumental" theory of knowledge and truth.

Dewey calls this doctrine "the continuity of nature and experience."[17] The "continuity" is so continuous that the two are indistinguishable. Nature *is* what is experienced. Things are the experience of them. They *are* the human reaction to them. A stone is something to throw or to build with. An object is what it is "good for" in human terms. It is something discriminated out of experience because it is useful or joyful, and it *is* the use or the joy to which it gives rise. Thus Dewey says: "For things are objects to be treated, used, acted upon and with, enjoyed and endured, even more than things to be known. They are things *had* before they are things cognized."[18]

We do not know the world as it is in itself, independent of us. We know only our reaction to the world, the use we make of it. To say that things are "had" first and that we know them only later, is to hold that the object of knowledge is not the natural world but the world as reacted to. We do not know trees as they exist, we know only the uses to which they are put and the emotions they evoke.

This is what Dewey meant when he referred to experience "penetrating continually further into the heart of nature." He merely introduces a variation on Berkeley's theme "to be is to be perceived." He holds that "to be is to be had, treated, used, enjoyed." It is clear that in either case, objects are dependent on man. From the point of view of reality, knowledge and truth, it makes no difference whatever *how* the world is dependent on man. The only essential question is dependence or independence. If the world depends for its existence on man in any way, then the outcome is subjective idealism. For the essence of this philosophy is the denial of objective reality, the denial that the world exists independently of man.

To deny this "continuity of nature and experience" is, according to Dewey, "the denial to nature of the characters which make things lovable and contemptible, beautiful and ugly, adorable and awful."[19] On the other hand, to affirm such continuity is to realize that "what is experienced, since it is a manifestations of nature, may, and indeed, must be used as testimony of the characteristics of natural events."[20] And he draws the inference from such a position: "Upon this basis, reverie and desire are pertinent for a philosophic theory of the true nature of things. . . . The features of objects reached by scientific or reflective experiencing are important, but so are all the phenomena of magic, myth, politics, painting, and penitentiaries."[21]

If usefulness to man is to be the criterion of "the true nature of things," then it follows that anything at all, however fantastic or super-stitious, if only it is useful to man or some class of men, belongs to the true nature of things. Here we see that Dewey's "continuity of nature and experience," like James' "radical empiricism" opens wide the way to obscurantism.

A thing, for Dewey, is useful if it elicits consequences in human activity, if it evokes habitual responses. He cites an example from social life first and then goes on to natural phenomena. He asks what a whistle blown by a policeman signifies. What is the essence of this event? He answers that "Its essence is the rule, comprehensive and persisting, the standardized habit, of social interaction, and for the sake of which the whistle is used."[22] A whistle is what it is used for. Or a whistle is what consequences it entails for human activity. An object is a name predicting certain consequences for people.

Dewey extends this conception to natural events: "The case is the same with the essence of any non-human event, like gravity, or virtue, or vertebrate. . . . Fire burns and the burning is of moment. It enters experience; it is fascinating to watch swirling flames; it is important to avoid its dangers and to utilize its benefitcial potencies. When we name an event, calling it fire, we speak proleptically [in anticipation, *e.g.,* of consequences, H.K.W.]. . . . We employ a term of discourse; we invoke a meaning, namely, the potential consequences of the existence."[23] He then goes on to repeat the example of the policeman's whistle, and con-tinues with regard to fire: Similarly the ultimate meaning, or essence, denominated fire, is the consequences of certain natural events within the scheme of human activities, in the experience of social intercourse, the hearth and domestic altar, shared comfort, working of metals, and other such affairs."[24]

Fire is what it means to people. It is not a name for an object or process which exists independently of people.

This points to the utter fraudulance of the device Dewey is employ-ing. Only if the essence is seen as a reflection in the human mind of objective existence, only, for example, if the essence of fire is combustion with its properties of heat, etc., can man come to know fire and therefore control and use it. If man could not know something of the essence of the object as it exists independently of him, he could never know how to use it. Thus when Dewey insists that the essence of an object is its use in the hands of human beings, he is at the same time, in reality, denying the very usefulness which he makes central. Could fire have become useful to man before he knew anything about fire? It is clear that usefulness depends in large measure on knowledge. Such knowledge requires that there be a more or less accurate reflection in the human mind of the object as it exists independently of that knowledge. To deny such existence and such knowledge amounts to the denial of usefulness of things.

It is, however, a fact that the essence of Dewey's philosophy of experience is to be found in its usefulness to the dominant power in the United States today. For if nature *is* experience, and if experience is the doings and undergoings, the suffering and joy, the use and treatment, the consequences in human activities, then there can be no question of truth or falsity. Ideas are not true or false; they are useful or useless as instruments to attain a goal. Dewey defines reality as anything which has consequences in human behavior. Therefore there can be no criteria of correspondence of ideas to objective existence. Existence, nature, is dependent on human experience. It is fabricated from experience, according to Dewey. Thus his theory of experience has no place for reality, knowledge or truth. In their place he puts usefulness, instrumentality, and workability. The essence of such a philosophy is in fact its usefulness to those for whom reality, knowledge and truth have become subversive.

Dewey's philosophy of experience, his doctrine of the continuity of nature and experience, constitutes the first step in his three-step argument. It is his argument against objective reality and the substitution of subjective experience in its place. By this means he would clear the way for his instrumental theory of truth.

Dewey's Instrumental Theory of Truth

The second step in Dewey's three-step argument is the substitution of the pragmatic or instrumental method of expediency in means and ends for the true method of science.

The particular form this second step takes is the substitution of *intelligence* for *reason*. But Dewey once more conceals what he is doing by an apparent attack on a genuine evil. In this case the evil he sets out to destroy is the split between theory and practice. The classic tradition in philosophy has glorified theory and held practice in contempt. Dewey calls this "dualism between theory and practice" the "chief fortress of the classic philosophical tradition."[25] We would expect, however, that his attack is a mere sham to cover his own efforts to perpetuate the "dualism" although in a different form. Such is in fact the case; for he does just the opposite of the classic tradition. Instead of glorifying theory and debasing practice, he glorifies practice and holds all theory in contempt. And he does it in the name of the unity of theory and practice.

In order to have a real unity of theory and practice, theory must be a guide to practice and practice must be the test of the truth of theory. For theory to be a guide to practice it must be scientific theory; it must be a correct reflection of processes in the objective material world. Theory must grow out of social practice and be tested back again in it. It is clear from the first step in Dewey's argument that theory for him cannot be correct reflection of the world, and therefore that it cannot be a guide to practice. We know ahead of time that he cannot produce the unity of theory and practice. What, then, does he actually do?

Dewey starts with the classic conception of theory as pure reason completely separated from practice. Reason separated from practice becomes dogmatic myth-making or logic-chopping. Identifying reason with this classic idealist conception of it. Dewey rejects reason and puts "intelligence" in its place. "Reason and law," he writes, "were held to be synonyms"; and this identification of reason and law "served to provide an intellectual justification or 'rationalization' of subordination of individuals to fixed and ready-made universals, 'principles,' laws."[26] So when Dewey rejects reason he is rejecting laws and principles. What the real enemy becomes for Dewey is not "pure" reason as a self-constituted governing principle—a worthy enemy indeed—but reason as a reflection in the mind of objectively existing law in the universe. It is true that so-called "pure" reason reduced itself to myth-making. But true reason, reason that is valid and scientific in character, can only be such if it is a reflection in thought of the logic of the world itself. But denying objective law in the world is the heart of pragmatism and of Dewey's theories. For to allow it is to cut the ground from under subjectivism. Thus Dewey's notion constitutes an attack on all scientific theory and particularly on Marxist science, which latter Dewey, along with all bourgeois ideologists, labels dogma because of its defense of the laws of change of the world and society.

Having rejected reason, as law and principle, Dewey substitutes his conception of intelligence. What does he mean by "intelligence?" He tells us: "Concrete suggestions arising from past experiences, developed and matured in the light of the needs and deficiencies of the present, employed as aims and methods of specific reconstruction, and tested by success or failure in accomplishing this task of readjustment, suffice. To such empirical suggestions used in constructive fashion for new ends the name intelligence is given."[27]

"Intelligence" is the use of past experience to reconstruct, not the world, but experience itself. "Now, old experience," Dewey says, "is used to suggest aims and methods for developing a new and improved experience."[28] Past experience of aims and methods, or ends and means, which have succeeded or failed, is used to guide present practical activity in order to change or reconstruct future experience. Past experience does not give rise to laws or principles which are true reflections of reality. The latter Dewey brands as dogmas. Rather, past experiences act as tentative hypotheses to guide experience. Thus there is no scientific theory to guide practice; there are no laws of nature or society, there are only hypotheses which must be tested as to whether they *work* in each and every case. As Dewey puts it: "The plans which are formed, the principles which man projects as guides or reconstructive action, are not dogmas. They are hypotheses to be worked out in practice, and to be rejected, corrected and expanded as they fail or succeed in giving our present experience the guidance it requires."[29]

Conditions and events, as part of gross experience, are not objective but are either obstacles or means to the accomplishment of desired ends. Knowledge, for Dewey therefore, is simply a matter of practical memory as to which means have been successful in the past, and *may* be successful in the present. Knowledge is thus practical, not real knowledge of the objective world: "Conditions and events are neither to be fled from nor passively acquiesced in; they are to be utilized and directed. They are either obstacles to our ends or else means for their accomplishment. In a profound sense knowing ceases to be contemplative and becomes practical."[30]

Here "contemplative" is a euphemism for knowledge of reality, and thus is part of the camouflage. For he has identified knowledge of objective reality with contemplation, rejected the latter and along with it has "destroyed" knowledge.

Knowledge for Dewey is intelligence, and intelligence is the *correct* selection of means to ends; where "correct" signifies means which work or are successful. Knowledge, thought, ideas, theories are *instrumental* in overcoming obstacles in the way of accomplishing goals. Ideas and theories are "true" if they work; if they lead to the goal. They are "false" if they do not. The central position of Dewey on pragmatic or instrumental "truth" is: "The hypothesis that works is the true one." The working of the hypothesis is not a test of the correspondence of the theory to the objective world; rather it signifies merely that the hypothesis has in this case succeeded in leading toward the goal. Dewey describes his own "theory of truth," which is the heart of his pragmatic method: "The hypothesis that works is the true one; and truth is an abstract noun applied to the collection of cases, actual, foreseen and desired, that receive confirmation in their works and consequences."[31]

Dewey calls this "the pragmatic conception of truth."[32] Any means that works is "good" and "true." As with James, it is sheer expediency in means to ends. "Truth," for Dewey, "is defined as utility."[33] Anything that is useful to human beings is true. He sees "the serviceableness of an idea or hypothesis as a measure of its truth."[34] Whatever serves a purpose is "true" and "good." "Utility" and "serviceableness" are simply other terms for expediencey. Whatever is expedient to a person or a class is "true" and "good." Compare this with James' statement: "The true, to put it very briefly, is only the expedient in the way of our thinking, just as the right is only the expedient in the way of our behaving."[35]

Dewey's "intelligence" is thus the ability to select useful, serviceable, expedient means to the ends which emotion and desire establish. The ends or goals are established by wish or by will, not by knowledge of objective necessity. And the means are selected solely on the basis of expediency and are justified by the goal, by their success or failure in reaching it.

The claim of producing the unity of theory and practice has turned into their further separation. Theory has become hypotheses generated in the doing which cannot guide practice because they have nothing to do with truth and because they have validity only *after* practice has succeeded or failed in reaching the goal. Thus practice is left to grope from moment to moment without guidance by real theory. Action becomes an end in itself; and action can proceed only on a trial and error basis, spontaneously and expediently. Thus Dewey rejects any genuine theory, and raises practice itself to the all-inclusive "principle." Practice separated from theory becomes something quite different; it becomes sheer improvisation guided solely by what appears at the moment to be propitious.

Reason, science, as the discovery of objective laws of nature and society, has been eliminated; and in its place Dewey has substituted his particular notion of intelligence in the use of means to ends. It should be clear now that "intelligence" is a synonym, in Dewey's lexicon, for expediency. Thus he has substituted sheer opportunist expediency in means to ends for the method of science and reason. And he has done it under cover of an attack on traditional "pure reason" and on the separation of theory and practice. Both of these are worthy of attack, but not as Dewey carries it out. Dewey reinstates what he supposedly set out to destroy. For he perpetuates the split between theory and practice by reducing the former to the latter. He perpetuates "pure reason" as myth-making by eliminating scientific method and substituting expedient "intelligence." If "intelligence" finds that myths are useful, that they work for certain purposes, then "intelligence" will certify that they are "true" and "good," and myth-making will be reinstated. This process of reinstating myths is Dewey's simple solution to the problems of "classic" philosophy. Having destroyed the objective basis of knowledge, and having substituted satisfaction for truth, there is no longer a conflict between mysticism and knowledge.

Dewey's Reconciliation of
Science and Religion

The third step in Dewey's three-step argument is the reinstatement of what had ostensibly been rejected in the first: the reconciliation of science and religion.

At the outset of this examination of Dewey's thought we saw that he condemned traditional philosophy for assuming the task of reconciling science and religion. He held that this task was necessary because religion and the philosophy which defended it claimed to reveal reality existing independent of human experience. His attack was then concentrated on independent reality whether natural or supernatural. In this way, under the cover of attacking supernatural being, he attacked the conception of the objective material world and the discovery of its laws by natural and social science. Thus the upshot of what he has done is to put science and religion on the same level, or in the same predicament. Neither is the discovery of the nature of objective reality. While seeming to center his attack on the disclosure of reality by religion, he has, in fact, cut the ground from under science by eliminating the objective material world as well as spiritual "reality." In this way he has stripped science of any power to challenge superstition and ignorance in any form, religious or other.

Science has come into conflict with religion and idealist philosophy, Dewey maintains, because all three claim to be disclosures of independent reality. His solution to the problem is not the elimination of obscurantism, the elimination of idealism and religion, and the defense of science and materialism. It is rather the willingness to sacrifice religion and idealism as disclosures of reality in order to treat science in an "equal" manner. By putting all three on the same level, he in effect defends idealism and religion while destroying the theoretical basis for genuine science.

Dewey holds that there is no need to reconcile science and religion if it is recognized that neither is the discovery of prior, antecedent and independent reality. What he is really saying, of course, is that once the two have been reconciled there is no further need to reconcile them. For if science as discovery of the nature of the real world is eliminated, then science has already been reconciled with religion. Dewey states the case over and over again: "All that is required in order to apprehend that scientific knowledge as a mode of active operation is a potential ally of the modes of action which sustain values in existence, is to surrender the traditional notion that knowledge is possession of the inner nature of things and is the only way in which they may be experienced as they 'really' are."[36]

In short, all that is required to transform science into an ally of moral and religious values is the surrender of science. Once this surrender is made, all talk of reconciliation is superfluous. The reconciliation has already taken place.

Dewey's Theoretical "Equality of Sacrifice"

To maintain that science is the disclosure of the properties of reality or existence, claims Dewey, is to hang on to the old metaphysical notions of absolute idealism: "The notion that the findings of science are a disclosure of the inherent properties of the ultimate real, of existence at large, is a survival of the older metaphysics."[37] It is because such notions still persist, that science and the "realm of values" come into conflict. Eliminate the notion, and the conflict disappears, and along with it science. Dewey says:

> It is because of injection of an irrelevant philosophy (materialism) into interpretation of the conclusions of science that the latter are thought to eliminate qualities and values from nature. Thus is created the standing problem of modern philosophy: the relation of science to the things we prize and love and which have authority in the direction of conduct. . . . Drop the conception that knowledge is knowledge only when it is disclosure and definition of the properties of fixed and antecedent reality; interpret the aim and test of knowing by what happens in the actual procedures of scientific inquiry and the supposed need and problem vanish.[38]

He finds it "ridiculous and disconcerting" that the "old habit" of materialist thinking that science is the discovery of the nature of the world is so persistent:

> There is something both ridiculous and disconcerting in the way men have let themselves be imposed upon, so as to infer that scientific ways of thinking of objects give the inner reality of things, and that they put a mark of spuriousness upon all other ways of thinking of them, and of perceiving and enjoying them. It is ludicrous because these scientific conceptions, like other instruments, are handmade by man in pursuit of realization of a certain interest. . . . The disconcerting aspect of the situation resides in the difficulty with which mankind throws off beliefs that have become habitual.[39]

Not even Dewey's formula that scientific laws are merely instruments made by man rather than discoveries of the nature of reality can beguile the common-sense materialism of mankind. The philosophy of materialism is hard to destroy. Ruling class ideologists have been working at the task for 2500 years. That there is an objective material world and that it can be known is the essential foundation of materialism. Dewey is out to prove that there is no objective reality and that if there were it could not be known anyway. It is a big job for a man to tackle, so Dewey tries to make science itself preach idealism: that ideas or theories are not statements of what is in the world, but only of "acts to be performed." He says: "A genuine idealism and one compatible with science will emerge as soon as philosophy accepts the teaching of science that ideas are statements not of what is or has been but of acts to be performed."[40]

It is precisely such a "genuine idealism" that Dewey is trying to construct. But science does not teach that ideas are "acts to be performed." This is Dewey's particular attempt to deal a "death-blow" to science and materialism.

Religion as well as science has fallen into the "erroneous assumption" that knowledge is the disclosure of reality. So religion has been "metaphysical" like science. It is because both religion and science have been rooted in the "illusion" of reality and truth that they have come into conflict. If neither are discoveries of the truth about the universe, then there is no conflict—there is no science. The reader will observe however that religion remains intact. Dewey says: "Religion has also been involved in the metaphysics of substance, and has thrown in its lot with acceptance of certain cosmogonies. It has found itself fighting a battle and a losing one with science, as if religion were a rival theory about the structure of the natural world. . . . Were it not for this underlying assumption there could be no conflict between science and religion."[41]

Philosophy, too, must sacrifice the "underlying assumption" that knowledge is the disclosure of the inner nature of the objective world. This is the theoretical counterpart of the capitalist doctrine of equality of sacrifice. Science must sacrifice reality and truth, but it is not an exception. Religion and idealist philosophy must make the same sacrifice. The only difference, of course, is that they are not losing anything, for they never had reality or truth. Only science is destroyed. Idealism and religion gain, rather than lose, for they gain an ally from what was an enemy. Science, Dewey version, goes over to the side of religion and idealism. But the sacrifice is made by Dewey to *appear* to be equal.

In this process of equality of sacrifice of reality and truth, philosophy plays the role of reconciler, mediator and "liaison officer" between science and religion. Thus Dewey reinstates the classic aim of philosophy which he had avowedly set out to overcome: "A philosophy which abandoned its guardianship of fixed realities, values and ideals, would find a new career for itself. . . . Philosophy under such conditions finds itself in no opposition to science. It is a liaison officer between the conclusions of science and the modes of social and personal action through which attainable possibilities are projected and striven for. No more than a religion devoted to inspiration and cultivation of the sense of ideal possibilities in the actual would it find itself checked by any possible discovery of science."[42]

Dewey's idealist philosophy of experience is assuredly a "liaison officer" between science and religion. Its function is to eliminate science as a threat to the obscurantist ideology the capitalist class requires in order to help maintain its exploitation and domination.

The third step in the three-step argument is complete: science and religion are reconciled and thus "the classic tradition of philosophy," the butt of the attack in the first step, is reinstated. Dewey's philosophy of experience with its vaunted "intelligence," its instrumentalism, turns out to be the reconstruction of subjective idealism in the familiar pragmatic version.

The preliminary analysis and the suspicion of Dewey's statements in the "intimate credo" article are substantiated and justified. The high-sounding phrases there employed were, indeed, bourgeois and social-democratic demagogy to conceal his true meaning. This would have been apparent from the outset had another passage from the article been cited.

Midway in that popular presentation of his philosophy Dewey asks a question: "How about religion? Does renunciation of the extra-empirical compel also an abandonment of all religion?"[43] And he answers, "I do not think that those who are concerned about the future of a religious attitude should trouble themselves about the conflict of science with traditional doctrines."[44] No need to "trouble themselves" at all; Dewey's philosophy of experience sees to that.

The term "experience" covers a multitude of sins for Dewey. This, however, is nothing new in bourgeois philosophy. It is not even "a new name for some old ways of thinking." Lenin exposed this intellectual hoax when dealing with the theories of Avenarius back in 1908. "At present," he wrote, "the professional philosophy of all shades conceals its reactionary tendencies under a mask of well sounding phrases about 'experience'."[45] Referring to Avenarius, he adds, "And he is, of course, neither the first nor the last to build toy systems of idealism on the word 'experience'."[46]

"Mankind," Dewey says, "has hardly inquired what would happen if the possibilities of experience were seriously explored and exploited."[47] What happens when Dewey, for one, exploits "experience" to reconstruct apologetics in social theory, ethics and religion, we will see in the chapters that follow.

X. DEWEY'S "HUMAN NATURE" THEORY OF SOCIETY

IN HIS "reconstruction" of social theory, Dewey makes a frontal attack on Marxism, but under cover of an attack on an outmoded bourgeois theory. In the end he reinstates the latter in a slightly revised form. He carries out this program in numerous works, but the chief of them is *Freedom and Culture,* published in 1939 on the eve of the second World War.

The bourgeois theory under cover of an attack on which he is going to "annihilate" Marxism is that freedom and democracy are inherent in human nature. It is the bourgeois revolutionary doctrine that men are born free and equal, and that they will produce and maintain free institutions once the oppressions exercised by church and state have been abolished. The trouble is that this theory is no longer adequate: "The view that love of freedom is so inherent in man that, if it only has a chance given it by abolition of oppressions exercised by church and state, it will produce and maintain free institutions is no longer adequate."[1]

This traditional view, he holds, is one-sided, for it puts all the emphasis on human nature and neglects "cultural factors." Dewey advances the thesis that the question of freedom and democracy will not be solved "until the problem has been placed in the context of the sided"; it is to be a "well-rounded" interaction of two factors, "native human nature."[2] Thus Dewey's social theory is not going to be "one-sided"; it is to be a "well-rounded" interaction of two factors, "native human nature" and "culture."

Already we can see how his attack on the traditional doctrine of human nature is going to be utilized for his main attack on Marxism.

He maintains that, while the old idea stressed one side, human nature, Marxism is equally one-sided in stressing culture, and not even all of culture but essentially the "economic factor." Dewey is going to take a "third course," one which unites the two and overcomes the "one-sidedness" of each. But, as we would suspect, the Deweyan alternative is not an alternative at all; it is rather a return to the human nature theory at a different level.

Dewey's "Native Human Nature"

Before we come to his attack on Marxism, however, we must investigate what he means by "culture" and by "native human nature." For in these concepts and their interaction he lays the basis for his own particular version of the human nature theory of social change.

What does Dewey mean by "native human nature?" He says "the make-up of human nature in its original state" is "the question of human psychology."[3] He speaks of "native constituents," "native tendencies," and maintains that "human nature in its native constitution is the relative constant."[4] He talks about the "raw or original human nature" which is there "from the moment of birth."[5] He nowhere in detail says what the "native constituents" or "native tendencies" of "raw or original human nature" are. But since he accepts James' psychology, we can assume that he refers to the emotions and instincts which according to it comprise the mental structure with which man is born. Dewey classifies these under two main tendencies: one toward individualism or differentiation and the other toward combination or association. Thus he says: "All that we can safely say is that human nature, like other forms of life, tends to differentiation, and this moves in the direction of the distinctively individual, and that it also tends toward combination, association."[6]

He also calls these "altruistic and egoistic tendencies in human nature."[7] The two tendencies are the "psychological constituents" of "raw or original human nature." As culture "interacts" with these tendencies, it develops one or the other, depending on what kind of culture it is. The problem, as Dewey would have the reader see it, is to build that culture which will develop both tendencies, the altruistic and the egoistic, the social and the individual, so that they might enhance one another: "Some cultural conditions develop the psychological constituents that lead toward differentiation; others stimulate those which lead in the direction of the solidarity of the beehive or anthill. The human problem is that of securing the development of each constituent so that it serves to release and mature the other."[8]

In making out human nature to be constituted of the two tendencies, Dewey is transforming the essential contradiction in capitalist society between the socialization of the forces of production and their private ownership and expropriation into subjective features. Not bourgeois society, but human nature is the seat of the contradiction. And this "original or raw human nature" is the "relative constant" in history. Thus it is going to be very, very difficult, and it is going to take a long, long time to change human nature so that society may be changed. We will see that this is in fact Dewey's conclusion. But first, what does he mean by "culture?"

The Role of Culture in Dewey's Theory

Society is the interaction of culture and human nature; and human nature is composed of a number of innate factors grouped around two inborn tendencies. Now we are told that "culture" is itself the interaction of many factors. Dewey says: "The state of culture is a state of interaction of many factors, the chief of which are law and politics, industry and commerce, science and technology, the arts of expression and communication, and of morals, or the values men prize and the ways in which they evaluate them; and finally, though indirectly, the system of general ideas used by men to justify and to criticize the fundamental conditions under which they live, their social philosophy."[9]

This is what is called "the factor theory" of culture, in which a plurality of factors, all on the same level and of the same importance, simply interact. No *one* is the determining element. It is an effective formula for the elimination of any possible way of understanding society. Dewey's social theory is a factor theory: a factor theory of society; a factor theory of human nature; a factor theory of culture. The mass of factor interactions is so complex that there is no way of bringing order out of the chaos. Dewey admits this when he says: "Today the influences that affect the actions performed by individuals are so remote as to be unknown. We are at the mercy of events acting upon us in unexpected, abrupt and violent ways."[10]

Society with all its factors is really unknowable. There can be no science of society. Experimentation in the social field is only trial and error, and legislation, therefore, cannot be based on science, but must rely on improvisation and patchwork expediency, as Dewey indicates: "What purports to be experiment in the social field is very different from experiment in natural science; it is rather a process of trial and error accompanied with some degree of hope and a great deal of talk. Legislation is a matter of more or less intelligent improvisation aiming at palliating conditions by means of patchwork policies."[11]

So many equally important interacting factors have to be taken into account that planning is impossible; and if there is an attempt at planning, it usually turns out not only different but the opposite of what was anticipated in the plan: "The economic situation is so complex, so intricate in the interdependence of delicately balanced factors, that planned policies initiated by public authority are sure to have consequences totally unforseeable, often the contrary of what was intended."[12]

The pluralistic factor theory is employed by Dewey as a weapon against Marxism. But he masks his attack on materialist working class science by *appearing* to be equally opposed to idealist theories. He carries on this double game under cover of an offensive against all monistic outlooks, whether materialist or idealist. Thus, he constructs a "third position" which, he would have us think, stands midway between the materialist and the idealist approach to society. That it is in no sense a third alternative but is in fact simply the old idealism we will see as Dewey unfolds his argument.

Dewey's Attack on Marxist Historical Materialism

The battle which was begun against the human nature theory of society, is now transformed into a struggle against any and all theories which are monistic, namely, which find any one factor so predominant that it becomes the ultimate causal element of which others are in the long run secondary and derived effects. Thus Dewey's straw man is enlarged to include Marxism as well as the human nature theory. He raises the main question: "The question is whether any one of the factors is so predominant that it is *the* causal force, so that other factors are secondary and derived effects."[13]

Traditional theories have stressed either human nature or culture, one to the exclusion of the other, Dewey holds: "Theories have simplified in exaggeration of either the human factor, the constituents derived from human nature, or the 'external' environing factor."[14] Those theories that stress the factor of human nature hold that "moral forces are the ultimate determinants of the rise and fall of all human societies."[15] Those that stress the environmental or cultural factor hold that "economic conditions are ultimately the controlling forces in human relationships."[16] Together, these comprise "two types of theory that carry one-sided simplification to extremes, extremes which are logical, given the premises, but which mislead action because of the absolute quality of the premises."[17]

In opposition to these two "extremes" of what he calls "monistic theories," Dewey advances his own "pluralistic theory" in which "social events are seen to be *interactions* of components of human nature on one side with cultural conditions on the other."[18] We will see that in the end he returns to the human nature idealist monism in which the question of social change is primarily a matter of changing of the individual through education, morality and religion. But before he can draw his own conclusions, he must "destroy" Marxism. In Chapter Four of *Freedom and Culture* he turns to this task:

> In this chapter, I shall criticize the type of social theory which reduces the human factor as nearly as possible to zero; since it explains events and frames policies exclusively in terms of conditions provided by the environment. Marxism is taken as the typical illustration of the absolutism which results when this factor in the interaction is isolated and made supreme. It provides a typical illustration both because of its present vogue, and because it claims to represent the only strictly scientific theory of social change and thereby the method by which to effect change in the future.[19]

The latter sentence is of course the reason why Dewey joins the endless number of bourgeois ideologists who for a hundred years have made a profession of "destroying" Marxism. The opening sentence indicates what is to be Dewey's line of attack. This line is no different from that employed by almost all apologists for the capitalist class. Its point of departure is a complete distortion of Marxist science of society into economic determinism. From there on, the attack is an "annihilation" of this straw man.

Dewey first covers his attack by making two points: first, that he is not criticizing the economic factor itself, but only the over-emphasis on it; and secondly, he is not defending the capitalist system by his attack on Marxism. The first is a corollary of the factor theory, while the second is a case of the foremost bourgeois apologist protesting too much: "With those not committed it may promote understanding if I say that the criticism is not aimed at denying the role of economic factors in society nor at denying the tendency of the present economic regime to produce consequences adverse to democratic freedom. These things are rather taken for granted. Criticism aims to show what happens when this undeniable factor is isolated and treated as *the cause* of *all* social change."[20]

These explanations behind him, Dewey sets out to erect his straw-man Marxism. This he does by making the social democratic "distinction" between Marx on the one side and Lenin and Stalin on the other. The latter, according to Dewey, transformed "pure Marxism" into Marxism-Leninism by changing an alleged "Marxist" factor theory into economic determinism. Thus Dewey tries to give the impression that he is defending Marx and Marxism from "Sovietism." This is, of course, the classic revisionist formula.

He sets out by characterizing the "Marxist doctrine" as "the doctrine that the state of the forces of production is the sole causal force."[21] He calls this alleged "Marxist doctrine" "economic determinism."[22] This one economic factor, he says, "determines all forms of social activities and relations, political, legal, scientific, artistic, religious, moral."[23] But he adds that in the original formulation by Marx there was a qualification to the effect that once political relations, science, etc., have come into being they act as causes and modify the economic factor. This qualification made by Marx was, according to Dewey, dispensed with by his followers, namely, by Lenin and Stalin. To maintain the "qualification" would be to agree with his own factor theory, he claims:

> The subsequent ignoring of this qualification, the relegation of it to a footnote, was not wholly accidental. For there were practical reasons for paying little attention to it. . . . To adopt and pursue (it) would be in effect to abandon the all-comprehensive character of economic determination. It would put us in the relativistic and pluralistic position of considering a number of interacting factors— of which a very important one is undoubtedly the economic.
>
> Marx would have a distinguished historic position if the qualification were admitted in even fuller extent than he allowed for it.[24]

Marx would have been assured of a "distinguished historic position" if only he had given up historical materialism and had agreed with Dewey's pluralistic-idealistic factor theory of social change!

It is not accidental that Dewey nowhere cites passages from Marx, Engels, Lenin or Stalin to buttress his charge of economic determinism. For there are no such passages. On the contrary, Marxism and Marxism-Leninism have carried on a sharp and consistent struggle against economic determinism, and therefore there could not be any question of "qualification" or "ignoring of this qualification." Dewey's assertions are bald lies designed solely to conceal the fact that he is denying the possibility of a science of society. The fact that he feels it necessary to hide behind Marx is a tribute to the power of the truth to attract the masses of the people.

Stalin in his *Dialectical and Historical Materialism* gives the lie to Dewey's statements, both as to economic determinism and as to the "qualification" of it. He shows that the material life of society is the determining element which brings spiritual life into being, but at the same time that consciousness has a great role to play. As a matter of fact, consciousness can only have causal efficacy through its origin as reflection of material life, through concrete social practice and through ideas gripping the masses. Dewey, not Marxism-Leninism, denies real power to ideas and institutions; for the heart of Dewey's instrumentalism is the denial that consciousness is the reflection of reality, which alone could make it an effective force.

Because he is writing to expose all bourgeois ideologists, Stalin writes as though he were answering Dewey's lies specifically:

Whatever is the being of a society, whatever are the conditions of material life of a society, such are the ideas, theories, political views and political institutions of that society.

In this connection, Marx says: "It is not the consciousness of men that determines their existence, but, on the contrary, their social existence determines their consciousness."

The strength and vitality of Marxism-Leninism lies in the fact that it does base its practical activity on the needs of the development of the material life of society and never divorces itself from the real life of society.

It does not follow from Marx's words, however, that social ideas, theories, political views and political institutions are of no significance in the life of society, that they do not reciprocally affect social being, the development of the material conditions of the life of society. We have been speaking so far of the *origin* of social ideas, theories, views and political institutions, *of the way they arise,* of the fact that the spiritual life of society is a reflection of the conditions of its material life. As regards the *significance* of social ideas, theories, views, and political institutions, as regards their *role* in history, historical materialism, far from denying them, stresses the role and importance of these factors in the life of society, in its history. . . .

New social ideas and theories arise precisely because they are necessary to society, because it is impossible to carry out the urgent tasks of development of the material life of society without their organizing, mobilizing and transforming action. . . .[25]

There is, thus, interaction between the material and spiritual life of society; but the interaction is dialectical, not mechanical. The interacting elements are not on the same level. The material life brings into being the spiritual life, but the latter reacts on the former to speed up or retard, to control and guide its development. This is quite different from Dewey's mishmash of equally interacting factors; at the same time it is opposed to his straw-man of economic determinism as a one-way street.

"Probability" and "Pluralism"

Thus Dewey attacks a caricature of Marxism, and having "demolished" it, sets up its opposite, complete indeterminism, which eliminates any possibility of a science of society. Once this has been accomplished, Dewey shifts his attack to what he considers the "single all-embracing law" set forth by Marxism, namely, "that class warfare is the channel through which economic forces operate to effect social change and progress."[26] To "destroy" the concept of class struggle, Dewey calls on his general philosophy which has previously "destroyed" the "metaphysical notion of laws of nature and society." Marxism is "dated" because it still maintains that there are such things as laws of the objective world. Dewey's pluralism and probability have taken the place of single laws and necessity.

Dewey begins the argument with the charge that Marx derived the law of conflict from Hegel and not from concrete observation of society: "This 'law' was not derived nor supposed to be derived from study of historical events. It was derived from Hegelian dialectical metaphysics. The method of its derivation is indicated by the saying of Marx that he stood Hegel on his head (sic!). . . ."[27]

That this charge is designed to conceal the attack on all science in order to deny Marxist science is made clear when Dewey continues: "As is said of literary products, Marxism is 'dated' in the matter of its claim to be peculiarly scientific. For just as *necessity* and search for a single all-comprehensive law was typical of the intellectual atmosphere of the 'forties of the last century, so *probability* and *pluralism* are the characteristics of the present state of science."[28]

This attack on Marxism is the attack on all science, and the attack on all science today has for its main objective the attack on Marxism. Dewey denies that Marxism is a science because "science" is not a matter of laws of necessity, but is simply the working hypotheses about the way complex factors interact leading to probabilities that events may turn out thus and so.

The chief argument against Marxism is that it is not rooted in analysis of conditions, but is based on authority; first the authority of Hegel and then the authority of Marx, Engels, Lenin and Stalin. Thus his charge is that Marxism is not a science but a "theology" with its "Inner Council to declare just what is the Truth,"[29] and with its "system of exegesis which rivals the ancient theological way of explaining away apparent inconsistencies."[30] This is the current main line of attack by bourgeois ideologists. It would try to "show" that Marxism and Catholicism are, in "their reliance on authority," one and the same thing. The rationale behind this argument shows where the seat of bankruptcy and degeneracy lies. For the argument rests on the denial of the objective material world and of scientific knowledge as a reflection of its laws and facts. Without objective reality and scientific knowledge, "law" and "truth" are reduced to articles of faith and can be maintained only by authority. What Dewey and the other bourgeois ideologists are depicting is the status of the lies they would disseminate as truth; these certainly have no other basis than the powerful authority of the ruling class with its state and mass media of communication.

Scientific knowledge, law, necessity, certainty and truth all are based on the materialist theory that there is an objective material world, and that it can be known and that it develops through its own laws. It is around this central position of materialism that the class struggle in ideology is fought out on the theoretical level. Dewey's attack on Marxism hinges on his idealist reactionary denial of this position. Both his factor theory and his repudiation of law and necessity, leading to the charge that Marxism is a "religion," are contingent on the rejection of materialism. The defense of materialism and science is the defense of Marxism; and the defense of Marxism is the defense of materialism and science.

The Moral Problem

Having "annihilated" Marxism through "destroying" science and materialism, Dewey sets out to put back what he claims Marxism leaves out of social theory. The social problem today, the problem of changing society, is primarily a moral problem, he maintains. It is a moral problem because of the lag of morality behind man's control over nature. Man has tremendous power but he does not know what to do with it; he does not know for what ends or goals to use the power. Thus the need is for a science, not of society, but of human nature. The issue is moral and religious, a matter of values, ends and goals, not scientific, a matter of means and methods. Dewey states the problem: "Human power over the physical energies of nature has immensely increased. . . . The thing still uncertain is what we are going to do with it. . . . What will be done with it is a moral issue."[31]

"A more adequate science of human nature" is what is now required to overcome the "lag."[32] Man must "face the issue of the moral ground of political institutions and the moral principles by which men acting together may attain freedom of individuals which will amount to fraternal associations with one another."[33] Cultural factors, then, depend on moral factors. So that human nature and its values are the determining element. Thus Dewey did not really mean what he said when he spoke of "interaction" of culture and human nature; for in fact he makes human nature the determining factor. This is the essence of idealism with regard to society. The solution of social, political and economic problems is the task of psychology, morality and religion. As Dewey states it: "That more adequate knowledge of human nature is demanded if the release of physical powers is to serve human ends is undeniable. . . . Anything that obscures the fundamentally moral nature of the social problem is harmful. . . ."[34]

Democracy, and especially "the American democratic tradition," is a moral matter and depends on faith in human nature, in its ability to achieve freedom. This is the same doctrine of freedom and democracy as rooted in human nature which Dewey was allegedly attacking at the outset of the book. Now, after getting rid of Marxism, he reinstates the human nature theory: "I have referred with some particularity to Jefferson's ideas upon special points because of the proof they afford that the source of the American democratic tradition is moral—not technical, abstract, narrowly political nor materially utilitarian. It is moral because based on faith in the ability of human nature to achieve freedom for individuals accompanied with respect and regard for other persons and with social stability built on cohesion instead of coercion."[35]

What does it mean to say that the social problem is moral, that democracy is a matter of faith in human nature? It means that the social problem, the problem of making society better, is a matter of choice of individuals. The individual must be changed before society can be changed. It all depends on what man *wants,* since there are no laws of motion of society which move independently of the wills of individuals.

Dewey himself tells what it means to say that the issue is a moral one: "To say that the issue is a moral one is to say that in the end it comes back to personal choice and action. It is individual persons who need to have this attitude substituted for pride and prejudice, for class and personal interest, for beliefs made dear by custom and early emotional associations. It is only by the choice and the active endeavor of many individuals that this result can be effected."[36]

Social change is to be a matter of individual choice and individual moral change. In this way social change is to be a slow day-by-day, almost non-temporal process. With no theory to guide it, it must tackle each problem as it arises. All methods must be individual, plural, partial and experimental. Man must grope blindly in a hit or miss manner. He can only hope and have faith, that somehow, some time, he will get some of the things that he may now think he wants. Dewey sums up his social theory in the following passage:

An American democracy can serve the world only as it demonstrates in the conduct of its own life the efficacy of plural, partial, and experimental methods. . . . We have every right to appeal to the long and slow process of time to protect ourselves from the pessimism that comes from taking a short-span temporal view of events. . . . Only thus can we be sure that we face our problems in detail one by one as they arise, with all the resources provided by collective intelligence operating in co-operative action.[37]

An experimental method which is "plural" and "partial" is an anti-scientific method. It is the theory of interacting factors which are so myriad and so complex that nothing can be known about them, no predictions can be made, and therefore no action is possible to make a better world through changing society. This is the theory and method of obscurantism, not science. It is the approach of reaction, not progress.

For Dewey all social problems are *moral* problems having to do with human nature and its instincts or "tendencies." To change society, human nature must be changed. This is the pure idealist approach to society. His "third position" collapses. His theory is monistic, but it is monistic idealism. His very multiplicity of factors combine to produce a single idealist view of society.

Since human nature is the key of social change, and since it is a slow, day-to-day process covering years and generations, if Dewey's theory has anything to do with it, capitalist exploitation and imperialist white supremacy are safe for Hitler's 1000 years. Thus Dewey has reestablished the bourgeois theory that human nature is central, that all problems are moral ones, and that you cannot change human nature, anyway; at least not very fast.

What Dewey means by saying that the problem of social change is a "moral problem," we shall see more fully when we follow him in his "reconstruction of morality."

XI. DEWEY'S
ETHICS OF GRADUALISM

DEWEY'S "RECONSTRUCTION" of ethical theory follows the general pattern of his other "reconstructions" of apologetics. In this case, the specific "bad theory" against which he carries on a militant struggle is the traditional absolute idealist and religious conception that there is a final "end or good" based on "loyalty or obedience to a higher power or authority," namely "Divine Will."[1] But, as usual, Dewey employs his initial attack as a feint to cover his main offensive. Here it is directed against all objective ethics, and specifically against Marxist ethical science. He is going to maintain that there is no objective criterion of what is good in human conduct; there are only plural, personal "goods" of individuals. His notion of "good" is therefore subjective in character. Good is whatever the individual prizes, values, desires; whatever he feels is good for him. In this way Dewey attacks the historical materialist conception of good as objective and as scientifically determinable. Once having "destroyed" materialist ethics and established the subjective approach, he reinstates the theory of a single final end in a slightly different form.

Veiled Attack on Materialist Ethics

Dewey begins his argument with an attack on traditional ethical theory: "Ethical theory ever since [the Greeks] has been singularly hypnotized by the notion that its business is to discover some final end or good or some ultimate and supreme law. This is the common element among the diversities of theories. . . . But they have differed from one another because there was one point in which they were agreed: a single and final source of law."[2]

166

The attack on the "final end or good" theory purports to be an attack on supernatural ethics. But this is to conceal an attack on materialist ethics which also holds that there is a single source of law. Materialist ethics, however, holds that the source of good is objective society with its laws of development. For the Marxist science of ethics, good has meaning only with regard to man in his struggle to know and control nature and society. Good is social, not simply individual. The determination of what is good in any particular society depends on a scientific analysis of what is rising and what is passing away in that society. What is rising represents the developing forces of production, man's control over nature; and in class society, there is a class representing what is rising. In capitalist society, what is good for the working class is good; good in its only meaning, namely, it advances man's control over nature and society. The good for all mankind is bound up with the good of the working class; for this class represents the forces of production as they burst through the old, constricting capitalist relations and their revolutionary transformation into socialist relations of common ownership of the means of production. It is against this only possible scientific ethical theory that Dewey is, in reality, fighting.

If there is no scientifically determinable meaning of "good," it becomes "a plurality" of "goods" or "individualized ends."[3] In this case, "every moral situation is a unique situation having its own irreplaceable good,"[4] depending on "conflicting desires and alternative apparent goods."[5] This is the heart of Dewey's reconstruction of ethics. It is a "reconstruction" of idealist ethics which above all must eliminate any genuine ethical theory which could be a scientific guide to action directed toward achieving a better life.

Dewey sees morality as a matter of "intelligence," and "intelligence" is the attempt of the individual to cope with his problems of desired ends, and the means to achieve them. We already know that "intelligence" is Dewey's substitute for reason. The latter is concerned with true reflection of the real world, including society. The former is concerned only with success or failure of ideas as instrumentalities, completely apart from any question of truth as correspondence with objective reality. In ethics, "intelligence" is solely concerned with determination of what it is that "I" desire and what will satisfy that desire. Anything that succeeds in satisfying it is good; anything that fails is bad. This is the pragmatic or instrumental method as applied to moral theory.

Nature and Role of "Intelligence"

Dewey substitutes his instrumental method for "source of law" theories: "It has been repeatedly suggested that the present limit of intellectual reconstruction lies in the fact that it has not as yet been seriously applied in the moral and social disciplines. Would not this further application demand precisely that we advance to a belief in a plurality of changing, moving, individualized goods and ends, and to a belief that principles, criteria, laws are intellectual instruments for analyzing individual or unique situations."[6]

Laws are not reflections of reality, they are merely instruments to help in the analysis of individual and unique situations. In truth, of course, laws can be effective instruments only when they are reflections of objective reality. What kind of instruments can they be when they are not reflections of reality? Without law or structure, morality is a matter of unique "goods" in unique situations. Dewey is afraid people will think he is eliminating moral principles, which, of course, he is, so he says: "The blunt assertion that every moral situation is a unique situation having its own irreplaceable good may seem not merely blunt but preposterous."[7]

The assertion may seem "preposterous" because it would "appear" to eliminate "guidance of conduct by universals," namely by laws or principles. In this way it "appears" to eliminate "moral responsibility." Dewey wants to apply the pragmatic rule. The pragmatic rule establishes the meaning of an idea by its consequences. Thus Dewey says: "Let us, however, follow the pragmatic rule, and in order to discover the meaning of the idea ask for its consequences. Then it surprisingly turns out that the primary significance of the unique and morally ultimate character of the concrete situation is to transfer the weight and burden of morality to intelligence. It does not destroy responsibility; it only locates it."[8] Responsibility is indeed located. Dewey is saying that morality is a matter of individual choice and decision in each unique situation. The responsibility is located in the individual. He alone is responsible for whatever choice and decision is made. Good and evil are not objective; they do not exist in society. They are made in the choices and decisions of the individual as he meets each unique situation. Thus according to Dewey, if there are evils in capitalism, they do not inhere in the nature of the system; rather they are the result of evil choices and evil decisions made by individual capitalists. To make capitalism "better" you would have to remodel each capitalist morally. This is the classic form of bourgeois moral theory backed by religious sanction.

Intelligence, according to Dewey, is the ability to choose means which will reach the end in view. What is there in this description of "intelligent" moral choices and decisions which could possibly guide action? There are no laws or principles, there is only blind "analysis" or "inquiry" taking into account all the complexities of interacting factors. Action can only be spontaneous expediency, the choice of ends I want and of any means which within the immediate and "unique" situation appear to promise success. Dewey draws the conclusion that you can never be *sure* of what you are doing until after it has been done, after the consequences of your action have occurred. The question of truth is not involved. The only question is whether or not the actual consequences "square" with what you "supposed" or guessed they might be. For Dewey, action is not a test of the truth of the idea. It *is* the meaning of the idea. It is either an idea that works, or one that does not work. It is a successful or an unsuccessful idea. If it works it is good, if not, it is bad. This is a formula for complete immorality, not for morality. What it really amounts to is that if you get away with something, then it has worked and your action is good. Dewey does not draw this conclusion, but it follows logically from his position. It is a perfect rationale for the rapine and murder which is capitalism in the era of imperialism. It is the morality of the gangster. The only evil is to "get caught."

Dewey says that he is only applying to moral questions what "science" has applied to physical subject-matter, namely, the operational denial of objective reality and truth. In science Dewey denies truth. In moral theory he denies any real meaning to good. Thus Dewey says: "After all, then, we are only pleading for the adoption in moral reflection of the logic that has been proved to make for security, stringency and fertility in passing judgment upon physical phenomena."[9] The logic that has proved so "secure" to the capitalist class in the realm of science, and proves just as "secure" in the field of morality, is the pragmatic logic, the instrumental logic of success in operations as constituting the meaning of ideas, laws, principles. Expediency in means to ends takes the place of objective good in moral theory, as it takes the place of truth in scientific theory. Thus Dewey fulfills the whole of William James' statement that: "The true, to put it very briefly, is only the expedient in the way of our thinking, just as the right is only the expedient in the way of our behaving."[10]

The pragmatic theory of the good as the expedient is sheer bourgeois apologetics in moral theory; for it correctly reflects the complete and utter moral degeneracy and bankruptcy of the capitalist system and class. Lynching, fascism and aggressive war are "good" if they are found to be expedient by the class to maintain itself in power.

Essence of Traditional Theory Reestablished

Having theoretically "annihilated" all objective "source of law" theories of ethics, and particularly materialist ethics, and having substituted his instrumental approach, Dewey sets about reestablishing what he had ostensibly set out to eliminate, namely the single *fixed end* doctrine. He is going to reinstate a single fixed end, but of a slightly different character from the theological systems. His single fixed end is the reformist, social-democratic one of "melioration" or gradual "making things better." The single fixed end of man is not to eliminate evils but to make them less evil, or better. Thus Dewey sets up "growth" as the final and fixed goal of mankind. "Growth" means "improvement," "progress" or quantitative change. The point is to prune and trim but never to change qualitatively. Not revolution but evolution is the goal of man. Not health, but improvement of health is the goal of medicine, for example. "Growth itself," says Dewey, "is the only moral 'end'."[11] Applied to capitalism, the point is not to transform it into socialism, but to make it "better." A bigger and better capitalism is the moral goal of society. Dewey describes this single final goal of the bourgeois reformist:

The process of growth, of improvement and progress, rather than the static outcome and result, becomes the significant thing. Not health as an end fixed once and for all, but the needed improvement in health—a continual process—is the end and good. The end is no longer a terminus or limit reached. It is the active process of transforming the existent situation. Not perfection as a final goal, but the ever-enduring process of perfecting, maturing, refining is the aim of living. Honesty, industry, temperance, justice, like health, wealth and learning, are not goods to be possessed as they would be if they expressed fixed ends to be attained. They are directions of change in the quality of experience. Growth itself is the only moral "end."[12]

By his use of health and illness as an example, Dewey is attempting to conceal the full meaning of what he is saying. Let us take a different example. What happens when his "theory" is applied to a social evil like white supremacy and a social good like full equality of the Negro people? Here is a paraphrase of the above passage but in terms of white supremacy:

> The process of growth, of improvement and progress, rather than the static outcome and result, becomes the significant thing. Not the elimination of white supremacy as an end fixed once and for all, but the needed improvement in the elimination of white supremacy—a continual process—is the end and good. The end is no longer a terminus or limit reached. It is the active process of transforming the existent situation. Not the perfect elimination of white supremacy as a final goal, but the ever-enduring process of perfecting, maturing, refining is the aim in the struggle against white supremacy. The elimination of white supremacy is not a good to be accomplished as it would be if it expressed a fixed end to be attained. The elimination of white supremacy is a direction of change in the quality of experience. Improvement in the elimination of white supremacy is the only moral end.

This obviously is a formula for the retention of white supremacy, not for its elimination. It is an evil which will always exist. The only thing that can be done is to chip away at it, making little improvements here and there. Such is the outcome of Dewey's moral theory when applied to social evil. And he maintains that making such little improvements is the "only moral end." Not the elimination but the "melioration" of jim crow is the moral end. The same for anti-semitism, exploitation, oppression, war, fascism, lynching, etc., etc. The point is not to get rid of them, but to make progress, to make improvements. Such a process is indeed an "ever-enduring" one. If it is "ever-enduring" then so is the evil. Thus gradualism, reformism, is a formula for maintaining things as they are.

Growth as "the only moral end" means that reform is the only moral end. And reform means the retention of the basic evil while mouthing phrases about lopping off its "worst" manifestations. Dewey defines what he means by "growth" or "meliorism": "Meliorism is the belief that the specific conditions which exist at one moment, be they comparatively bad or comparatively good, in any event may be bettered. It encourages intelligence to study the positive means of good and the obstructions to their realization, and to put forth endeavor for the improvement of conditions."[13]

There is nothing wrong with the day-to-day struggle to make things better. There is nothing wrong with reform providing one condition is insisted upon, namely, that it is not made an end in itself, a final, single fixed end. Only when day-to-day struggle is seen as quantitative change preparing the way for qualitative change, the change which is at once the destruction of the old evil and the leap to the new good, is there nothing wrong with reform. Reform is a progressive concept only when taken together with transformation. Just as evolution is a progressive concept when taken together with what it leads to, namely, revolutionary change.

But it is precisely this interpenetration of reform and transformation, of evolution and revolution, that is explicitly repudiated by Dewey. For him "growing, or the continuous reconstruction of experience, is the only end."[14] Thus the final and fixed end which Dewey reinstates is the static, the unchanging. But he reinstates it under the appearance of change in the form of quantitative change. Quantitative change, taken apart from qualitative change, is unchanging or static.

Marxism insists on the interpenetration of the day-to-day struggle with the revolutionary struggle for socialism. The former is the preparation of the working class and its allies for the accomplishment of the transformation of capitalism. To stress the day-to-day struggle apart from the struggle for socialism, is to work for the preservation of the *status quo.* Dewey lays the philosophical basis for reformism, for social democracy, for Fabian or Norman Thomas "socialism," with his doctrine of "growth" or quantitative change as the final and only goal.

To say, as Dewey does in his "reconstruction" of social theory, that social change is a "moral problem," is to say that to change society the individual must go through a moral "reconstruction." Now we know that by "moral reconstruction" he means that the individual must use his "intelligence" in choosing successful means in satisfying his desires. To develop the "intelligent" employment of expediency is the function of education. Thus "moral reconstruction" and education are, for Dewey, one and the same process. Both are the process of "continuous passage of experience from worse to better." Dewey says that "the educative process is all one with the moral process, since the latter is a continuous passage of experience from worse to better."[16] And the process of social change, being a "moral issue" is "all one" with "the educative process." To change society, individuals must be educated morally. This is a prescription for the preservation of the *status quo* of both individuals and society.

Dewey's social, moral and education theories form a three-step argument or syllogism: all social problems are moral problems; all moral problems are problems of education; therefore all social problems are problems of education. The school, by this argument, must be the instrument for bringing about social change. But what in fact is the central function of the schools under the capitalist system? Are they instruments for the changing of capitalism into socialism? To ask the question is to pose the absurdity of Dewey's argument. The schools have as their primary function precisely the preservation, not the transformation, of the *status quo*. Thus Dewey's entire argument is in effect an argument for 1,000 years of the capitalist system.

The only thing that is missing from this three-step argument is religious sanction. But he does not fail to supply this lack, for the crowning achievement of his career is his "reconstruction" of religion.

XII. DEWEY'S

RELIGION OF SUBMISSION

By NOW it should be clear that with Dewey "reconstruction" means the recasting of traditional reactionary idealist doctrines so that they can serve as weapons in the class struggle under the conditions of imperialism. In the "reconstruction" of religion, the task is to preserve its classic essence while appearing to attack it. What is the classic essence of religion in a class society? Marx said that the essence of religion as employed by a ruling class is "the opiate of the people." It is this essence which Dewey must preserve. But he can preserve it only under cover of an offensive against it. He does it in the familiar three-step argument.

"Natural" Religion

The first step is to attack that premise of religion which has been traditionally associated with it, the belief in the supernatural. Dewey does this in many places, but he wrote one entire book on religion, *A Common Faith,* and it is to that volume we now turn our attention. There he states: "Religions have traditionally been allied with ideas of the supernatural, and often have been based upon explicit beliefs about it. Today there are many who hold that nothing worthy of being called religious is possible apart from the supernatural."[1] Not only theists, Dewey maintains, but also atheists have accepted this definition of religion, for they both hold that if science destroys belief in the supernatural then religion itself is destroyed. Of traditional theism and atheism, he says, "There is one idea held in common by these two opposite groups; identification of the religious with the supernatural."[2] It is against this identification of religion with the supernatural that he is going to wage "militant struggle."

Dewey sets out to construct a "natural" religion, one stripped of supernatural "encumbrances." He states his intention: "In the discussion I shall develop another conception of the nature of the religious phase of experience, one that separates it from the supernatural and the things that have grown up about it. I shall try to show that these derivations are encumbrances and that what is genuinely religious will undergo an emancipation when it is relieved from them; that then, for the first time, the religious aspect of experience will be enabled to develop freely on its own account."[3]

His purpose in the reconstruction of religion is to "emancipate" it from the "encumbrances" of supernaturalism. Why is such reconstruction through emancipation necessary? Because traditional supernatural religion in large part is unacceptable to the masses of the people today. Many people will no longer be taken in by it, and therefore it is not by itself an adequate weapon. This in no sense means that Dewey rejects the established churches. On the contrary, what he professes to do is to add other forms of religious expression so that even those people who today are repelled by the "encumbrances" of organized religion can be brought under its influence.

To recast religion so that it will be "appropriate to present conditions" is Dewey's goal. The historical "encumbrances" must be eliminated, at least in their old form. How can they be eliminated and yet at the same time "the religious quality of experience" be retained?

Dewey begins by accepting the Oxford Dictionary definition of religion: " 'Recognition on the part of man of some unseen higher power as having control of his destiny and as being entitled to obedience, reverence and worship.' "[4] He accepts religion as being concerned with "unseen powers" and with "reverence and obedience." The point is to find what form of these concepts or beliefs is consonant with "present conditions." At the same time certain "inconvenient aspects of past religions" must be lopped off. In short, what Dewey is asking is how much of past and present religions can be retained and still receive general credence from the masses. He wants to know what form the "unseen," "reverence" and "obedience" must take if they are to be generally acceptable today. He puts the problem as follows: "It demands that in imagination we wipe the slate clean and start afresh by asking what would be the idea of the unseen, of the manner of its control over us and the ways in which reverence and obedience would be manifest, if whatever is basically religious in experience had the opportunity to express itself free from all historic encumbrances."[5]

It is at once apparent that Dewey has by no means "wiped the slate clean," for he already has "unseen powers," "obedience," and "reverence" written indelibly upon it. His attack on supernatural religion is already seen to be a pseudo one. The sole question at issue is concerned with what *form* of supernatural religion Dewey is going to reinstate.

Religion-Centered Society

But that is not all. Dewey is not only going to reinstate supernatural religion, he is going to reconstitute it at a level equal to what it was in mediaeval times, a theocracy in which religion is no longer peripheral but is the center of individual and social life. That this is in fact his real goal will become clear when we see how he characterizes the "revolution" that has taken place in religion since "the rise of modern science and industry."

It is not the challenge of science which causes the "revolution" in religion, according to Dewey. We remember that he has already eliminated science as a threat by theoretically eliminating knowledge, truth and reality. In dealing directly with religion he is not concerned with that problem. What he is concerned with is the change that has taken place with regard to "the social import," "the place and function," of religion. It used to be the "social center of gravity," now it is only a *"special institution within a secular community."*[6] Dewey calls this change "the greatest revolution that has taken place in religions during the thousands of years that man has been upon earth. For, as I have said, this change has to do with the *social* place and function of religion."[7]

There was a time when the revolutionary bourgeoisie fought against the central, pivotal "place and function" of religion. But a dying capitalist class, through the eyes of its leading ideologist, looks back with longing to a time when religion permeated all institutions and activities of the exploited and oppressed peoples.

Dewey describes the historic religion-centered theocratic society, the type, in somewhat altered form, he would like to reinstitute:

The more significant point as regards the social import of religion is that the priesthoods were official representatives of some community, tribe, city-state or empire. . . . Each social group had its own divine beings who were its founders and protectors. Its rites of sacrifice, purification and communion were manifestations of organized civic life. The temple was a public institution, the focus of the worship of the community; the influence of its practices extended to all the customs of the community, domestic, economic, and political. Even wars between groups were usually conflicts of their respective deities.[8]

The culmination of Dewey's entire philosophy is so to "reconstruct" religious experience that it will "permeate all the customs and activities of group life." He sees the fact that "everything that can justly be termed religious in value" has "grown up outside of organized religions" as either being calamitous or "it provides the opportunity for expansion of these qualities on a new basis and with a new outlook."[9] The latter alternative is of course the one he follows. He sees it as an opportunity for "religious experience" to permeate "throughout the length and breadth of human relations."[10]

Dewey sets up the alternatives: "Secular interests and activities have grown up outside of organized religions and are independent of their authority. . . . This change either marks a terrible decline in everything that can justly be termed religious in value, in traditional religions, or it provides the opportunity for expansion of these qualities on a new basis and with a new outlook."[11] Secularization can either signify the final decline and eclipse of religion, or it can, through liberation from institutionalized religion, mark the reinstatement of religious experience as pivotal in social life. The latter alternative would mean that religious experience would permeate human relations, and would once again, as in the Church era, become the center of gravity. The "expansion" of "everything that can justly be termed religious in value" is Dewey's goal. Dewey states his goal: "Were men and women actuated throughout the length and breadth of human relations with the faith and ardor that have at times marked historic religions the consequences would be incalculable. To achieve this faith and *elan* is no easy task."[12]

To permeate all human relations with religious "faith and ardor" *is* a difficult task, but Dewey makes the attempt. How does he propose to accomplish it? The answer lies in his "reconstruction" of supernatural religion in such a way that "unseen powers" and "obedience and reverence" will constitute an integral part of all human experience.

Religious Experience

Dewey is going to separate the "religious elements of experience" from the historically constituted "encumbrances" of particular religions. Such a separation "would operate to emancipate the religious quality from encumbrances that now smother or limit it."[13] To do this he transforms *religion as a noun* into *religious as an adjective*: "The heart of my point is that there is a difference between religion, *a* religion, and the religious; between anything that may be denoted by a noun substantive and the quality of experience that is designated by an adjective."[14]

Religious as an adjective "denotes attitudes that may be taken toward every object and every proposed end or ideal."[16] In short, all aspects of experience may be taken as "religious." In this way, the "elements of religious experience" can permeate the whole of life, and Dewey's goal of making religion the "center of gravity" would be well on the way to realization in theory. But let him tell us in more detail what he means by the distinction between "religion" and "religious": "To be somewhat more explicit, a religion (and I have just said there is no such thing as religion in general) always signifies a special body of beliefs and practices having some kind of institutional organization, loose or tight. In contrast, the adjective 'religious' denotes nothing in the way of a specifiable entity, either institutional or as a system of beliefs. . . . It denotes attitudes that may be taken toward every object and every proposed end or ideal."[16]

The central point is that "religious," unlike "religion" is not a special *kind* of experience, but is a quality that may belong to all experiences; esthetic, scientific, moral and political. Thus Dewey says: "Those who hold to the notion that there is a definite kind of experience which is itself religious, by that very fact make out of it something specific, as a kind of experience that is marked off from experience as esthetic, scientific, moral, political; from experience as companionship and friendship. But 'religious' as a quality of experience signifies something that may belong to all these experiences."[17]

If Dewey can somehow lay a theoretical basis for the "religious" as "belonging to all these experiences," he will have fulfilled the most exacting requirements of the bourgeoisie. He will have ideologically justified a return to the religion-centered theocratic society, which revival at this time would be a fitting ideology for a fascist corporate state. As a matter of fact, Dewey throughout his philosophy and throughout its application to other realms of ideology, has already laid the theoretical basis for the reintegration of religion as the central and all-pervasive feature of human life. After all, if there is no objective material world, if there is no scientific knowledge, no truth, then what remains but faith in the submission to "unseen powers" with "obedience and reverence?" The unknown "unseen" is full of fearful terrors and each step is a life-in-hand risk. What is left but to pray and proceed on the basis of trial and error expediency?

Submission to Unseen Powers

What are the "religious elements of experience" and what is their function as they permeate all phases of experience? Dewey says there are two basic religious elements inherent in experience: "submission" and "unseen powers." "Obedience" and "reverence" flow from these.

"Submission" is a "generic and enduring change in attitude" and whenever such a change occurs it is religious in quality. It means gladly submitting to "the buffetings of fortune." "Thus," says Dewey, "we accommodate ourselves to changes in weather, to alterations in income when we have no other recourse."[18] Such "accommodations" are made through "a composing and harmonizing of the various elements of our being such that, in spite of changes in the special conditions that surround us, these conditions are also arranged, settled in relation to us."[19] This is the classic "Thy Will be done" of traditional religion; but for Dewey it is to be a quality of all experience, including the scientific and political. Don't rebel, accept life as it comes with all its vicissitudes, its evils, its hard knocks. Don't struggle against exploitation and oppression; compose and harmonize your being; adjust to the world, don't try to change it.

Dewey has been speaking of "accommodation" and "adaptation," and goes on to say: "There is a composing and harmonizing of the various elements of our being such that in spite of changes in the special conditions that surround us, these conditions are also arranged, settled, in relation to us. This attitude includes a note of submission. But it is voluntary, not externally imposed; and as voluntary it is something more than a mere Stoical resolution to endure unperturbed throughout the buffetings of fortune. It is more outgoing, more ready and glad, than the latter attitude, and it is more active than the former."[20] "Voluntary" submission to the "vicissitudes of fortune" is far more valuable to the ruling class than submission achieved by force, particularly if it is "ready and glad!" Just such submission has always constituted the value of religion to the class in power.

He makes the point that it is not religion which brings about the change in attitude from defiance to submission, but rather whenever there is such a change, the experience is "religious" as an adjective. Thus the change can take place not only inside but outside of churches with their rites and priesthoods. It can take place in the public schools and in other public institutions. It can even take place in misled unions, political parties and organizations. *Whenever and wherever submission occurs, it is religious.* Any change in attitude from defiance to submission, any composing and harmonizing in the face of adverse conditions, is religious. To make this clear beyond doubt, Dewey says: "It is the claim of religions that they effect this generic and enduring change in attitude. I should like to turn the statement around and say that whenever this change takes place there is a definitely religious attitude. It is not *a* religion that brings it about, but when it occurs, from whatever cause and by whatever means, there is a religious outlook and function."[21]

This is a formula for transforming the decline of religion into a revival. But in order to lay the theoretical basis for the widest possible expansion of the religious attitude, Dewey must show that no other attitude is in fact possible. This is done through his "reconstruction" of the traditional doctrine of "unseen powers."

He makes a transition between "submission" and "unseen powers" by pointing out that the former comes about not through a conscious act of will but from "sources beyond conscious deliberation and purpose."[22] The "sources beyond" are the "unseen powers." But what is meant by these terms? Dewey begins his explanation by pointing out that voluntary submission does not mean submission by an act of will. Speaking of the change in attitude from defiance to submission, he says: "And in calling it voluntary, it is not meant that it depends upon a particular resolve or volition. It is a change *of* will conceived as the organic plenitude of our being, rather than any special change *in* will."[23] What is meant by saying that the change of will comes from the "organic plenitude of our being?" Dewey answers that: "The religious attitude signifies something that is bound through imagination to a *general* attitude."[24] The change of will from defiance to submission is brought about by a *"general* attitude." What *"general* attitude?" Dewey answers: "All religions, marked by elevated ideal quality have dwelt upon the power of religion to introduce perspective into the piecemeal and shifting episodes of existence. Here too we need to reverse the ordinary statement and say that whatever introduces genuine perspective is religious, not that religion is something that introduces it."[25]

The *"general* attitude" which brings about the change from defiance to submission is an attitude which introduces "perspective," and any such perspective is religious, as an adjective. But what perspective has the power to change defiance to submission? Dewey answers:

> There can be no doubt of our dependence upon forces beyond our control. . . .
> Some optimistic souls have even concluded that the forces about us are on the whole essentially benign. But every crisis, whether of the individual or of the community, reminds man of the precarious and partial nature of the control he exercises. *When man, individually and collectively, has done his utmost, conditions that at different times and places have given rise to the ideas of Fate and Fortune, of Chance and Providence, remain.* . . .
> *The fact that Human destiny is so interwoven with forces beyond human control* renders it unnecessary to suppose that dependence and the humility that accompanies it have to find the particular channel that is prescribed by traditional doctrines. (My italics.—H.K.W.)[26]

Now we have it: the "organic plenitude of our being," the *"general* attitude," the "perspective" which can change defiance into submission is "the sense of dependence,"[27] namely, that "human destiny is so interwoven with forces beyond human control" that it gives rise to "ideas of Fate and Fortune, of Chance and Providence." This "sense of dependence" on the unseen "forces beyond human control" is the "religious quality of experience." Economic crises, war, fascism, insecurity, unemployment, poverty, sickness—these are not caused by the exploitation and oppression exercised by the capitalist class; they are rather due to "forces beyond human control," to "Fate and Fortune," "Chance and Providence." In the face of such "forces" the human being can only render "submission," "obedience and reverence."

Dewey's entire philosophy has been leading up to this final crowning point. For the import of the general system is that man cannot know anything with certainty and truth; that therefore he is dependent on unseen "forces beyond his control." Dewey is above all a "salesman of theology."

A Perilous World

For Dewey, the religious quality is the "harmonizing of the self with the universe."[28] By "universe" he means "the totality of conditions with which the self is connected."[29] Since "the self" cannot know these "conditions," the process of "harmonization" can take the form only of the "sense of dependence" leading to the "*general* attitude" of submission.

The pragmatic philosophy is designed to make this conclusion inevitable. In essence, the philosophy attempts to convince the working class and its allies that there has in fact been no progress in knowledge in all history; that we are still subject to the unseen forces beyond our control and that superstition, though in slightly different form, is still the basic character of our outlook and mode of thought. The central thesis of pragmatism is that the world is unknowable and that people are therefore buffeted by chance and hedged in by risk and uncertainty. Life is dangerous, for you never know what is going to happen next. It is precarious and perilous, and you travel at your own risk. Religion is the product of this fact. It is man's only answer to his plight: submit, be obedient and reverent toward the unknown, unseen, capricious world.

Dewey's philosophy is an attempt to reestablish superstition at a time when all the conditions but one are present for its complete eradication—the elimination of that predatory class which has a stake in the perpetuation of superstition in any and all forms.

In a passage from his major work, *Experience and Nature,* he makes this fact perfectly plain for all to see. His central point is that despite all apparent "progress" man is still as superstitious as he was in primitive society. Since the world is precarious and perilous, he has every reason to be so:

We confine ourselves to one outstanding fact: the evidence that the world of empirical things includes the uncertain, unpredictable, uncontrollable, and hazardous. . . .

Man fears because he exists in a fearful, an awful world. The world is precarious and perilous.

Everything that man achieves and possesses is got by actions that may involve him in other and obnoxious consequences in addition to those wanted and enjoyed. His acts are trespasses upon the domain of the unknown; and hence atonement, if offered in season, may ward off direful consequences that haunt even the moment of prosperity—or that must haunt that moment. While unknown consequences flowing from the past dog the present, the future is even more unknown and perilous; the present by that fact is ominous. If unknown forces that decide future destiny can be placated, the man who will not study the methods of securing their favor is incredibly flippant. . . . Goods are by grace not of ourselves. He is a dangerous churl who will not gratefully acknowledge by means of free-will offerings the help that sustains him.

These things are as true today as they were in the days of early culture.

The visible is set in the invisible; and in the end what is unseen decides what happens in the seen; the tangible rests precariously upon the untouched and ungrasped. . . .

We have substituted sophistication for superstition, at least measurably so. But the sophistication is often as irrational and as much at the mercy of words as the superstition it replaces. Our magical safeguard against the uncertain character of the world is to deny the existence of chance, to mumble universal and necessary law, the ubiquity of cause and effect, the uniformity of nature, universal progress, and the inherent rationality of the universe. These magic formulae borrow their potency from conditions that are not magical. Through science we have secured a degree of power of prediction and of control. . . . *But when all is said and done, the fundamentally hazardous character of the world is not seriously modified, much less eliminated.* (My italics.—H.K.W.) [30]

Such is the sum and substance of Dewey's philosophy. The only thing that man can be sure of is that the world is "hazardous," "perilous," "uncertain," "full of risk," "invisible," "unseen," "ominous," "unpredictable," "precarious," "uncannily unstable," "dangerous," "inconstant," "irregular," "irrational," "fearful," "awful," "unknown forces," "untouched," "ungrasped." In such a world man's acts "are trespasses upon the domain of the unknown" which "involve him in other and obnoxious consequences in addition to those wanted and enjoyed." Whatever happens is "by grace not of ourselves." It is a world in which "The visible is set in the invisible and in the end what is unseen decides what happens in the seen."

The only real difference between primitive and modern superstition is that today men "mumble universal and necessary law" instead of making sacrifices. They believe in "cause and effect, the uniformity of nature, universal progress, and the inherent rationality of the universe," in all those things which Dewey, with his subjective idealist philosophy, has "demonstrated" do not exist. In short, modern man believes in the *superstition* of "science" and "truth" rather than in magic and myth. Thus would Dewey reduce man to ignorance and perpetuate slavery.

Human beings are all in the same boat, in the same "precarious and perilous" world; it follows that an integral part of experience is the religious quality of resignation to that fact. This is the religious significance of Dewey's entire system. It is his method of reestablishing the theoretical base for putting religion at the center of gravity of social life. He says: "Whether or no we are, save in some metaphorical sense, all brothers, we are at least all in the same boat traversing the same turbulent ocean. The potential religious significance of this fact is infinite."[31] The "potential religious significance" of Dewey's philosophy of life as a "turbulent ocean" of "unseen forces" is indeed "infinite."

The Divine Restored

We have seen how Dewey "reconstructs" religion in the form of the opiate of the people, in the form of "submission" with "obedience and reverence" to the "unseen"; and how he "extends" it so that it is to become the central element in all experience. It remains to see how he reinstates what he ostensibly set out to fight against, namely, "God" or "the Divine."

There are two essential elements of religion as it is employed as a weapon in the class struggle: the first is the element of submission to unseen powers, the element of resignation that is incorporated in the classic religious attitude of "Thy Will be done"; the second is the element of compensation through emphasis on an ideal realm, heaven. Both elements are essential to the class role and function of religion. Dewey introduces the element of submission to unseen powers into his "reconstruction" of religion without explicitly labeling these powers as divine. He does it, as we have seen, through his doctrine that the world is unknowable, perilous and precarious. But as an apologist and ideologist of the ruling class he does not omit to introduce the other element, the element of compensation or heavenly reward for poverty and suffering. To do this he has to name names; he has to call on "God" or the "Divine." He has to make some connection between the ideals which are held up before the people and the actuality of their daily life. The working masses must be told that even though the connection between the ideal and the actual is not immediately apparent, it nevertheless does exist. They are to have faith that there *is* such a connection. Some day, somewhere, in some world or other, life will be ideal. Dewey gives the name "God" or "divine" to "the union of actual with ideal."[32]

The exploited and oppressed masses can be kept "from a sense of isolation and from consequent despair or defiance" only by "use of the words 'God' or 'divine' to convey the union of actual with ideal."[33] The working class and its allies can be kept from "defiance," not only by the force and violence of the state, but also by the promise, certified by "God," that everything will come out all right in the end. Appearances to the contrary notwithstanding, there is in divine reality a connection, a union of actual with ideal. It is the doctrine that all the evil is worth suffering through because it leads to good in the long, very long, run.

Dewey develops his argument:

> It is this *active* relation between ideal and actual to which I would give the name "God". . . .
>
> There exist concretely and experimentally goods—the values of art in all its forms, of knowledge, of effort and of rest after striving, of education and fellowship, of friendship and love, of growth in mind and body. These goods are there and yet they are relatively embryonic. Many persons are shut out from participation in them; there are forces at work that threaten and sap existent goods as well as prevent their expansion. A clear and intense conception of a union of ideal ends with actual conditions is capable of arousing steady emotion. It may be fed by every experience, no matter what its material.
>
> In a distracted age, the need for such an idea is urgent. . . .
>
> Use of the words "God" or "divine" to convey the union of actual with ideal may protect man from a sense of isolation and from consequent despair or defiance.[34]

There is no mistaking the line of Dewey's argument. There are actual goods which *some* people are in a position to enjoy; but there are many more people who are prevented by forces beyond their control from enjoying these good things of life. To protect the few who possess the goods from the "defiance" of the many who do not possess them, it is "urgently needed at the present time" to convince the many that "God" is "the union of the actual with the ideal." The many must be convinced that there will be "pie in the sky bye and bye." The militant working class for generations has known the answer to that one, namely, "that's a lie."

Just as Dewey's entire philosophy is designed to "reconstruct" the religious doctrine of *submission*, so it is also designed to "reconstruct" the doctrine of *compensation*. For if the world is unknown and unknowable, if it is perilous and precarious, if it is a complex of unseen forces, then there can be no theoretical ground for an actual connection between ideals, goals or ends with day to day living, with the world. The only possible connection on the basis of Dewey's system between the ideal and the actual is the supernatural, is "God" or the "divine."

Thus the "reconstruction" of traditional religion with its class function and role of opiate of the people, including both essential elements, submission and compensation, is the logical outcome of Dewey's philosophy as a whole. The entire philosophical edifice is built with the primary objective of "reconstructing" the religious doctrines which the bourgeoisie requires, and requires more than ever in the era of imperialism. The religion is not simply "tacked on," as some would have people think. It is not in any sense "detachable" from the system as a whole. Rather it is an integral part of it. But more than that, it is the determining element within the system. It is at once the core and the culmination. Even had Dewey himself not drawn the religious implications of his philosophy, they would have been there to be extracted. As Lenin pointed out, the essence of subjective idealism in any and all forms is clericalism. The "reconstruction" of religion is the reason for the "reconstruction" of philosophy, of science, etc. And the reason for all Dewey's "reconstructions" lies in his role of apologist for U.S. imperialism.

Dewey is indeed the high priest of bourgeois apologetics in the United States. He is the head salesman of theology.

XIII. PHILOSOPHY OF IMPERIALISM

IN CLASS society, the dominant ideas of an age are the ideas of the dominant class of that age. Today in this country the dominant way of looking at the world and at society is the pragmatic way of the bourgeoisie. Pragmatism is the reactionary idealist view of life of a bankrupt class. Pragmatic philosophy permeates the thought, policies and institutions of this class and system, and from there spreads its corroding poison over all strata of the population, including the labor movement. Above all, pragmatism is a weapon in the attack on the working class science of Marxism-Leninism. The center of this struggle has shifted to the United States, and the obscurantist philosophy of pragmatism is a standard bearer in the ideological offensive.

Pragmatism is the main-line philosophy of U.S. imperialism. It is the world outlook, the theory and method, of the capitalist class.

What are the principal features of pragmatism as they have been exhibited in the analysis of Peirce, Fiske, Holmes, James and Dewey?

Philosophical pragmatism is both a method and a theory. We begin our summary with the principal features of the pragmatic method. They are four: a. empiricism; b. individualism; c. spontaneity; and d. opportunism.

The Pragmatic Method

EMPIRICISM. The pragmatic method is an empirical, in opposition to a rational, method of thinking, of knowing and of making decisions.

Now there is nothing, in itself, wrong with an empirical method. The method of Marxist materialism is empirical, as is that of all true science.

But to be scientific, a method cannot be *exclusively* empirical; it must be both empirical and rational: it must unite action with knowledge, practice with theory. A method which is empirical to the exclusion of reason, which embraces action and rejects knowledge, which puts all its emphasis on practice and holds theory in contempt, is no longer simply an empirical method but has become wholly one-sided; it has passed over into *empiricism*.

The first feature of the pragmatic method is empiricism.

Empiricism is by no means just one-sided over-emphasis on action and practice, a healthy counter-balance to a one-sided over-emphasis on rational knowledge and theory. It is, rather, a complete distortion which has its reason for existence solely in the requirements of the ruling class. It is a form of apologetics, not a form of knowledge.

In the real process of knowing, practice leads to theory, and theory guides and is tested by practice. A genuine scientific method moves from practice to theory to practice at a new level, and again to developed theory.

It is this dialectical relation between theory and practice, between empirical and rational knowledge, which empiricism in general and pragmatism in particular deny and repudiate. In essence, it is the denial and repudiation of scientific method.

But pragmatism attempts to conceal this rejection of scientific method by pressing a super-militant offensive against the direct opposite of pure empiricism, namely pure rationalism. Rationalism is the completely one-sided and distorted stress on reason to the exclusion of experience, on theory to the exclusion of practice. Where empiricism limits its attention to sensations, rationalism pays little attention to them and instead proceeds to spin myths out of "pure" mental threads.

Thus empiricism and rationalism are simply alternative routes to the same destination. Both lead to the fictions required by the ruling class. The empirical method is the dominant method of bourgeois ideology, for it lends itself to the demagogy required in an attempt to mislead the modern working class.

Pragmatic method bows down before practice and despises theory, but in the end turns out to be an attack on practice as well.

Empiricism is not simply *a* principal feature, it is *the* principal feature. The others follow logically, serving only to draw the inferences inherent in it.

INDIVIDUALISM. The exclusive stress on sensuous experience leads to a distorted emphasis on individual, as opposed to social, practice.

Now there is nothing in itself wrong with individual practice. All practice is in the first place, practice of individuals. But at the same time the individual aspect of practiced experience can be understood only when it is seen in relation to the social. To stress the individual at the expense of the social is to turn the former into individualism.

The second feature of the pragmatic method is individualism. Starting from the basic position of empiricism, that all knowledge is limited to immediate sense experience, it follows that such experience is the property of the experiencing individual, that all he knows is his own experience. What is this experience of the individual when it is isolated from the social? It is composed of his own disconnected sensations and impressions. Each experience is particular and unique. Particularity and uniqueness are inevitable corollaries of individualism. Particularity is the denial of universality; while uniqueness is the repudiation of similarity. The pragmatic method denies that particular instances are expressions of universal laws of nature and society. It likewise denies that "unique" situations may be unique only in detail while they are the same in essence.

The pragmatic method would condemn human experience and knowledge to individualism, particularism and uniqueness. For example, it would have the worker who is layed off or evicted think that his situation is particular and unique, that he, himself, is responsible, and that he should in consequence suffer a guilty conscience of shame as well as hunger and cold. It would prevent the worker from understanding that his situation, while uniquely his own in one sense, is essentially the same as that of all workers under capitalism; that his being fired or evicted is an expression of the general laws of U.S. capitalism which in turn are expressions of the universal laws of capitalism as a whole. If the worker understood this, he would not blame himself nor suffer with a bad conscience. He would put the responsibility squarely where it belongs, on the economic system, and he would join forces with fellow workers to organize and struggle.

The pragmatic method treats each individual as an isolated case, and each sensuous impression as itself isolated. Whatever connections are made between the sensations, and between the individuals who have the sensations, are made not as reflections of objective interconnections in the external world, but as the result of subjective habits, desires, instincts, or behavior patterns. Thus human thought is not a reflection of the objective world, but is an organizer of sense experience to meet emotional and practical needs.

With this approach, the pragmatic method carries further its attempt to eliminate scientific knowledge. The facts and laws discovered by science are reduced to prescriptions which have in past experience been found to be useful.

Individualism, together with its corollaries of particularism and uniqueness, comprises the second feature of the pragmatic method. It leads directly to the third.

SPONTANEITY. If knowledge is always experience, never theory, and if experience is always individual, particular and unique, never social, general and similar, it follows that there can be no long range plans or projects. Planning and projecting require theoretical knowledge based on social experience embodying general laws which hold for similar cases. It is such knowledge that pragmatism condemns.

The third feature of the pragmatic method is the direct opposite of plans and projects; it is the glorification of spontaneity and improvisation. Without general social theory to guide it, individual practical activity can only meet each situation as it arises. The method of pragmatism is anarchic; it advocates the fire brigade technique of rushing from crisis to crisis.

There can be no real planning beyond the immediate situation at hand. Thus improvisation, trial and error, are the approved procedures.

Spontaneity refers to something which appears suddenly from nowhere, without labor and without preparation, and without being expected. It implies complete novelty. Now it is true that at times of sudden transformation a thing *appears* to change spontaneously, appears to change qualitatively without having undergone a relatively prolonged period of gradual or quantitative change which fully prepared the way for the sudden leap. But one of the primary tasks of Marxist scientific method is to ascertain about any given process both the way in which it changes gradually and how and at what point it changes suddenly and qualitatively. Given such knowledge, it is not necessary to proceed by guess work, by trial and error, by improvisation; one can proceed by prediction, planning and projecting.

The anarchy of the pragmatic method, exemplified in its features of spontaneity and improvisation, is on one side a reflection of the anarchic character of capitalist production and distribution, and on the other a weapon against the people. A class which cannot plan beyond the limits of single corporations, and which periodically plunges nations into economic crises of overproduction, and the world into war, creates a philosophical method in its own image. But at the same time, the class requires a method designed to prevent the workers from predicting, planning and projecting their own future.

The pragmatic method fills the bill. It preaches to the workers that they cannot know and predict that the very growth of capitalism is leading to the point at which it will burst asunder, that the working class and its allies are rising to throw off the oppressors and build a new world. It preaches that they cannot work out strategy and tactics to cooperate with and speed up this historical process. It says to the workers that they must rely on their day-to-day experience within the trade unions, working for reforms, for a fair day's pay for a fair day's work, for a bigger slice of the capitalist pie. It tells the workers that there is no such thing as certain knowledge, therefore prediction is impossible. You never know what will happen until it has happened. So the only thing to do is to keep your nose to the grindstone, and meet each new demand of the boss with whatever methods seem best at the time. If you don't get what you want one way, try another, and keep on trying this and that. Guess, don't predict; act spontaneously, don't plan; improvise, don't lay out projects; such is the advice of the pragmatic method to the workers. This kind of advice is calculated to mislead the working class away from its real class interests.

Marxism-Leninism teaches that tested knowledge is objective and true, and that on this basis predictions can be made with regard to the over-all course of historical development; that the workers can know the direction of development and can work with it to eliminate exploitation and oppression and to build socialism; that plans can be made, both short- and long-range, and that on the basis of these plans, projects can be devised and carried to successful conclusion. The Marxist method opposes scientific strategy to pragmatic spontaneity, scientific knowledge and prediction to pragmatic anarchy, scientific tactics to pragmatic improvisation. The one method guides the working class in a unity of struggle for day-to-day needs and for socialism. The other would have the proletariat stop at the day-to-day struggle within the framework of capitalism and forever reject the struggle for socialism.

The third feature of the pragmatic method, spontaneity, together with its corollary of improvisation, prepares the way for the last. The fourth is the culminating characteristic, toward which the others lead. It finally lays bare the full implications of empiricism.

EXPEDIENT OPPORTUNISM. The first three features are essentially negative; they are designed to undermine genuine scientific method. Empiricism, individualism and spontaneity do not by themselves constitute a method which can be employed in action. They do, however, lay the groundwork for the practical side of the pragmatic method, for the pragmatic substitute for the method of science.

If, as pragmatism holds, there is no theory to guide practice, if there can be no plans and projects based on scientific knowledge and prediction, then how can man function? How can he think, judge and act? If there is no such thing as truth, what can be the criteria for discriminating between various ideas, judgments and actions? On the basis of the first three features the pragmatic method would answer that people should rely on their own experience, meet each novel problem as it arises, and improvise solutions as best they can. This is of course no help at all. It merely says in effect that above all people must avoid the use of scientific method; that they must avoid theory, social experience, planning and projecting as guides to practice. It tells them what not to do, but presents no alternative.

Pragmatism, however, does not stop with admonitions alone. It goes on to offer an alternative, as a guide to practical activity.

Pragmatism offers expedient opportunism as the alternative to the scientific method. *Opportunism is the taking advantage of opportunities or circumstances with little or no regard for principles or ultimate consequences.* It is the employment of any means whatever if only they succeed in attaining the desired end in view. A means is "good" if it is successful, if it "works"; bad if it fails, if it does not "work." Contrary to science, which holds that an idea is effective if it is true, the pragmatic method advances the notion that an idea is true if it works. In the one case, truth means correspondence with objective reality; thus an idea, according to science, will be effective to the degree that it reflects the way things really are. In the other case, "truth" means success; thus it is a label tacked on to any idea which appears at the moment to lead toward a desired goal.

The fourth and final feature of the pragmatic method is expedient opportunism: expedient because pragmatism is concerned solely with adaptation of means to ends; opportunism because it advocates the use of any means which appear to promise success. *Any means to the end in view is the essence of the pragmatic method.*

Such a method is eminently suited to the ideological requirements of a class which in fact employs any and all means which appear to be successful in maintaining and extending exploitation and oppression: strike-breaking, union-busting, red-baiting, violence, frame-ups, spies, goons and stoolpigeons planted in the labor movement; doctrines of racial superiority, social and national discrimination, brutality, all-white juries, "legal" and "illegal" lynching; aggression, atomic bombs, germ warfare, mass murder, genocide. The pragmatic method is perfectly adapted to apologize for, and advocate, ideological lies and murderous force. Expedient opportunism accurately reflects the character of the dying, desperate capitalist class. Knowledge, science, principles of true and false, right and wrong can no longer serve this class.

There is of course nothing in itself wrong with means and ends. In point of fact, one of the distinguishing features of the human species is its ability consciously to establish ends or goals and to proceed in a purposeful and planned fashion to work for their realization. In this process, man cooperates with nature. He discovers the internal structure of a phenomenon and on the basis of this knowledge works with it to produce changes which are possible and desirable. The *possibility* depends on the objective structure of the natural or social process; the *desirability* depends on the needs and interests of man. But if desire it not to be capricious it must coincide with what is possible of achievement.

For example, the desire for steam-driven engines was rooted in the knowledge that water could be transformed into steam and that steam under pressure was a great source of power. Thus genuine desire does not come from within, solely, it is not the spontaneous product of individual consciousness. It is rather, if it is effective desire, a reflection of the world in relation to man at a certain level of historical development, at a certain level of possibility. Desire establishes ends or goals for man, but these goals are not spun out of whole cloth. To be real goals they must be possible of achievement; they must represent some change which can be brought about if certain intervening tasks are carried out. The "certain intervening tasks" refer to the means for achieving the end. What means must be employed to realize the goal? Obviously, the means, like the goal and the desire, must reflect truths about nature; they must correspond, not primarily to the desired end, but to the objective conditions which make the end a truly possible goal. Thus the means to attain the goal of a steam engine center around the known contradiction between the law of expansion of gases, in this case steam, on the one hand, and the known tensile strength of steel boilers and cylinders on the other. Achievement of the goal depends on the utilization and control of this contradiction through keeping steam within a boiler under just enough pressure and allowing it to expand inter-mittently into cylinders in order to drive pistons which in turn drive wheels.

Means and ends based on knowledge of the laws of motion of the objective world are a necessary and vital part of human life. Dialectical materialism recognizes this fact and makes it a keynote of method. Marxism requires that both means and ends, goals and methods, be established on the basis of correspondence with the concrete conditions existing in the material world. Means and ends are based on the scientific discovery of objective truth.

Pragmatism, however, denies the existence of scientific knowledge and objective truth. In that case, what happens to the question of means and ends, methods and goals? It is clear that for the pragmatic method neither means nor ends can be rooted in real, objective possibility: they can therefore only be based on desirability. A certain goal is desired because it is opportune for the individual, the group or the class. What, according to pragmatism, will determine the selection of means? With knowledge and truth eliminated, means can be selected solely on the basis of expediency, on the basis of "any means that may work." Expedient opportunism is substituted for scientific knowledge in the selection of both means and ends. An example will help clarify the difference between the two methods. Could the capitalist class in the epoch of imperialism, after the manner of the proletariat, establish its long range objective and its means primarily on the basis of scientific knowledge of the course of history? Could it know and will the revolutionary transforma-tion of capitalism into socialism? Could it know and will the necessity of its own destruction as a class? Obviously it could do none of these things. The means and ends of the capitalist class must be established primarily on the basis of desirability and only secondarily and derivatively on the basis of historical conditions. Thus the capitalist class must set its means and ends according to the pragmatic rather than the scientific method.

Far from being in conformity with what is coming into being in history, the capitalist goal is in direct contradiction to it. Rather than desiring and willing its own destruction as a class, it insists on its own eternal existence. The one thing the class wants above all is to continue forever in the role of exploiter and oppressor of the working masses. But history moves counter to this goal. It moves inevitably toward elimination of the class. It is clear that the bourgeoisie cannot afford to have a science of history, for history is not on its side today. Thus the class objective of perpetual rule is founded exclusively in its own desire and will. The latter are determined by the position and character of the class.

What means does the capitalist class employ to achieve its goal of eternality? Obviously it employs any and every available means with no regard for principles, scientific or moral. The end determines the means. Objective conditions simply limit the possibilities. The only "principle" recognized by the class is success.

All four features of the pragmatic method are in direct opposition to the features of materialist dialectics. They are in each case specific forms of the general features of idealist metaphysics. The first feature of the pragmatic method, empiricism, reveals its idealist character. The second, individualism with its corollary of particularism, takes sides with the metaphysical feature of isolation in opposition to dialectical interconnection. The third, spontaneity, is a form of the metaphysical feature of the static in opposition to the dialectical unity and transformation of quantitative and qualitative change. The fourth, expedient opportunism, is the denial of the inner structure of change and thus is identical with the final feature of metaphysics, namely, the denial of contradiction.

The pragmatic method is a form of pure empiricism, relying on spontaneous and improvised, expedient and opportunist means to ends.

It is anti-theoretical, anti-social, against plans and projects, anti-scientific, and utterly devoid of principle.

In sum, *it is an opportunistic method advocating any means to success.* Its most appropriate dictum is "nothing succeeds like success."

The pragmatic method is indeed adapted to the character and role of the capitalist class in the era of imperialism.

The Pragmatic Theory

Pragmatism is not only a method. It is likewise an interpretation, a conception, a *theory* of the world. What is the theory of pragmatism and what are its principal features?

The theory of pragmatism is subjective idealism of the positivist type. Positivism is fully developed subjective idealism without either sceptical or agnostic reservations. It views the mind as being so *active* that it can know only its own *activity*. Thus the activist route to subjective idealism, first laid out by Hume, Kant and Comte is followed through with full consistency by the modern positivists from Ernst Mach to Bertrand Russell, Wittgenstein, Carnap, James and Dewey.

There are many contemporary versions of positivism which, however, fall into a few main types. Among these types the best known and most influential are: logical positivism; semantical positivism; and pragmatic positivism. All have in common the central position that man creates his own world out of the "primordial chaos" of sensations through the agency of some aspect of mental activity. They differ primarily on what particular aspect of mental activity does the organizing of "raw" sense experience. Logical positivism holds that the logical structure of mind does it. Semantical positivism maintains that the meaning and grammatical syntax of language do it. While pragmatic positivism holds that practical advantage and usefulness do it.

There is considerable demagogy in the three main versions of positivism. This is by no means purely accidental, for the positivists developed their philosophical theories late in the history of capitalism and at a time when the working class and the national liberation movements were shaking the foundations of imperialism. The challenge to the bourgeoisie was crucial in all spheres, economic, social, political and ideological. If its philosophical theories were to have any hope of successful penetration into the ranks of the challengers, they must have a liberal coat of demagogic camouflage. Thus one version of positivism insists that thought must be rigorously logical; another that it must be expressed in clearly defined terms and must follow strict syntactical rules; still another insists that thought must be practical and useful. Everybody would agree at once. Almost nobody openly advocates thinking which is illogical and irrational, which is expressed sloppily and in a self-contradictory manner, and which is impractical and useless. To think logically, clearly and practically is universally acclaimed. Positivism rides the band-wagon of popular conceptions.

For thought to be logical, clear and practical, however, it must truth-fully reflect the interconnections and laws of the objective world. The logic, the structure, of thought must reflect, and correspond to, the logical structure of the world; the meaning and syntax of language must reflect, and correspond to, externally existing phenomena and their interconnections; to be practical and useful, thought must reflect, and correspond to, reality. Dialectical materialism is logical, clear and practical because it is a true reflection of the external world. The philosophy of the working class puts great stress on logical consistency, clarity and definition of terms, and on practical application through social practice. But this is something quite other than the one-sided, distorted treatment of the three concepts at the hands of positivism.

Logical, clear and practical thinking is transformed into its opposite when, as is the case with positivism, the logic, the clarity of terms, and the practicality are man-made, mind-made relations between sensations having no reference to natural phenomena and their interconnections as they exist in the objective material world. For the positivists, the "world" is created by man out of his welter of experience by forcing it into pre-fabricated molds, either logical, semantical or practical. Ideas are con-structed and tested, not on the basis of reflection of, and correspondence to, reality, but solely according to their logical self-consistency, their conformity to the meanings and rules of language, or simply according to their usefulness.

Whether of the logical, semantical or pragmatic type, the essence of positivism is the doctrine that the human mind imposes its own structural pattern on sense data and thus organizes the previously unorganized sensations. From this the conclusion is inescapable that man cannot know the external world but only the results of his own mental activity. He fabricates a "world" and knows only his own fabrication. Thus positivism would erect an impenetrable iron curtain between man and reality and thereby seek to embargo, extradite and outlaw the scientific knowledge by the aid of which man can free himself from bondage.

There are three principal features of the positivist form of idealism: a. subjectivism; b. obscurantism; c. fictionalism. Positivism subscribes to subjectivism and obscurantism because it maintains that the world is unreal and unknowable; and it subscribes to fictionalism because, without reality, knowledge and truth, man is free to invent such fictions as are ostensibly required by "logic," "semantics" or "pragmatics" but which in fact are dictated by the requirements of the ruling class.

Such are the general features of positivism as a whole. But let us summarize how they are expressed in the particular pragmatic form.

SUBJECTIVISM. Mental activity, according to pragmatic positivism, is neither primarily logical nor semantical; it is instinctive, emotional, volitional, behavioral, practical and utilitarian. The "blooming, buzzing confusion" of sensations presented by the nervous system is organized by the drives and instincts, the emotions and habits which constitute the innate structure of the mind. Thus thought can deal only with what the instincts and emotions have already organized. "Things" are not of this or that nature objectively; they are what they are feared to be, or what they are desired to be; they are what they are used for in human experience. This is obviously only a variation of the well-known Berkleyian doctrine that "to be is to be perceived." To be is to be useful or harmful in human behavior; in this way the pragmatic positivists reduce the world to dependency on human nature. It is their road to subjectivism.

The inevitable corollary of subjectivism is solipsism. Subjective idealism in any form always thrashes in the morass of solipsism, and pragmatic positivism is no exception. Since all "things" are what they are utilized for, it follows that everything, including all other selves, as the construct of the self. The conclusion is unavoidable that the self is the only existent thing. It creates its own world and lives alone in it.

Subjectivism, together with its corollary of solipsism, is the first feature of pragmatic positivism.

OBSCURANTISM. If all that man can know is the product of his own emotional and practical activity, it follows that the external material world is completely unknown and unknowable.

With its repudiation of scientific knowledge and truth, and with its acceptance of any belief as long as it has some verifiable effect on people, pragmatic theory opens the floodgates of superstition, from ghosts and table-tipping to mysticism and religion. It includes in its essence the feature of obscurantism. "Obscurantism" is the doctrine of the unknowability of the world coupled with superstition as a substitute for knowledge.

The second feature of pragmatic positivism is obscurantism.

FICTIONALISM. If the world as it really exists is unknowable, and if superstition is substituted for knowledge and truth, it follows that pragmatic positivism is an apology for the invention of fictions which may be serviceable for a given purpose. If such fictions prove useful, they will be "true" in the pragmatic sense, and there will be no genuine truth within the framework of the theory which can possibly contradict them. Fictions, ranging from the psycho-analytical and theological to the economic, social and political, are furnished their *rationalization* by this theory. Fictions of the Unconscious Id and the Divine Will, fictions of "racial" superiority and inferiority, fictions of sun spots as the cause of economic crises, fictions designating capitalist nations as "Western Civilization," war as peace, aggression as defense, mass murder as liberation, fascism as democracy—all these find their rationale in pragmatic positivism. If they produce the desired effect, if they are successful, if they work, they are counted as "true" and "good."

Perhaps some of the pragmatists would not follow their theory quite so far. The logic is there none the less. The theory offers no touchstone, no objective measure for truth; it offers only the useful, expedient and opportune. Conscious fictions may not be to the taste of a Dewey, for example, but his instrumentalism furnishes no ground whatever for combatting the lies, big and little, of U.S. imperialism. Indeed, the theory furnishes apology for, not criticism of, such methods.

Fictionalism is the third and final feature of pragmatic positivism.

Pragmatic theory is thus a form of positivism which in turn is a consistent form of subjective idealism; it is a subjectivist, obscurantist, fiction-making theory well adapted to meet the requirements of the class it serves.

We have summarized the principal features of the method and the theory of pragmatism and are now in a position to advance a concise characterization.

Characterization of Pragmatism

A complete definition of pragmatism can only be formulated through full knowledge of its history in decisive interconnection with the development of capitalism in the United States. The beginnings of such a definition have been attempted in the body of this book. A full definition must await further, and collective, work. At this juncture we can, however, present a preliminary, descriptive characterization based on the summary of the general character and the principal features of pragmatism.

Pragmatism is the main-line philosophy of U.S. capitalism in the era of imperialism. It is the idealist world outlook of the entrenched bourgeoisie. It includes both a method and a theory. The pragmatic method is pure empiricist, relying on improvised, expedient and opportunist means to ends. The pragmatic theory is subjective idealism of the type of positivism. It is a subjectivist, obscurantist, fiction-fabricating view of life. Altogether, pragmatism is a class weapon in apology for brutality, ignorance and superstition. In method and in theory it is the opposite of dialectical and historical materialism, and is directed against the working class and its allies in their struggle for liberation.

The pragmatic method is the direct opposite of materialist dialectics.[1] First, contrary to dialectics, pragmatism does not regard nature as a connected and integral whole, in which things are organically connected with, dependent on, and determined by, each other, but as an accidental agglomeration of things, of phenomena, unconnected with, isolated from, and independent of, each other. The pragmatic method therefore holds that a phenomenon in nature can be understood if taken by itself, isolated from surrounding phenomena.

Second, contrary to dialectics, pragmatism holds that nature is not a state of continuous movement and change, of continuous renewal and development, where something is always arising and developing, and something always disintegrating and dying away, but a state of rest and immobility, stagnation and immutability. The pragmatic method therefore requires that phenomena should be considered not only from the standpoint of their isolation and independence, but also from the standpoint of their rest, their immobility and their immutability.

Third, contrary to dialectics, pragmatism does not regard the process of development as one which passes from insignificant and imperceptible quantitative changes to open fundamental changes, to qualitative changes. The pragmatic method therefore holds that the process of development should not be understood as an onward and upward movement, as a transition from an old qualitative state to a new qualitative state, but as movement in a circle, as a simple repetition of what has already occurred.

Fourth, contrary to dialectics, pragmatism does not hold that internal contradictions are inherent in all things and phenomena of nature, nor that the struggle of opposites, the struggle between the old and the new, between that which is dying and that which is being born, constitutes the internal content of the process of development; rather, pragmatism holds that the process of development takes place as a harmonious unfolding of phenomena. The pragmatic method therefore holds that the process of development from the lower to the higher should be understood not through a disclosure of the contradictions inherent in things and phenomena, but through revealing their harmonious unfolding.

In sum, the pragmatic method apprehends things as isolated and static, and would understand them in terms of simple growth and harmonious unfolding. This method fully meets the requirements of, and has certain obvious advantages for, an entrenched exploiting class. Interconnection and change are abhorrent to such a class; dearly would they love to abolish these features of the world, to abolish them in particular from the thought of the oppressed masses. The relation between evolutionary and revolutionary change terrifies them; they would like to limit change to simple growth in which a phenomenon, for example, the capitalist system, could grow bigger and more profitable forever without changing into something else. Finally, the struggle between opposites, between the old and the new, in particular the struggle between rising and dying classes, must be banished from the ideology, though by no means from the practice, of the ruling, oppressing class. Class collaboration, not class struggle, must be preached: a harmonious unfolding of interests of workers and owners.

The pragmatic method is the philosophical method required by the entrenched exploiting class.

The pragmatic theory is the direct opposite of Marxist materialism.

First, contrary to Marxist materialism, which holds that the world is by its very nature *material,* that the multifold phenomena of the world constitute different forms of matter in motion, and that the world develops in accordance with the laws of movement of matter and stands in no need of a "universal spirit," pragmatism regards the world as the embodiment of human activity and usefulness.

Second, contrary to Marxist materialism, which holds that matter, nature, being, is an objective reality existing outside and independent of our mind, that thought is a product of matter, with the brain as the organ of thought, and that therefore one cannot separate thought from matter without committing a grave error, pragmatism asserts that only our mind and our activity really exist, and that the material world, being, nature, exists only in our mind, our sensations, ideas and perceptions.

Third, contrary to Marxist philosophical materialism, which holds that the world and its laws are fully knowable, that our knowledge of the laws of nature, tested by experiment and practice, is authentic knowledge having the validity of objective truth, and that there are no things in the world which are unknowable, but only things which are still not known, pragmatism denies the possibility of knowing the world and its laws, does not believe in the authenticity of our knowledge, does not recognize objective truth, and that the world can ever be known to science.

In sum, pragmatism holds that the world depends on man, that it is subjective, and that at any rate it is unknowable.

What are the sources of power which allow this philosophy to penetrate and contaminate the consciousness of the American people?

Sources of Power of Pragmatism

The main source of power of pragmatism is the organized power of the capitalist class. All the power of the state, all the force and violence, all the mass media of communication are behind it. It is on the air, in the press, on the screen. It is in all bourgeois institutions. It is in the schools. It is in all phases of ideology. The power of pragmatism lies primarily in the economic and political power of the ruling class to foster it.

No member of society, including the worker, can avoid exposure to the corrupting influence of pragmatism. It enters his consciousness through an infinite variety of channels. It invades his home through the radio, the press, the education of his children. It penetrates his union through the misleaders and hired agents. It confronts him at work through the entire process of production for profit in which skilled labor is subordinate to "getting the job done" somehow and as fast as possible. It poisons him through the cynical corruption and graft inherent in bourgeois politics.

The vicious ideology of white supremacy, fostered by the imperialist oppressors, is a prime source of the pragmatic virus, for it leads to unprincipled practice. It leads to expedient adjustment to the special oppression of the Negro people, and thus undermines principle in all aspects of life. The ideology of male supremacy is likewise a major source of the pragmatic outlook as it penetrates the working class in the home and in the factory. Here again there is compromise with principle and adjustment to the special oppression of women, which further heightens the corruption of theory and the transformation of practice into opportunistic expediency.

The fact that under capitalism labor power is a commodity, and that workers meet in the market as competing sellers of that commodity, is a virulent source of the power of pragmatism as it penetrates the working class. The capitalist system breeds individual opportunism in which personal expediency takes precedence over principle, and personal immediate success measured by bourgeois dollar values takes precedence over long range class effects. This tendency comes into direct conflict with the solidarity and organization of the workers. The breeding ground for such pragmatic opportunism is in the upper strata of labor, the aristocracy of labor, bought off with the crumbs of imperialist superprofits.

Another source of power of pragmatism as it invades the working class is found in certain historical factors. An unprecedented rate of capitalist development laid emphasis on getting things done, accompanied by an impatience with theory in the form of book-learning. This was particularly true when available books were out of touch with the material reality of life, whether on the frontier or in industrial centers. "Results are what count" became something of a national slogan, expressing what amounted to a psychological characteristic embodied in a common cultural feature. So-called "Yankee ingenuity" and "American efficiency" expressed this "go-getting" emphasis on success and turning the job out.

The merging of "American efficiency" with theoretical understanding, with imaginative grasp of long range developments, is the direction in which the U.S. working class must move if it is to break out of the pragmatic trap. Other peoples, notably the Russian, have been confronted, through their national culture, with more or less the opposite situation, namely, they had the imaginative grasp in the form of revolutionary sweep, but were lacking in immediate efficiency. This was due in large measure to the relatively retarded development of capitalism in Russia, which in turn was due to feudal institutions and imperialist domination at the hands of Germany, France and Britain.

As it affects the U.S. working class, pragmatism is the separation of practical work from revolutionary theory. It is narrow practicalism. The capitalist class in this country has attempted to transform a great asset of the working class, its practical efficiency, into a weapon against the development of the class. It has sought to do it through concentrating on this single aspect to the exclusion of its opposite, scientific theory, thus giving a wholly one-sided and distorted outlook. Through it all, there is the appeal to what *appears* as the best tradition of the U.S. working class, its efficiency in overcoming obstacles and producing results. Tenacious day-to-day practice, however, taken apart from the guidance of long-range theory and planning based on scientific principles, leads to more speed-up, more exploitation for maximum profits. It becomes economism, pure and simple trade-unionism, binding the labor movement within the capitalist system.

The U.S. working class must break through the huge fraud of pragmatism and unite its great efficiency in practice with Marxist-Leninist theory as an indispensable step toward putting itself on the main road to socialism.

All these sources of power of pragmatism have prepared the working class and its allies to accept a one-sided and distorted view in which practice is stressed to the exclusion of theory. They have prepared the American people for the acceptance of pragmatism. With regard to the working class, pragmatism has acted to heighten the opportunism fostered by the labor aristocracy. It has made the work of the misleaders easier. Lenin cites Bernstein's opportunist doctrine that "The final aim is nothing, the movement is everything" and goes on to characterize this pragmatic approach in the labor movement as "determining its conduct from case to case, in adapting itself to the events of the day and to the chops and changes of petty politics; it consists in forgetting the basic interests of the proletariat, the main features of the capitalist system as a whole, and of capitalist evolution as a whole, and of sacrificing these basic interests for the real or assumed advantages of the moment."[2] Pragmatism helps to truss the labor movement in the straitjacket of pure and simple trade-unionism with its narrow practicalism, and thus aids the "labor statesmen" in their task of tying union policy to the foreign and internal policies and programs of Wall Street.

Pragmatism and Official Policy-Making

The monopoly capitalist class is a dying class representing a moribund system. There is no future for the class or the system. Both are in the deepening throes of their general crisis. Could this class have a scientific theory of history and political economy? Such a theory would demonstrate the futility of all the efforts of the class to maintain itself in power beyond its time. Above all, the imperialist class has to reject historical materialist theory. It cannot afford to predict the future, for it has none. Therefore it has to repudiate scientific theory which alone could make prediction possible. Only a revolutionary class can have a science of the laws of development of capitalism. For these laws include the transformation of capitalism into socialism. Only the working class can predict the future, for it alone has one.

A Soviet scientist, F. V. Konstantinov, noted this condition of the ruling class: "It is not given to the ideologists of the bourgeoisie to foresee the course of events. The future terrifies them, for it holds out no good for capitalism. The actual course of historical development contradicts the interests of the bourgeoisie, since its day is over."[3]

A lead editorial in *The New York Times* agrees with this characterization: "It is more difficult today than at almost any time in modern history to forecast—or even imagine—the future."[4]

A philosophy that reflects the outlook and the requirements of the monopoly capitalist class must inevitably have as its ground the repudiation of even the possibility of a scientific theory of historical development. But to deny the possibility of a science of society, it must deny that there is any such thing as *necessity* in social development. It must reject any notion that there is a structure of change. If there were such structure it would mean that it could be known and acted upon. It would mean that it could be reflected in scientific theory which could then guide social practice.

Objective structure of social change and its reflection in scientific theory is an enemy of the imperialist class. For this class has as its burning aim its own self-preservation beyond its time. The class wills its continued dominance, while at the same moment its material life rushes it toward its doom. It is mortally sick with insoluble contradictions, crises and wars, and yet it has hallucinations of indomitable power and eternality. It cannot commit suicide. It can only attempt to turn back the tide of history by force of arms, while in its ideology it denies the inevitable.

To continue to exist at all, the ruling class in the imperialist era, and particularly in the era of the general crisis of capitalism, must set its *will* against what cannot be checked. It must hold to the notion that its desire and will are the determining factors, rather than the objective motion of historical forces. The class goal is to perpetuate the class power. But this goal has no basis in the direction of social development. Its aim is a class aim, generated solely out of the position of the class in monopoly capitalism. And the aim or goal determines the means to be employed to achieve it. Any means to the class end, anything in the immediate situation which appears to lead toward the class goal, is grasped at in the desperation of the imperialists.

Thus pragmatism, with its anti-theoretical orientation and its central doctrine of expediency, is a faithful reflection of the character of the monopoly capitalist class. The class can proceed only on the basis of sheer opportunist expediency in means and ends. Neither the goal nor the means of moving toward it can be "chosen" on the basis of scientific analysis of objective conditions. Both are established by the will and desire of the class, which in turn are determined ultimately by the character of the class and the nature of capitalist society.

For this class and its philosophy, things seldom turn out the way they were expected to. As a matter of fact they usually turn out just the opposite. Hence the risk, the uncertainty, the crisis to crisis character with its fire-brigade technique. Events appear to happen spontaneously because there can be no long range prediction and no long range planning. The class seldom knows what is going to happen until it has happened. Therefore the thinking of the imperialists often takes the form of hindsight, as witness the interminable "hearings" and "inquiries" *ex post facto,* to try to discover how and what happened. They never know what road they are really on until it is too late, or until they arrive at some strange destination.

Pragmatic expediency, not scientific knowledge, forms the basis for the policy decisions of capitalist governments in domestic and foreign affairs. The politicians and statesmen of imperialism must rely on what has worked in the past to achieve the class goal, and which may work again, "God willing." Pragmatic experience plus hunches to meet new situations are the intellectual equipment of the executive committee of the ruling class.

The magazine section of the *New York Times* published an article some years ago on "How the President Makes Decisions." Obviously this subject is of more than passing importance to each and every person in or out of the United States in this critical period of history. So how *does* the president make his fateful decisions? "Mr. Truman's decisions," we are told, "represent the sum of three influences—the researches and recommendations of his advisors, his own pragmatic experience and his willingness in moments of crisis to give heed to his own deep hunches."[5] This is reassuring, and particularly so when we recognize that the presidential advisors likewise arrive at conclusions on the basis of "pragmatic experience" and "hunches." Thus the president relies, not on scientific understanding and analysis, but on pragmatism to guide the internal and external affairs of the nation. The author of the *Times* article recognizes this when he concludes that "Mr. Truman is a pragmatist."[6]

Mr. Truman, however, is a pragmatist not primarily because of the intellectual limitations of the individual man. On the contrary, the president, whoever he be, could function only on this basis. He represents a class which can proceed only in a pragmatic fashion. The same holds throughout the state apparatus from the cabinet, the Congress and the Supreme Court to the police precinct. *Action* without theoretical guidance and rooted in pragmatic experience, *spontaneity* in the form of hunches, *expediency* of any means to the class end, such is the philosophy underlying the making of state policy.

There is no question of principle involved, but only one of expediency. The suppression of the rights of the people proceeds in direct ratio to what can be "gotten away with." The lengths to which white supremacy, Jim Crow, lynch law and police brutality go is determined primarily by the amount of opposition on the part of the people, Negro and white. There is no limit to the vicious means employed except the united struggles of the masses. Only the united front of an aroused people can check and reverse the drive to war and fascism. There is no such thing as the good will or the enlightened self-interest of the ruling class. There is only expedient adjustment to immediate circumstances.

This fact gives the lie to those who preach to the working class and its allies that they must not be militant, for in that way they only provoke fascism and war. Such advice would prepare the way for fascism and war by breaking the will to resist. Without militant struggles to oppose them, the imperialists would enmesh the peoples in fascism and a new world war at once. The threat of fascism and war comes from the inevitable drive toward them, inherent in the character of the imperialist class and their system. The same is true of the drive to crush the labor movement. Taft-Hartley legislation is brought on not by labor militancy but by the lack of it. The drive to crush labor is always present and only militant struggle prevents its success. The same holds for rent and price increases. The imperialists will use any means and go to any lengths that they can get away with to reach their goal.

The Communist Parties of each and every nation the world over establish their policies on the basis of working class scientific understanding of concrete historical circumstances. In so far as the circumstances within different nations are similar, and there is an over-all sense in which they are, namely liberation from imperialist oppression and war as the central task, the policies are similar. The truth of these policies is continuously tested in action and evaluated through criticism and self-criticism. Because they reflect the objective situation and the laws of motion of history, they are in the best interest of the working class and the great mass of toiling humanity. This does not mean that these policies are "expedient." They meet the needs of the toiling masses because they correspond to the progress of society. They work because they are true. And because they are true and work they meet the needs and interests of the people and are sooner or later accepted and acted upon. Propaganda lies cannot for long conceal the truth and mislead mankind.

Pragmatism and Dialectical Materialism

Dialectical and historical materialism, the philosophy of the working class, is the precise opposite of the imperialist philosophy of pragmatism. Each is the world outlook and method of a class. Pragmatism is the philosophy of a class whose only mode of existence is to exploit and oppress, to make profits and war. It is the philosophy of a class with no future. Pragmatism is the reflection of this class character and condition, and has not other basis for existence. It is a Nietzschean superman philosophy; beyond good and evil; beyond truth and falsity; beyond humanity. It is a dead-end philosophy of a dead-end class.

Opposed to this reactionary idealist philosophy of pragmatism, the working class has its own progressive, materialist philosophy which is the backbone of the science of Marxism. Dialectical and historical materialism is the scientific world view and method of the proletariat and the Communist Party. It is a class, partisan, party philosophy which embodies the generalized experience and the aspirations of the working class. It is a philosophy created by the entire class. The class creates the philosophy, but not out of whole cloth. It creates it out of its material life, out of its class position, out of its revolutionary historical role, out of its knowledge of the world and of life as garnered from its productive activity and out of its struggle against exploitation and oppression. It creates its philosophy out of the wisdom of head and hand passed from generation to generation, from the mothers and fathers to the sons and daughters of the working class, throughout centuries of struggle against poverty and exploitation, against oppression and war; and throughout centuries of long hard hours and days, grappling with the forces of nature to produce the necessities and luxuries of life, only to see them expropriated for the use and enjoyment of others, and to receive at best a bare subsistence in return.

Out of such experience does the working class create its view of life, its mode of thought, its philosophy. But even this is not all. The working class draws for its philosophy not only on the generalized experience of all toiling peoples. It is at the same time the inheritor of all the knowledge, all the science and great art, all that is progressive in human history. Where the imperialist class returns to the obscurantist darkness of the past to create its philosophy of pragmatism, the working class goes, not to the discarded forms of ignorance and superstition, but to the accumulated knowledge, beauty and truth won in the long course of mankind's struggle to raise itself above the level of animal existence.

Dialectical and historical materialism is the outgrowth of these two roots: the generalized experience of the working class and the accumulated fund of human knowledge. But when these two mainstreams of history came together at long last, the result was not simply one more step in progressive development. It marked a tremendous leap forward, a great revolution, a qualitative change in human knowledge which raises it to an entirely new level. It is not only built on what went before, but is a sharp break with all previous forms of knowledge. The reason is not far to seek. For the first time in the life of man, knowledge becomes the property of those who do the work, those who are exploited and oppressed.

When the generalized human productive experience, the experience in struggle of the exploited working masses, was finally united with the accumulated knowledge of the ages, there was bound to be a world-shaking transformation. It meant above all the unity of theory and practice, the uniting of head and hand, after thousands of years of separation by a class division of labor. From then on, all forms of knowledge, technology, art and science, were to be carried forward by those who put them to the test of practical activity. This great fact means a new kind of technology, a new kind of art, a new kind of science, a new society and new individual human beings.

Dialectical and historical materialism is the living, progressive philosophy of the rising, revolutionary class, the working class, whose historic destiny it is to liberate itself and all people for all time from exploitation and oppression, from fascism and war, and to establish peace, democracy and socialism. For a third of the peoples of the world it is already the philosophy of socialism in the process of building; and for the Soviet peoples it is a philosophy of the transformation of socialism into communism. It is a great leap forward in the consciousness of mankind, making possible the planned development of the environment and the social forces, which heretofore worked blindly, spontaneously and independently of the knowledge and will of people. Dialectical and historical materialism is the philosophy of the working class, but it is not simply a reflection of the class character. It is at the same time, and by that very fact, the reflection of the objective natural and social world. It is this double feature which gives it its tremendous power of transformation, its power to transform nature and society. Its power lies in its truth.

REFERENCES

CHAPTER I

1. Maxim G o r k y , *Articles and Pamphlets,* Moscow, 1951, p. 80.
2. *New York Times,* March 12, 1951.
3. Karl Marx, *The Eighteenth Brumaire of Louis Bonaparte,* New York, p. 40.
4. Charles S. Peirce, "How To Make Our Ideas Clear," *Popular Science Monthly,* January, 1878. Reprinted in *Chance, Love and Logic, ed.* Morris R. Cohen, New York, 1949, p. 45.
5. V. I. Lenin, *Imperialism, The Highest Stage of Capitalism,* New York, 1939, p. 22.
6. *Ibid.*
7. Karl Marx, *Capital,* Vol. I, New York, 1939, p. xxiii.
8. Charles S. Peirce, fragment quoted in *Evolution And The Founders Of Modern Pragmatism,* Cambridge, Mass., 1949, p. 21.
9. Philip P. Wiener, *Evolution And The Founders Of Modern Pragmatism,* Cambridge, Mass., 1949, p. 11.
10. *Ibid.* p. 14.
11. *Ibid.,* p. 11.
12. *Ibid.,* pp. 41-42.
13. *Ibid.,* p. 174.
14. *Letters of Chauncey Wright, ed.* James B. Thayer, Cambridge, Mass., 1878, p. 111.
15. *Ibid.,* pp. 111-112.
16. *Ibid.,* p. 132.
17. *Ibid.,* p. 131.
18. *Ibid.,* p. 133.
19. Immanuel Kant, *Critique Of Pure Reason,* pp. 647-648.
20. Wiener, work cited, p. 19.
21. *Ibid.*

CHAPTER II

1. See Note 4, Chapter I.
2. Peirce, *Chance, Love And Logic,* p. 41.
3. *Ibid.,* p. 15.
4. *Ibid.,* p. 16.
5. *Ibid.*
6. *Ibid.,* p. 38.
7. *Ibid.,* p. 16.
8. *Ibid.,* pp. 17-18.
9. *Ibid.,* p. 19.
10. *Ibid.,* p. 20.
11. *Ibid.,* pp. 20-21.
12. *Ibid.,* p. 21.
13. *Ibid.*
14. *Ibid.*
15. *Ibid.*
16. *Ibid.,* p. 22.
17. *Ibid.,* p. 28.
18. *Ibid.*
19. *Ibid.*
20. *Ibid.,* p. 25.
21. *Ibid.*
22. John Dewey, "The Pragmatism Of Peirce," *Chance, Love And Logic,* p. 308.
23. *Ibid.,* p. 45.
24. *Ibid.,* p. 43.
25. *Ibid.,* p. 25.
26. *Ibid.,* p. 26.
27. *Ibid.*
28. *Ibid.*
29. *Ibid.*
30. *Ibid.,* p. 53.
31. *Ibid.*
32. *Ibid.,* pp. 53-54.

33. *Ibid.*, p. 57.
34. *Ibid.*
35. William James, *Pragmatism,* New York, 1907, p. 47.

CHAPTER III

1. Wiener, work cited, p. 149.
2. Karl Marx, *A Contribution To The Critique Of Political Economy,* Chicago, 1904, pp. 11-12.
3. *Ibid.*, p. 12.
4. John Fiske, *American Political Ideas,* New York, 1885.
5. *Ibid.*, p. 6.
6. *Ibid.*
7. *Ibid.*
8. *Ibid.*, p. 101.
9. *Ibid.*, pp. 9-10.
10. *Ibid.*, p. 101.
11. *Ibid.*, p. 129.
12. *Ibid.*, p. 132.
13. *Ibid.*, p. 133.
14. *Ibid.*
15. *Ibid.*, pp. 140-141.
16. *Ibid.*, p. 141.
17. *Ibid.*, p. 143.
18. *Ibid.*, pp. 151-152.
19. Arthur M. Schlesinger Jr., *The Age Of Jackson,* New York, 1945, p. 522.
20. H. S. Commager, *The American Mind,* New Haven, 1950, p. 304.
21. *Ibid.*, p. 308.
22. *Ibid.*

CHAPTER IV

1. Commager, work cited, p. 385.
2. *Holmes-Pollock Letters, ed.,* Mark DeWolf Howe, Cambridge, Mass., 1941, Vol. I, p. 105.
3. Holmes Letter to Otto, *Journal Of Philosophy,* Vol. XXXVIII, p. 391.
4. *Illinois Law Review,* Vol. X.
5. *Holmes-Pollock Letters,* Vol. II, p. 252.

6. *Ibid.*, p. 22.
7. A. Y. Vyshinsky, *The Law Of The Soviet State,* New York, 1948, p. 50.
8. *Ibid.*
9. Oliver Wendell Holmes, *The Common Law,* Boston, 1881, p. 1.
10. *Ibid.*, p. 2.
11. *Ibid.*
12. *Ibid.*, p. 35.
13. Noble State Bank *v.* Haskell, 219 U.S. 110.
14. Holmes, *The Common Law,* p. 108.
15. Oliver Wendell Holmes, *Speeches,* Boston, 1934, p. 18.
16. Holmes, *The Common Law,* p. 35.
17. Oliver Wendell Holmes, "The Path Of The Law," *Collected Legal Papers,* New York, 1921, p. 195.
18. *Ibid.*, p. 187.
19. *Ibid.*, p. 182.
20. "The Path Of The Law," *Collected Legal Papers,* p. 200.
21. Holmes, *The Common Law,* p. 213.
22. Holmes, *Collected Legal Papers,* p. 258.
23. Max Lerner, *The Mind And Faith Of Justice Holmes,* Boston, 1943, pp. 50-51.
24. *Ibid.*, p. 432.
25. Holmes, *Collected Legal Papers,* p. 169.
26. *Ibid.*
27. *Ibid.*, p. 173.
28. *Ibid.*
29. *Ibid.*, p. 174.
30. *Ibid.*, p. 69.
31. Peirce, *Chance, Love And Logic,* p. 56.
32. Oliver Wendell Holmes, *Dissenting Opinions,* p. 50.
33. Holmes, *Collected Legal Papers,* p. 295.
34. Holmes, *The Common Law,* p. 1.
35. Lerner, work cited, p. 50.

36. Commager, work cited, p. 378.
37. *Ibid.*
38. *Ibid.*, p. 379.
39. *Ibid.*, pp. 379-380.
40. *Ibid.*, p. 381.
41. *Holmes-Pollock Letters,* Vol. I, p. 81.
42. *Ibid.*, p. 139.

CHAPTER V

1. William James, *Principles Of Psychology,* New York, 1890, Vol. I, p. 1.
2. *Ibid.*
3. *Ibid.*, p. 2.
4. *Ibid.*, p. 3.
5. *Ibid.*, pp. vi-vii.
6. *Ibid.*, p. vi.
7. *Ibid.*, p. 4.
8. *Ibid.*, p. 5.
9. *Ibid.*, p. 28.
10. *Ibid.*, p. 129.
11. *Ibid.*, p. 288.
12. *Ibid.*, p. 239.
13. *Ibid.*, p. 243.
14. *Ibid.*, p. 402.
15. *Ibid.*, pp. 288-289.
16. *Ibid.*, Vol. II, p. 283.
17. *Ibid.*, Vol. II, pp. 295-297.
18. *Ibid.*, pp. 321-322.
19. *Ibid.*, p. 322.
20. Mao Tse-tung, *On Practice,* New York, 1951, p. 3.
21. *Ibid.*
22. *Ibid.*
23. V. I. Lenin, *Materialism And Empirio - Criticism* (*Collected Works,* Vol. VIII), p. 83.
24. James, *Principles of Psychology,* Vol. II, p. 628.
25. *Ibid.*, p. 629.
26. *Ibid.*, p. 631.
27. *Ibid.*, p. 632.
28. *Ibid.*, p. 392.
29. *Ibid.*, p. 383.
30. *Ibid.*, p. 390.

31. *Ibid.*, p. 422.
32. *Ibid.*
33. *Ibid.*, p. 414.
34. *Ibid.*, pp. 409-410.
35. *Ibid.*, p. 442.
36. *Ibid.*, pp. 449-450.
37. Joseph Wortis, *Soviet Psychiatry,* Baltimore, 1950, p. 271.
38. James, *Principles Of Psychology,* Vol. II, p. 463.
39. *Ibid.*, p. 402.
40. *Ibid.*, p. 121.
41. *Ibid.*, p. 121.
42. *Ibid.*, p. 287.
43. *Ibid.*
44. *Ibid.*, pp. 285-286.
45. *Ibid.*, p. 641.
46. *Ibid.*, p. 686.
47. John Dewey, "From Absolutism To Experimentalism," *Contemporary American Philosophy,* Vol. II, New York, 1930, pp. 23-26. This essay is the closest Dewey ever came to writing an intellectual auto-biography.

CHAPTER VI

1. John Dewey, *The School And Society* (First published, Chicago, 1899; edition cited is Chicago, 1949).
2. *Ibid.*, p. 9.
3. *Ibid.*, pp. 22-28.
4. *Ibid.*, p. 26.
5. *Ibid.*, p. 28.
6. *Ibid.*, p. 12.
7. *Ibid.*
8. *Ibid.*, p. 11.
9. *Ibid.*, p. 10.
10. *Ibid.*, pp. 21-22.
11. *Ibid.*, p. 22.
12. *Ibid.*, p. 35.
13. *Ibid.*
14. *Ibid.*, pp. 53-55.
15. *Ibid.*, p. 123.
16. *Ibid.*
17. *Ibid.*, p. 124.

18. *Ibid.*, p. 125.
19. *Ibid.*
20. *Ibid.*, p. 126.
21. *Ibid.*, p. 127.
22. *Ibid.*, p. 90.
23. *Ibid.*, p. 88.
24. *Ibid.*
25. *Ibid.*, pp. 88-89.
26. *Ibid.*, p. 135.
27. *Ibid.*
28. *Ibid.*, p. 90.
29. *Ibid.*
30. *Ibid.*
31. *Ibid.*, pp. 92-93.
32. *Ibid.*, pp. 94-96.
33. A. N. Leontiev, "The Most Important Tasks of Soviet Psychology," *Benjamin Rush Bulletin,* Summer, 1950, p. 13.
34. *Ibid.*
35. Dewey, *The School And Society,* p. 97.
36. *Ibid.*, p. 135.
37. *Ibid.*, pp. 97-98.
38. *Ibid.*, p. 99.
39. *Ibid.*
40. *Ibid.*, p. 100.
41. N. K. Goncharov, "The School and Pedagogy in the U.S.A. In The Service Of Reaction," *Sovietskaia Pedagogika,* November, 1949. Translated and published by Teachers College, Columbia University, in a pamphlet entitled *A m e r i c a n Education Through the Soviet Looking-Glass,* with anti-Soviet slanders by George S. Counts, New York, 1951, p. 50.
42. Dewey, *The School and Society,* pp. 99-100.
43. *Ibid.*, p. 100.
44. *Ibid.*, pp. 101-102.
45. *Ibid.*, p. 102.
46. *Ibid.*, p. 103.
47. *Ibid.*
48. *Ibid.*, p. 111.
49. *Ibid.*, p. 112.
50. *Ibid.*, p. 114.

51. *Ibid.*, p. 147.
52. N. K. Goncharov, work cited, p. 41.

CHAPTER VII

1. William James, *Pragmatism,* New York, 1907, p. 222.
2. *Ibid.*, p. 75.
3. *Ibid.*, p. 28.
4. *Ibid.*, pp. 28-32.
5. *Ibid.*, p. 32.
6. *Ibid.*, pp. 32-33.
7. Ralph Barton Perry, *The Thought And Character of William James,* Boston, 1935, Vol. I, p. 165.
8. *Ibid.*, Vol. II, p. 11.
9. James, *Pragmatism,* p. vii.
10. *Ibid.*, p. 6.
11. *Ibid.*, pp. 7-8.
12. A. A. Zhdanov, *Essays on Literature, Philosophy, and Music,* New York, 1950, p. 47.
13. James, *Pragmatism,* p. 12.
14. *Ibid.*, p. 9.
15. *Ibid.*, p. 13.
16. *Ibid.*, p. 15.
17. *Ibid.*
18. *Ibid.*, pp. 15-17.
19. *Ibid.*, p. 19.
20. *Ibid.*, pp. 18-20.
21. *Ibid.*, p. 20.
22. *Ibid.*, p. 40.
23. *Ibid.*
24. *Ibid.*, pp. 65-66.
25. William James, *Essays In Radical Empiricism,* New York, 1912, pp. 40-41.
26. James, *Pragmatism,* p. 53.
27. *Ibid.*, pp. 53-54.
28. James, *Essays In Radical Empiricism,* p. 10.
29. *Ibid.*, p. 42.
30. *Ibid.*
31. V. I. Lenin, *Materialism and Empirio-Criticism,* p. 19.
32. *Ibid.*, pp. 11-12.
33. *Ibid.*, p. 23.
34. *Ibid.*

35. *Ibid.*
36. *Ibid.*, p. 296 *n.*
37. *Ibid.*, pp. 296-297.
38. James, *Pragmatism,* p. 93.
39. *Ibid.*, p. 93.
40. *Ibid.*
41. *Ibid.*, pp. 89-90.
42. James, *Essays In Radical Empiricism,* p. 28.
43. *Ibid.*, p. 29.
44. *Ibid.*, p. 37.
45. *Ibid.*, p. 4.
46. *Ibid.*, p. 15.
47. *Ibid.*, p. 23.
48. *Ibid.*, p. 24.
49. *Ibid.*, p. 25.
50. *Ibid.*, p. 59.
51. *Ibid.*, p. 23.
52. *Ibid.*, pp. 9-10.
53. *Ibid.*, p. 42.
54. *Ibid.*, p. 193.
55. *Ibid.*, p. 59.
56. *Ibid.*, p. 196.
57. *Ibid.*, p. 57.
58. *Ibid.*, p. 198.
59. *Ibid.*, p. 60.

CHAPTER VIII

1. William James, *Essays In Radical Empiricism,* pp. 203-204.
2. *Ibid.*, p. 202.
3. James, *Pragmatism,* pp. 57-58.
4. *Ibid.*, p. 58.
5. *Ibid.*
6. *Ibid.*, p. 222.
7. *Ibid.*, p. 68.
8. *Ibid.*, p. 64.
9. *Ibid.*
10. *Ibid.*, p. 218.
11. *Ibid.*, p. 75.
12. *Ibid.*, p. 76.
13. *Ibid.*
14. *Ibid.*, p. 58.
15. *Ibid.*, p. 76.
16. *Ibid.*
17. *Ibid.*, pp. 77-78.
18. *Ibid.*, p. 14.
19. *Ibid.*, p. 79.
20. *Ibid.*, p. 77.
21. *Ibid.*, p. 51.
22. *Ibid.*, pp. 72-73.
23. *Ibid.*, p. 299.
24. *Ibid.*, p. 73.
25. *Ibid.*, pp. 73-74.
26. *Ibid.*, p. 74.
27. *Ibid.*
28. *Ibid.*, p. 75.
29. *Ibid.*, pp. 79-80.
30. *Ibid.*, p. 80.
31. *Ibid.*, p. 200.
32. *Ibid.*, pp. 54-55.
33. James, *Essays in Radical Empiricism,* p. 185.
4—References — Pragmatism .. ..
34. *Ibid.*, pp. 183-184.
35. James, *Pragmatism,* p. 52.
36. *Ibid.*, p. 57.
37. *Ibid.*, p. 53.
38. *Ibid.*, p. 217.
39. *Ibid.*, p. 122.
40. *Ibid.*, pp. 288-289.
41. *Ibid.*, p. 54.
42. William James, *The Will To Believe,* New York, 1897, p. 3.
43. *Ibid.*, p. 15.
44. *Ibid.*, p. 29.
45. *Ibid.*
46. *Ibid.*, p. 25.
47. *Ibid.*
48. *Ibid.*, pp. 18-19.
49. James, *Pragmatism,* p. 121.
50. *Ibid.*, p. 122.
51. James, *The Will To Believe,* p. 25.
52. *Ibid.*, p. 300.
53. *Ibid.*, pp. 302-303.
54. *Ibid.*, p. 304.
55. James, *The Will To Believe,* pp. 318-372.
56. James, *Pragmatism,* p. 64.
57. *Ibid.*
58. Benito Mussolini, in an interview with the press in April, 1926. Quoted in R. B. Perry, *The Thought and Character of William James,* Vol. II, p. 575.

CHAPTER IX

1. *New York Times,* June 3, 1952.
2. *Living Philosophies,* New York, 1931.
3. *Ibid.,* p. 31.
4. *Ibid.*
5. *Ibid.*
6. *Ibid.,* p. 22.
7. *Ibid.,* p. 26.
8. *Ibid.*
9. *Ibid.*
10. *Ibid.*
11. *Ibid.,* p. 30.
12. *Ibid.,* p. 34.
13. John Dewey, *The Quest For Certainty,* New York, 1929, p. 43.
14. *Ibid.,* p. 45.
15. *Ibid.*
16. John Dewey, *Experience And Nature,* Revised edition, New York, 1929, p. iii.
17. *Ibid.,* p. 8.
18. *Ibid.,* p. 21.
19. *Ibid.*
20. *Ibid.,* p. 19.
21. *Ibid.,* p. 20.
22. *Ibid.,* p. 190.
23. *Ibid.,* p. 191.
24. *Ibid.*
25. Dewey, *Quest For Certainty,* p. 77.
26. John Dewey, *Reconstruction In Philosophy,* New York, 1920, p. 91.
27. *Ibid.,* p. 89.
28. *Ibid.,* p. 88.
29. *Ibid.,* p. 89.
30. *Ibid.,* pp. 102-103.
31. *Ibid.,* pp. 128-129.
32. *Ibid.,* p. 130.
33. *Ibid.,* p. 129.
34. *Ibid.*
35. James, *Pragmatism,* p. 222.
36. Dewey, *Quest For Certainty,* p. 100.
37. *Ibid.*
38. *Ibid.*
39. *Ibid.,* p. 131.
40. *Ibid.,* p. 133.
41. *Ibid.,* p. 288.
42. *Ibid.,* p. 26.
43. *Living Philosophies,* p. 28.
44. *Ibid.,* p. 28.
45. Lenin, *Materialism and Empirio-Criticism,* p. 119.
46. *Ibid.,* p. 120.
47. *Living Philosophies,* p. 22.

CHAPTER X

1. John Dewey, *Freedom And Culture,* New York, 1939, p. 7.
2. *Ibid.,* p. 23.
3. *Ibid.,* p. 13.
4. *Ibid.,* pp. 18-19.
5. *Ibid.,* p. 19.
6. *Ibid.,* p. 21.
7. *Ibid.,* p. 29.
8. *Ibid.,* p. 22.
9. *Ibid.,* p. 23.
10. *Ibid.,* p. 45.
11. *Ibid.,* p. 64.
12. *Ibid.,* p. 62.
13. *Ibid.,* p. 13.
14. *Ibid.,* p. 75.
15. *Ibid.,* p. 12.
16. *Ibid.,* p. 14.
17. *Ibid.,* p. 75.
18. *Ibid.*
19. *Ibid.*
20. *Ibid.,* p. 76.
21. *Ibid.,* p. 98.
22. *Ibid.,* p. 77.
23. *Ibid.*
24. *Ibid.,* pp. 77-78.
25. Joseph Stalin, *Dialectical and Historical Materialism,* New York, 1940, pp. 21-23.
26. Dewey, *Freedom and Culture,* p. 79.
27. *Ibid.,* pp. 79-81.
28. *Ibid.*
29. *Ibid.,* p. 97.
30. *Ibid.,* p. 30.
31. *Ibid.,* p. 165.
32. *Ibid.,* p. 171.
33. *Ibid.,* p. 164.

34. *Ibid.*, p. 171.
35. *Ibid.*, p. 162.
36. *Ibid.*, p. 151.
37. *Ibid.*, pp. 175-176.

CHAPTER XI

1. Dewey, *Reconstruction In Philosophy,* p. 131.
2. *Ibid.*, pp. 131-132.
3. *Ibid.*, p. 132.
4. *Ibid.*
5. *Ibid.*
6. *Ibid.*
7. *Ibid.*
8. *Ibid.*
9. *Ibid.*, p. 134.
10. James, *Pragmatism,* p. 222.
11. Dewey, *Reconstruction In Philosophy,* p. 140.
12. *Ibid.*, p. 141.
13. *Ibid.*, p. 142.
14. *Ibid.*, p. 148.
15. *Ibid.*, p. 45.

CHAPTER XII

1. John Dewey, "A Common Faith," *Intelligence In The Modern World,* p. 1003.
2. *Ibid.*, p. 1004.
3. *Ibid.*
4. *Ibid.*, p. 1005.
5. *Ibid.*, p. 1008.
6. *Ibid.*, p. 1031.
7. *Ibid.*, p. 1032.
8. *Ibid.*, p. 1030.
9. *Ibid.*, p. 1035.
10. *Ibid.*, p. 1034.
11. *Ibid.*, p. 1035.
12. *Ibid.*, p. 1034.
13. *Ibid.*, p. 1010.

14. *Ibid.*, p. 1005.
15. *Ibid.*, p. 1010.
16. *Ibid.*
17. *Ibid.*, p. 1011.
18. *Ibid.*, p. 1014.
19. *Ibid.*, p. 1015.
20. *Ibid.*
21. *Ibid.*
22. *Ibid.*, p. 1016.
23. *Ibid.*, p. 1015.
24. *Ibid.*, p. 1019.
25. *Ibid.*, p. 1020.
26. *Ibid.*
27. *Ibid.*, p. 1021.
28. *Ibid.*, p. 1016.
29. *Ibid.*
30. Dewey, *Experience And Nature,* pp. 41-44.
31. Dewey, "A Common Faith," work cited, p. 1036.
32. *Ibid.*, p. 1027.
33. *Ibid.*
34. *Ibid.*, pp. 1025-1027.

CHAPTER XIII

1. The apposition of the pragmatic and dialectical methods and theories is a paraphrasing of Stalin's *Dialectical and Historical Materialism,* pp. 7-17.
2. V. I. Lenin and Joseph Stalin, *Marxism and Revisionism,* New York, 1946, p. 11.
3. F. V. Konstantinov, *The Role of the Individual in the Development of Soviet Society,* p. 21.
4. *New York Times,* December 10, 1950.
5. *New York Times,* October 30, 1950.
6. *Ibid.*

INDEX